The Normative Constitution:

Essays for the Third Century

The Normative Constitution: Essays for the Third Century

Edited by

Richard Sherlock
Kent E. Robson
Charles W. Johnson

ROWMAN & LITTLEFIELD PUBLISHERS, INC.

ROWMAN & LITTLEFIELD PUBLISHERS, INC.

Published in the United States of America
by Rowman & Littlefield Publishers, Inc.
4720 Boston Way, Lanham, Maryland 20706

3 Henrietta Street
London WC2E 8LU, England

Chapter 2: Robert Bork, "Neutral Principles and Some First Amendment Problems." *Indiana Law Journal,* vol. 47 no. 1 (1987): 1-35. Used with permission.

Chapter 3: Harvey C. Mansfield, "Tocqueville and the Future of the American Revolution," in *Three Beginnings: Revolution, Rights and the Liberal State; Comparative Perspectives on the English, American and French Revolutions,* edited by Stephen Englehart and John A. Moore, Jr. (New York: Peter Lang, 1994), 9-30. Used with permission.

Chapter 6: Portions of this chapter appeared in Joel Feinberg, *Freedom and Fulfillment* (Princeton University Press, 1992), 245-49. Used with permission.

Typesetting by Robin K. Sterns

British Cataloging in Publication Information Available

Library of Congress Cataloging-in-Publication Data

ISBN 0–8476–8048–7 (cloth : alk. paper)
ISBN 0–8476–8049–5 (pbk. : alk. paper)

Printed in the United States of America

™ The paper used in this publication meets the minimum requirements of American National Standard for Information Sciences—Permanence of Paper for Printed Library Materials, ANSI Z39.48–1984.

Contents

Preface

The American Constitution will soon enter its third century, yet explications of its normative character remain extremely controversial. Theorists, judges, public leaders and ordinary citizens refer to it constantly, read it infrequently, and ponder its meaning interminably. Disputes besetting the Constitution have been addressed in Jefferson's attacks on federalist "abuses," the Lincoln/Douglas debates, and the recurring complaint that certain laws are inconsistent with the document's letter or spirit. Debates among conservatives, liberals and libertarians are reflected in a rich and balanced way in the essays contained in this volume.

These essays are derived from a series of lectures given at Utah State University. The lecture series was funded by the Joseph Marion Tanner Lecture Fund. This series was established by the late Mr. Obert C. Tanner of Salt Lake City, Utah, in honor of his father, who was the third president of USU. Mr. Tanner was a philosopher, businessman and philanthropist whose generosity has enriched the civic, artistic and intellectual life of the state, the nation, and the world. The editors are deeply grateful to Mr. Tanner and his family for their support.

All but one of the lectures are presented here as expanded articles. Readers may find they provide significant contributions to the ongoing dialogue concerning interpretations of the Constitution. We hope the scholarly, yet vigorous, dispute among the authors will add to the understanding of our unique founding document and enrich the various debates regarding its interpretation.

The editors thank Peter Macnamara for his valuable comments on an earlier draft of the introduction. Robert Bork appeared as a speaker in the Tanner Lecture Series; however, previous commitments prevented him from providing an article based on his remarks for this anthology. He granted us permission to reprint here his seminal article "Neutral Principles and Some First Amendment Problems," which initially appeared in the *Indiana Law Journal* 47 (1971) 1.

Introduction: The Normative Constitution

Richard Sherlock
Utah State University

Constitutional interpretation has always been a vexed question, even more so in our day when partisans of unpopular positions in all political camps seek a constitutional mandate for policies that they are otherwise unable to achieve in the ample forums of republican democracy.[1] Activists of all stripes have always sought the ear of the powerful and supposedly "enlightened" few to do what the "unenlightened" many will not. From abortion rights, to homosexuality, to balancing the federal budget, we are repeatedly implored to have the least amendable text, the Constitution, and the least democratic of its guardians, the judiciary, relieve us of the burden of democratic government.

But while activists and politicians demand that the Constitution do their work for them, they ignore the deepest and most fundamental of questions: What is a constitution to begin with and why, two hundred years later, should it still bind us as citizens within its ambit? Before anyone can demand that the Constitution and its special guardians perform the work of daily governance, *sub silentio*, the various partisans must first recognize the normative force of the Constitution itself. Inevitably the question of the normative character of the Constitution will be intrinsically connected to the more well-known and pervasive controversies over the means and modes of constitutional interpretation. Interpretive theories such as "original intent" or "fundamental rights" inherently imply a teaching about the normative character of the Constitution and the proper roles of the various branches of governance that it establishes. The reverse is just as true. Starting with an answer to the question of constitutional authoritativeness will lead forthwith to a teaching about interpretation. Robert Bork's "originalism," for example, implies a contractual view of the Constitution in which the text is merely a contract among Americans much like a contract between two private parties.[2] The text is then to be read with a close eye to what the parties meant when they entered into it. The moral rectitude of any particular reading is irrelevant. If I knowingly agree, in a proper contractual form, to sell you land for a certain price I may not now go to court to have the deal revoked because I have subsequently come to believe that the agreement is "unjust" and/or the price "unfair." Moral considerations are beside the point. The text is clear, the intent of the signatories ascertainable, and their competence to sign the agreement is uncontested. The deal stands.

By contrast, liberal theorists see the Constitution as being normative for all Americans as a vehicle for securing their individual rights even where these liberties were not originally contained in the text either explicitly or even implicitly. Thus, the Constitution becomes normative for later generations of Americans because it allows "justice to be done" in their generations, in ways that are only visible in their generation. It achieves its normative force for later eras of Americans by winning their allegiance, as it were, through the ways it offers special opportunities to protect the liberties that they believe are so important that they must be placed "off limits" to the ebb and flow of democratic political activity.[3]

Comprehending the normative character of constitutions and the proper interpretations of foundational texts are among the oldest and most central tasks of political philosophy. All of the foreign and domestic policies with which politics is concerned on a daily basis are policies of regimes whose essential, animating principles are seen most clearly in the founding charter. Policies follow from the principles embodied in the founding of the regime. The aggressive, expansionist foreign policy of the Soviet Union in the 1950s and 1960s was powerfully influenced by the universalistic character of its founding marxist orthodoxy. Similarly America's long struggle over civil rights for African-Americans was one inherent fruit of our founding commitment to legal and civil equality.[4]

1.

Since this concern with founders and their constitutions is coeval with the study of politics, we might gain some insight into the understanding of constitutional founding by examining a rich discussion by one of the most important founders of political philosophy itself: Aristotle's description in *The Constitution of Athens* of the laws and deeds of the Athenian founder Solon. In fact Aristotle's rich but admirably compressed discussion of Solon may be a model of the nature and complexity of constitutional interpretation itself.[5]

Much like the American founders Solon was entrusted with leadership when all factions in Athens trusted no one else, i.e. "when the strife was severe and the opposition longstanding." Solon's task was to found the Athenian regime in a manner that would long endure, assuring that domestic tranquillity and foreign independence from which prosperity and individual liberty would follow. By his laws and deeds he had to found the Athenians as a regime and establish a constitution that they would regard as normative.

Aristotle describes Solon's founding as essentially threefold. First and foremost Solon made of Athens one nation not two. This was accomplished by canceling all previous debts and forbidding new loans to be secured by the freedom of the one to whom the loan had been made. The old system in which loans could be repaid by a form of slavery had resulted in the perpetual strife associated with a system in which the many "were slaves of the few."[6] In order for Athens to long endure it must first be a whole people who can be constituted as a regime. "We the people" form regimes whose governing principles are found in constitutions. Solon first had to bring forth this "we" from "us" and "them" before he could establish the means of governing this "we" in founding laws.

Having first founded a people, Solon proceeds to set forth in written form the various offices of the state by means of which Athens will be governed. These offices and the laws governing them are reflective of the pre-political division of wealth in the city. Solon noted four such classes divided by wealth and allotted various governing offices to each, especially the upper three. He never attempted to eliminate differences in wealth or family background. Foolish attempts to do so only alienate those whose support is essential in founding. He had just made some of them poorer by canceling debts and freeing the indebted. He needed no further hostility from that quarter. What he could do was to modify or tame some of the worst political effects of such a division.[7]

Recognizing many of their concerns and their influence, Solon reserved many of the positions of daily governance for the upper three classes. This prudent maneuver allowed the real core of the founding to proceed in a profoundly democratic fashion. The lowest class of citizens was given an equal vote in the ecclesia which passed on all laws and, even more crucially, in the courts which interpreted, enforced and sat in judgment in the shadow of the laws. Aristotle notes the perennial truth that in all law "obscurity arises...from the impossibility of including the best solution for every instance in a general provision."[8] Courts, therefore, must always interpret the law in the act of judging the case at hand. Hence, Aristotle believes that Solon made a crucially correct decision in taking this enormous power of interpretation and judgment out of the hands of the upper classes and entrusting it to courts comprised of the many as well as the few. This gave the many a control over the constitution that brought them into the regime. They were not only subjects of the constitution but its protectors as well.

Furthermore, the courts were open to all, especially the many, to have their cases heard. This and its companion move of letting many serve in the courts had the effect of securing the allegiance of the many as part of the regime and as its guardians. Hence, as Aristotle shows, when Psistratus attempted to set himself up as a tyrant he was unsuccessful at the crucial moment. He could be a dictator, but he couldn't dictate. He governed "moderately and constitutionally... both because moderation was his character and because governing in accordance with the laws" were the only secure means of governing.[9] The many had secured their place in the regime at the time of Solon's founding and were not about to be enslaved again.

Solon's constitution became normative for the Athenians in a threefold manner noted by Aristotle. To begin with, one notes its properly legalistic origin in Solon who was authorized by the Athenians to establish a regime of stability and peace. Much like the formalistic contractarians of our day, Solon had the proper authorization since "the state had been entrusted to him." One may therefore conclude by implication that the people of Athens had agreed to abide by the laws he set forth.

This sort of contractarian formalism, however important at the outset, does not fully account for the fact that later supposed tyrants like Psistratus could not act tyrannically, that others who tried like Cleomenes and Isagorus were thrown out by the many "who had taken control of their affairs," and that reformers like Cleisthenes could only make the regime more democratic, not the reverse. Thus the Athenian constitution became normative not merely because properly authorized delegates or founders wrote it but also because of the rights, powers, and responsibilities it articulated and the ends or way of life to which it pointed; a way of life that ennobled the many so that they could take control of affairs when tyrants threatened.[10]

Solon's constitution became the normative foundation of the Athenian regime in complex and nuanced ways. It was a contract real and implied, it established the various offices of the state through which governance was conducted and finally it became normative for the many because of the ends of liberty and dignity to which it pointed them.

Aristotle's rich discussion of constitutionalism shows the complexity of constitutional interpretation even at the beginning of the enterprise. This complexity and the controversy it engenders has remained and even intensified in our day. Liberals bemoan executive appeals to an unspecified authority to conduct foreign and military policy, preferring instead rigid adherence to a written text that specifies the extent and character of executive authority.[11] Many of these same liberals, however, applaud when the judiciary articulates an implied series of rights and assumes an unwritten authority to enforce these rights against Congress, the executive and the states.[12] Conservatives, by contrast, have typically despaired at the plethora of penumbral rights discovered by an activist judiciary. But some of them do want an activist judiciary to vigorously defend the textually based rights of property owners against the activities of states and local governments and most conservatives defend the inherent (penumbral?) authority of the executive to conduct foreign policy largely free of constitutional or congressional restraint.[13]

2.

The essays in this volume fully reflect this debate across disciplines, points of view and methods of argument concerning constitutional interpretation. In subsequent pages of this volume are essays of legal scholars, political theorists and moral philosophers that reflect this rich diversity. Robert Bork's skeptical majoritarianism represents one rather conservative version of contractarianism. For Bork the Constitution is a contract among Americans past and present. Its provisions are to be read with close fidelity to the written text and to the ascertainable intentions of the writers and signatories of the original contract. If the framers would not have given constitutional protection to consensual sodomy we should not do so now except by the nearly impossible route of specific amendment. To do more is to have the judiciary enforce its private moral judgment over a democratic electorate. Since moral beliefs are nothing more than a private opinion, the judiciary cannot possibly do better than the electorate in such matters of moral choice. Since the judiciary cannot do better, the electorate remains as the only legitimate forum of constitutional interpretation, except where that same electorate has presumptively decided the issue and authorized judicial activism in a specific, narrowly read, constitutional text.[14]

While generally sharing Bork's disdain for a liberal, textually disconnected interpretation of the Constitution, Mansfield, Epstein, and Barrus dispute his moral skepticism and partially his despair over interpretative activism in defense of national security and/or individual liberty. For Barrus, the Constitution's Lockean ancestry and textual ambiguity with respect to foreign military and diplomatic policy both require the president to have and permit him to find in the Constitution broad interpretive powers to conduct those foreign relations necessary to the survival of the republic with a minimum of legislative or judicial restraint. Since foreign affairs are conducted largely in the Lockean state of nature, constitutional provisions which create civil, not natural, society do not bind a president in foreign relations the same way that they bind both president and Congress in domestic affairs.[15] Rather, the Constitution implicitly empowers the president to adopt possibly unpopular measures in support of his fundamental responsibility to "preserve, protect and defend the constitution" and the republican institutions it creates.

Epstein shares Bork's dislike of judicial legislation that is only loosely connected to the constitutional text, e.g. *Roe v. Wade*'s right to abortion. But like Barrus he finds timidity on the part of the institutions created by the Constitution to be a similarly serious threat to liberty. Epstein is often referred to as the leading proponent of what some have called "conservative judicial activism."[16]

For him, the Constitution must protect the liberty of private citizens, entrepreneurs, and groups, irrespective of how marginal their beliefs or unpopular their activities. Statism in the drag of benevolence is still statism whether it was known as such by the founders or not. In his seminal work on property rights Epstein has argued that even though the founders did not know of governmental regulations that would deny a property owner a financially profitable use of his property because of such concerns as zoning, protection of wetlands or environmental degradation, we see it constantly. It is every bit as much of a taking of property by the state as was the king's seizure of land for military fortifications with which the framers were concerned. A traditionalist might conclude like the court once did that since the Fourth Amendment does not mention wiretapping, police may eavesdrop without concern for the formalities set forth therein. In the same manner, perhaps, since regulatory "takings" are not specified in the Fifth Amendment and were unknown to the framers, they are not matters of constitutional concern. For Epstein this would miss the forest and see the trees. The state can take property in many ways, only some of which were recognized by the founders. But they did specifically note the generic evil of "taking" by the state without just compensation. It is the special task of the judiciary to be expansive in its vision and activist in its pursuit of such encroachments to individual liberty.[17]

In his contribution here, Epstein extends his activist concern for individual liberty to the interplay between economic and business regulation and religious liberty. He explores in a rich and nuanced way issues which the framers never foresaw but that now require thoughtful vigilance from a judiciary that is faithful to the text of the Constitution but not so limited in its vision that it cannot see new dangers to liberty at every hand. The Constitution becomes normative for Americans because it protects their liberties, past, present and future, not because of real or implied votes taken in 1788 or 1993. The judiciary enhances this liberty and ensures its own legitimacy not by blind obeisance to narrowly read textual wording but by vigilant enforcement of textually based principles.

Mansfield too disputes the moral skepticism of Bork and the sort of textual skepticism of the left (i.e. we don't know what the text means *per se* so it can mean what we want). But Mansfield stresses that the Constitution is first and foremost a text that establishes a means of republican self-government, not a vehicle for promoting special views of public rectitude. Thus the Constitution is fundamentally concerned with setting forth a form or structure of self-government and not with securing to various public factions the satisfaction of their desires in the guise of textual interpretation. It becomes normative because of the manner in which it creates and is, in turn, legitimated by the institutions of republican self-government. The most essential right, the principle which preserves all other rights, is the right of self-government, what the founders called "popular government." Thus, Mansfield agrees with Hamilton that the true bill of rights is the original Constitution itself.[18] Without the original organization of self-government, the amendments are no more than vague statements of principle that will have no more lasting influence than the contemporaneous French Declaration of the Rights of Man, which being disconnected to a specific form of self-government was impotent in the face of revolutionary turmoil. Mansfield sees the threats to constitutional government from the skepticism of the right and the left and the need to order and control the factious popular passions of the moment as the Constitution originally sought to do on behalf of self-government. Conservatives have often promoted the view that the Constitution would be perfect if only their special amendment were added. However salutary the policy such proposals embody, amending the Constitution to include them is a notion that actually discourages republican government by writing into the founding document the policies of the moment. Liberals on the other hand wish to exploit the text and its special, deliberately nonrepresentative guardians, i.e. the courts, to silently amend the Constitution to achieve specific policies and enforce extratextual rights. They both disparage republican institutions by demanding that the founding should prevent later generations from exercising, in the most contested of cases, the very self-government that the founders so passionately sought to encourage.

Liberals like Feinberg and Nickel profoundly disagree with both the moral skepticism of Bork and the textual conservatism of Mansfield and to some extent Epstein and Barrus as well. Like Athenian reformers after Solon, they believe that our Constitution can secure new forms of liberty and justice in our age and in our terms, not just the age and terms of two centuries past. In varying ways both Feinberg and Nickel hold that moral philosophy is at the heart of proper constitutional deliberation, especially the most contested current deliberations over rights and conflicts among rights. They hold that a real fabric of rationally justifiable rights and correlative obligations must form the backdrop of constitutional interpretation. The Constitution itself gives a broad voice to these rights but each generation must divine the specific applications that are relevant to its own moral/political controversies. The framers could not see our world but they knew the essential rights that must be part of any just political world. It is for us to interpret their broad language in such a manner as to bring these rights vividly to bear on the threats to liberty and justice which exist in our day.

The founders were not Borkean skeptics. They believed the eminently plausible proposition that real rights exist, independently of personal opinion, social convention, or historical context.[19] It was precisely because the British parliament and crown were together consistently violating these rights that they felt compelled to resist with force of arms. It was to secure individuals in the enjoyment of this extratextual fabric of moral rights that the legal fabric of constitutional rights was created. To properly comprehend the latter we must have recourse to the former. But this recourse will illuminate more than just the dry words of an eighteenth-century text. It will also cast light on new threats to those rights to which the Constitution itself gives a legalistic voice. Thus the Constitution becomes a vehicle for securing moral rights, i.e. justice which is real and justified in every age against new encroachments in any age. The Constitution is normative for Americans today not because it is a contract of the past to which they now implicitly agree but because it establishes fabric rights which are truths of the past, present, and future.

For this reason Feinberg especially rejects the whole idea of "value free" or neutral interpretation both as dangerous to individual rights and as impossible in any event.[20] To make any sense of phrases like "cruel and unusual punishment" or "due process of law" is to engage in a fundamentally moral, non-neutral, enterprise. If Bork's own skepticism is granted, then why should Americans find a contract from the past to bind them today? Bork seems to hold the Constitution as a sort of contract. But if so then its binding character seems to follow from a more fundamental and fundamentally moral premise about obeying the terms of a contract or a promise. Hence, Bork's supposedly neutral interpretation rests on a nonskeptical, moral premise about the authoritative character of the document itself.

Feinberg's essay here, as with most of his work in social philosophy and ethics, defends an expanded set of liberty rights, expanded from the same genus as those already found in the Constitution.[21] He has always seen negative or liberty rights as the archetype of real rights and so-called positive or welfare rights as statements of social goals or ideals. One has a fundamental right to practice a religion of one's choice in Feinberg's view but while it would be nice if everyone had an adequate diet or house, no one has a right against other persons or groups to see that such material goods are provided.[22]

In our volume James Nickel dissents from this neat distinction in a modest but powerful way. Once we regard the Constitution as normative today because of the manner in which it "secures the blessings of liberty" today, then we might properly ask how those rights are secured today and what foundations are required for their being secured adequately to all citizens. Viewed in this light, Nickel like a number of contemporary theorists regards the distinction between liberty rights and welfare rights as unpersuasive and narrow.[23]

Individual liberty cannot be secured to anyone if the citizenry who must be its guardians do not know of their rights and the constitutionally legitimate means of protecting them. One cannot hire an attorney to defend in court rights of which one is ignorant. To hire the attorney is to know that one has rights that might be being violated and that a constitutionally legitimate means of protecting such rights exists. To secure even the liberty rights noted in the original Constitution requires an educated populace. Education provided by the state is thus constitutionally mandated if the equal liberties articulated in the Constitution are not to be regarded as a sham. Nickel regards this sort of argument as a proper and, in fact, necessary extension of the concern for liberty rights with which Feinberg and many civil libertarians have been historically concerned. Without at least two crucial parts of human welfare, education and minimum economic sustenance, individuals cannot know of their rights or properly resist encroachments thereupon.

Like Cleisthenes in Aristotle's account of Athenian constitutionalism, liberals such as Feinberg and Nickel, believe that our Constitution like Solon's can be updated and rendered more democratic in ways that are consistent with the spirit that animates the works of the founders without requiring strict fidelity to the textual expression of those principles in our founders' greatest achievement, the written constitution. Today's democratizers like those of ancient times seek a constitutional mandate for the redistribution of power and to some extent wealth as well. They have learned of the socialist dictum that the freedom of the press belongs to the one who owns a press and they have concluded that democracy cannot be successful when large numbers of citizens lack the material conditions necessary for real participation in the democratic process. Unlike conservatives, they conclude that a "constitution of process" requires by implication a "constitution of results." In mandating some means, the Constitution tacitly mandates some ends.

3.

The debate among conservatives, liberals and libertarians which is reflected in these pages is a uniquely modern struggle over the normative character and meaning of the constitutional text. The Constitution is said to be authoritative and thus to require certain actions if it is read this way or that. But the uniquely modern and hence limited character of this struggle only comes to light if we return to the very founder of constitutional study itself, Aristotle. At the core of Aristotle's teaching is the connection between constitutions and regimes or "ways of life." Constitutions both arise out of certain habits of mind and heart in the people and nurture certain ways of life by the principles set forth in the founding text. Constitutions do not just represent past agreements or articulate the fashions of current individualism. They give rise to distinctive ways of life, grounding certain pursuits firmly in their soil and discouraging others less noble or less suited to the regime they establish.

Ralph Lerner's splendid contribution with which we begin our examination of constitutional questions renews this classical and Tocquevillian understanding of constitutional founding. What is at stake for Lerner is not the specifics of textual meaning but the capacity of constitutional governance itself to establish a way of life, a character of the people that is at once "authentically national and genuinely worthy." What is in doubt, profoundly in doubt in this age of relativism, deconstructionism, and fragmentation, is not the terms of a contract written in 1787 or 1868 but whether the living fruits of that contract shall be known as good today. Rights are only a disconnected series of claims unless they are embedded in a way of life that is itself virtuous and worthy of respect. As this is written Russia is enduring a prolonged struggle to see if a parchment list of rights, which were always extensive and elaborate, can bring forth the noble fruit that will transform a bare list into a way of life that truly respects both liberty and virtue.

Just as Professor Lerner tries to examine the import of constitutional government in a way different from much of the current discussion, so it may be useful to think of new possibilities or reformulations of forgotten possibilities if we are to transcend the conundrum of constitutional interpretation that has divided liberals, conservatives and moderates for half a century.

Liberals have generally taken the view that Feinberg does: there are real rights not just opinions or social conventions. Governments may invade these rights under the cloak of factional pressures or simple majoritarianism. When they do, it is the special provenance of the judiciary to restrain such tyranny, that these rights and the liberty they protect might flourish.

In this age of skeptical relativism it is refreshing to have a nonrelativist view set forth so clearly by a number of constitutional scholars.[24] While one may disagree with the details of the liberal theory of nonrelative moral claims, the primary difficulty for liberals has always been to connect their attractive moral theory to the constitutional text. Liberals are fond of quoting Chief Justice Marshall's dictum about the necessary breadth of constitutional interpretation: "It is a constitution we are expounding, a constitution designed to endure for ages to come." Though certainly eloquent and apt, this begs the liberal point. For liberals still must show how their moral claims are connected to the Constitution itself, which, as Marshall noted, was the text being interpreted. Judges are not being asked to interpret the texts of Locke or Jefferson or Mill. Nor are they confirmed as teachers of natural law. However broadly, it is a specific text that is being interpreted, not the moral sentiments of humankind.

How, then, critics ask, do you find such rights as "privacy" in this specific text? Surely some sense of privacy is implied in the Fourth Amendment's limits on searching private homes, papers and "effects." But the right of privacy which liberals celebrate is not this sort of limit on how government may conduct the business of law enforcement. What liberals see is a prohibition against making and enforcing certain sorts of laws at all. They claim to find in the Constitution a prohibition against making certain sorts of intimate, personal lifestyle choices a matter of legal restriction at all.[25] Certain areas of personal behavior are off limits to the state. This may be a defensible philosophic proposition, but where is it found in the Constitution?

Over the past two decades leading liberals have repeatedly turned to continental theories of interpretation, broadly denoted by the term "hermeneutics" for an apparent solution to their difficulties on this point.[26] But this solution may prove more troubling than the original problem. Deriving fundamentally from the inspiration of post-Kantian historicism, especially as articulated by Heidegger and his student Gadamer, hermeneutics' principal claim is that no reading of a text is a value-free exposition of a preexisting meaning, either derived from authorial intention or some other source. All reading is interpreting by a reader who brings his own pre-understanding to the text. Hence, the meaning of a text is always a meaning for this or that reader, in light of his or her pre-understanding of the world around them. Meaning is fundamentally a product of the reader, a meaning driven by his horizon of pre-understanding, not the always opaque intentions of the author.[27]

For example, a reader of the Bible in the Middle Ages may have actually believed that when mention is made of the sun standing still in the sky for a period of hours some actual recorded miracle is being referred to. A reader steeped in modern science will simply ignore any such literalistic meaning. He may read it as a myth or fable. He may read it as a dramatic device that is part of a larger literary of philosophic work. He may believe that a kernel of history is being recorded because the constant sunlight may refer to an exploding supernova. But the interpretive horizon of modern science will simply filter out the most literal reading at the outset. For this modern reading the most literal possible reading is actually "meaningless," i.e. not possible or sensible.[28] Hence this reader and every reader creatively draws a meaning from the text in light of his interpretive horizon.

Leading liberal constitutional scholars have found in post-Heideggerian hermeneutics a means of drawing from the constitutional text new meanings that are more acceptable to the horizon of moral beliefs that dominates the last half of the twentieth century than those possibly intended by the original authors of the constitutional text. For example, many of the framers held the common eighteenth-century belief in the practical utility of religion for teaching civic morality and motivating adherence thereto. As such, they sanctioned a greater public support for mainstream Protestantism than we might find acceptable today in a vastly more religiously pluralistic society and one in which the supposed utility of religion is not as widely accepted.[29] The framers and their countrymen may read the First Amendment one way and we may properly read it another given our situation as readers in a different time and place. It will mean one thing to an eighteenth-century jurist and may, quite properly, mean something very different to us.

Raoul Berger, in another example, has richly documented the racial prejudice of the members of Congress who drafted and passed the Fourteenth Amendment.[30] In particular he has shown how they assured other, wavering, members that this amendment would not lead to the abolition of legally segregated school systems in their states and districts. Viewed in terms of intentionalist theories of interpretation, such evidence casts a dark pall on *Brown v. Board of Education* and its massive progeny.[31] But newer, hermeneutical theories appear to bypass this difficulty easily. Since courts today must read the amendment in a contemporary setting, they are permitted and even encouraged to do justice in terms recognizable in our era, not that of 1868.

But this seems to throw the baby out with the bathwater, so to speak. If no text has a fixed meaning, if all interpretations are the artifact of the reader's history, then the same is true of the reading given by current courts as well. When we consider the immense social upheaval attendant on seminal decisions like *Brown* and *Roe*, it is hard to conceive of any justification for such decisions that does not ultimately rest on a conviction that America is a more just regime after a decision like *Brown* than before.[32] But if hermeneutics is correct in its fundamental teaching about the historicity of all thought, then this very assumption of a principle of justice which is better embodied after *Brown* than before is difficult, if not impossible, to defend. In effect the moral foundation of the liberal's position is severely undermined by the most common method of connecting this moral conviction to the constitutional text.

The typical conservative argument appears to have a similar problem in reverse. Conservatives establish the meaning of the text by referring to the intentions of the framers as revealed in word and deed. Thus the text has a relatively determinate meaning, which may persuade, please, enrage, or dismay readers. Its meaning is set by authorial intention, while its "significance" may be determined by the responses of various readers.[33] It has never proven sufficient at this point to retort either that we do not know authorial intention, especially of a many-authored text like the Constitution or that the broad phrases of the Constitution are an intentional invitation to sweeping and modernizing interpretive maneuvers. On most of the hotly contested issues of recent times the courts have gone much further than any plausible review of the thought and actions of the framers would sustain, a point tacitly admitted by leading liberals.[34]

But conservatives then must answer one fundamental query: why is the Constitution normative for us today? If the text does not establish justice, why is it binding on us? To which, Bork and company usually reply with some version of contract theory, i.e. because our forbears explicitly agreed to these terms of social agreement and we implicitly do so by living in and enjoying the benefits of this regime today. But this makes constitutional commitment a matter of contractual fiat, divorced from the noble or ignoble character of its provisions and the institutions it establishes.

It appears, therefore, that the constitutional text has a relatively determinate meaning, ascertainable in most cases by established, eminently sound interpretive methods. But justice, the establishment of which is among the first purposes of the document, is a shifting collection of personal opinions determined by individual history and social circumstance. Conservatives who read the constitutional text with sober, careful analytical skills deny that the philosophical and religious traditions of the West can be read in this same sober, thoughtful manner which would lead to some teaching about justice that is more than a collection of vacuous appeals and personal opinions. In a way this is a mirror image of the liberal tradition which regards the actual text of the Constitution as a pastiche of vague phrases and eighteenth-century opinions, while regarding the moral tradition behind it as capable of providing the clear, careful teaching about justice which the text itself appears incapable of.

We might begin to envision a way past this impasse by considering first the sort of query that Professor Lerner presses: to what end does the work of the framers point? More pointedly, what is the purpose of the Constitution and the regime which grows from it? If it was primarily to teach or enact "justice" we might have expected a much fuller discussion of the principles of this "justice" and the policies it requires. But the Constitution never aimed at an impossible politics of pure justice. Rather, the founders' Constitution is first and foremost a means of establishing the one thing that astounded their European contemporaries: governance "of the people, by the people, and for the people." Europeans knew of justice in a thousand variations in the philosophic traditions of ancient and modern times. What they knew nothing of was a republican regime that would aim at its own full measure of justice and foster a genuinely worthy character that would sustain republican institutions in times of trial.

Seen in this light both conservative skepticism and liberal expansiveness are at odds with republican self-government. Grant the skeptic his premises and the possibility of a genuinely worthy republican self governance collapses. Contractual fiat replaces republican virtue. By demanding that the least democratic of our institutions resolve our most contested issues, from race relations, to abortion, to gay rights, liberals, too, denigrate the possibility of self-government that they otherwise demand in its most individualistic forms, i.e. "nobody can tell me how to live."

Perhaps of any supposed reading of the Constitution we ought to ask how it furthers republican governance and nurtures the individual character necessary to sustain this governance.[35] Constitutional interpretation should not demean democratic process by being made to bear the weight of solving every contested area of public affairs. If on the most crucial issues we must go from self-government to "philosopher kings" on the bench, then we might as well declare the American experiment over and failed. But neither should interpretation be conducted in such a mechanical fashion that the larger ends of self-government are imperiled. Claims that gun control, or foreign aid, or various regulatory or tax schemes are unconstitutional because they are not explicitly provided for in the original document or would have been regarded as unwise by Madison or Jefferson appear to entail a profound distrust of the capacity of ordinary democratic governance to sort out, over time, the wheat from the chaff.[36]

One example from the past might help to make the general outlines of this suggestion somewhat clearer. In the well-known "school prayer" case of *Abington Township v. Schempp*, the Court struck down local practices of Bible reading and recitation of the Lord's Prayer to start the school day. In a revealing concurring opinion Justice Brennan admits that the Court is going beyond what the framers would have thought reasonably required by their test. Brennan regards the search for their intentions as "futile and misdirected." Though he makes the obligatory references to the imprecision of the historical record, it is readily apparent that Brennan knows the Court is going beyond what the framers would have deemed as required by their efforts. Rather, Brennan advises, we should inquire "whether the practices challenged here threaten those consequences which the framers deeply feared," whether they promote the entanglements which the framers sought to prevent. The task of the Court is to translate the "majestic generalities" of the Bill of Rights into concrete restraints on twentieth-century public policies. For this, the Court must look at twentieth-century history and politics, not eighteenth-century intentions.

Justice Brennan concludes that the modern public school, with required attendance of all children, and the vastly more pluralistic society of twentieth century America make it unwise and unconstitutional in today's context to require an admittedly Christian religious practice at the start of school. But if this context requires a new reading of our founding document and a new application of its principles, why is the Court best situated to give it? It would seem that of the divisions of government in America, those best situated to recognize the very diversity that Justice Brennan speaks of would be local school officials who are required by the nature of their office to accommodate the diversity of their patron families and children. Is there any reason to suppose that this most fundamental form of local self-government is so backward in its capacities that it cannot recognize the changes that Justice Brennan notes, if they are as important as he alleges, and take steps to alter their school policies accordingly?

Suppose local school officials decided to have every religious group in the community, Christian, Jewish, Muslim or any other, offer, on a rotation basis, a short, sincere devotional once a week as a means of teaching about other faiths and encouraging respect for religious diversity and toleration. Justice Brennan would undoubtedly find this practice too "entangling" and thus constitutionally infirm. But it is hard see why this might not be as sound an attempt to respond to the very circumstances that he concludes must now govern constitutional interpretation on this matter. Whatever the framers may have thought of the specific practices challenged in *Abington*, their own greatest achievement, "self-government," suggests that they would have been far more reluctant to declare self-government void at the most local level and on the most complicated of topics, than Justice Brennan.

Two centuries ago Americans embarked on a bold experiment in self-government, with faith in its possibilities that Europeans regarded as foolish. If our experiment and the text by which we constituted its foundations remain binding on us today perhaps that is most fundamentally because by it we, citizens of the same republic in a different century, are still sufficiently empowered for and nurtured in the arts of self-governance that we may justly claim a constitutional inheritance. If the constitutional republic is to survive for another century it will surely be because we have refused to demean its nobility with skepticism and abdicate its responsibilities to mechanical amendments or judicial gurus, but have found in constitutional institutions and processes the same possibilities of character and empowerment that our forbears once proudly claimed.

Notes

1. For some useful introductions to the problems and issues see Chris Wolfe, *The Rise of Modern Judicial Review* (Littlefield Adams, 1993); Eugene Hickock, ed., *The Bill of Rights: Original Meaning and Current Understanding* (University Press of Virginia, 1986); for an excellent collection of primary texts, judicial and otherwise, see Walter Murphy et al, eds., *American Constitutional Interpretation* (Foundation Press, 1986).

2. See the selection from Bork reprinted below and the further reflections in Robert Bork, *The Tempting of America: The Political Seduction of the Judiciary* (Free Press, 1989).

3. See generally Ronald Dworkin, *Taking Rights Seriously* (Harvard, 1977); idem, *Laws Empire* (Harvard, 1986); Michael Perry, *The Constitution, the Courts and Human Rights* (Yale, 1982); Jesse Choper, *Judicial Review in the National Political Process* (Chicago, 1980). A vast array of other books and articles can be cited here but these are seminal works in this vein that must be taken account of by any serious writer.

4. For some discussion of America's founding commitment to equality see Harry Jaffa, *Equality and Liberty* (Oxford, 1962) and idem, *How to Think About the American Revolution* (Carolina Academic Press, 1978).

5. Aristotle, "The Constitution of Athens" in J.M. Moore, ed., *Aristotle and Xenophon on Democracy and Oligarchy* (Berkeley, 1975).

6. Constitution of Athens, 5:1.

7. Ibid. 7:1-4.

8. Ibid. 9:2.

9. Ibid. 16:6-8.

10. Ibid. sec 21.

11. For a review of these issues see Clinton Rossiter, *The Supreme Court and the Commander in Chief* (Cornell, 1976); Abraham Soafer, *War, Foreign Affairs, and Constitutional Power* (Ballinger, 1976). The liberal critique of presidential authority in foreign affairs was most powerfully codified in the famous "war powers resolution" (1973), 50 *U.S. Code* par. 1541-1548; for an analysis see Robert Scigliano, "The War Powers Resolution and the War Powers" in Jeffrey Bessette and Jeffrey Tullis, eds., *The Presidency in the Constitutional Order* (Louisiana State University Press, 1981).

12. This notion of implied or "penumbral" rights as Justice Douglas called them is a mainstay of liberal interpretation as is the companion concept of a "living constitution"; for a seminal view of the former see *Griswold v. Connecticut* 381 U.S. 479; for defenses of the general liberal theory of a living constitution see Thomas Grey, "Do We have an Unwritten Constitution?" *Stanford Law Review* 27(1975) 703-735; Stephen Munzer and James Nickel, "Does the Constitution Mean What It Always Meant?" *Columbia Law Review* 77(1977) 1029-1082.

13. See the discussion of Epstein below.

14. See Bork, *The Tempting of America* op. cit. Also see Bork, "The Impossibility of Finding Welfare Rights in the Constitution" *Washington University Law Review* 1979(3) 695-701.

15. The classical contract theorists Hobbes and Locke both considered foreign relations to be one of three examples of the state of nature and of human behavior in

it. The other two were civil war and the state of the native peoples of the new world; Hobbes, *Leviathan*, chap. 13; Locke, *Second Treatise of Government*, chap. 3

16. Richard Epstein, *Takings: Private Property and the Power of Eminent Domain* (Harvard, 1985). Others frequently linked to this school are Stephen Macedo, *The New Right and the Constitution* (Chicago, 1980); idem, *The Supreme Court's Constitution* (Transaction, 1987); Two major edited collections also reflect this view, Richard Wagner and James Gwartney, eds., *Public Choice and Constitutional Economics* (Cato Institute, 1988); Henry Manne, ed. *Economic Liberties and the Judiciary* (Cato Institute, 1987); for a critical analysis of these issues see Lino Graglia, "Judicial Activism: Even on the Right It Is Wrong" in Ellen Frankel Paul, *Economic Liberties and the Constitution* (Basic Blackwell, 1990).

17. See Epstein *Takings*, op. cit. and Epstein, *Forbidden Grounds: The Case Against Employment Discrimination Law* (Harvard, 1991).

Epstein originally held that individual rights must be defended on some version of Kantian formalist grounds. In a recent paper he now believes that they can and should be defended on utility grounds, along with what I submit are largely the "rule utilitarian" approaches of contemporary moral theory.

18. This is Hamilton's comment in Federalist 84; for a discussion see Walter Berns, "The Constitution as Bill of Rights" in *In Defense of Liberal Democracy* (Gateway, 1984).

19. Versions of this view are a commonplace in histories of political thought and/or American government. For recent statements see Bernard Balyn, *The Ideological Origins of the American Revolution* (Harvard, 1972); Gordon Wood, *The Formation of the American Republic* (Chapel Hill, 1969); Forest MacDonald, *Novus Ordo Seclorum: The Intellectual Origins of the Constitution* (Kansas, 1985).

20. See the Feinberg selection below for one statement of this view.

21. See especially Feinberg's magisterial series on liberty rights, *The Moral Foundations of the Criminal Law*, 4 vols. (Oxford, 1984).

22. For Feinberg's view of the nature of this distinction and the problems of calling welfare claims "rights" see Joel Feinberg, *Social Philosophy* (Prentice Hall, 1973) and idem, "The Nature and Value of Rights" *Journal of Value Inquiry* 4 (1970), 243-257.

23. James Nickel, *Making Sense of Human Rights* (Berkeley, 1986); also see Frank Michelman, "Welfare Rights in a Constitutional Democracy" *Washington University Law Quarterly* 1973:3, 659-693 and Henry Shue, *Basic Rights* (Princeton, 1980).

24. See especially Michael Perry, *Morality, Politics and Law* (Oxford, 1989); David Richards, *Foundations of American Constitutional Theory* (Oxford, 1989) and Bruce Ackerman, *Social Justice and the Liberal State* (Harvard, 1981); for a more conservative but still nonrelativist view of the law see John Finnis, *Natural Law and Natural Rights* (Oxford, 1977).

25. The literature on privacy is much too vast to be reviewed here. For a few influential and representative titles see David Richards, "Sexual Autonomy and Constitutional Right to Privacy" *Hastings Law Journal* 30 (1979), 957-1021; Charles Fried, "Privacy" *Yale Law Journal* 77(1968) 475-531; Kenneth Karst, "Freedom of Intimate Association" *Yale Law Journal* 89(1980), 624-673; Louis Lusky, "Invasion of Privacy: A Clarification of Concepts" *Columbia Law Review* 72 (1972) 693-751; David O'Brien *Privacy, Law and Public Policy* (Praeger, 1979); John Chapman and Roland Pennock, eds., *Privacy* (Atherton, 1971).

26. For an excellent collection of key texts in the development of hermeneutical

theory see K.M. Vollmer, ed., *The Hermeneutics Reader* (Continuum, 1990).

27. Hans George Gadamer, *Truth and Method,* trans. Garret Barden and William Doerpel (Seabury, 1975); Martin Heidegger, *Being and Time,* trans. Edward Robinson and John Macquarrie (Blackwell, 1973); also Martin Heidegger, *An Introduction to Metaphysics,* trans. Ralph Mannheim (Oxford, 1959).

28. As this example suggests, hermeneutics has had an enormous influence in twentieth-century Christian theology; for an introduction to this usage, which is useful in its own right as an introduction to hermeneutics, see James Robinson and John Cobb, eds., *The New Hermeneutic* (Harper, 1964) and Edgar McKnight, *Meaning in Texts* (Fortress, 1978); David Hoy, *The Critical Circle: Literature, History and Philosophical Hermeneutics* (Berkeley, 1977); Richard Palmer, *Hermeneutics: Interpretation Theory in Schleieracher, Dilthey, Heidegger, and Gadamer* (Northwestern, 1969).

29. The attitude of the framers on the matter of religion is complex; for sense of the complexity one should consult: Michael McConnell, "The Origins and Historical Understanding of the Free Exercise of Religion" *Harvard Law Review* 103(1990) 1410-1517; Ton Lindsey, "James Madison on Religion and Politics: Rhetoric and Reality" *American Political Science Review* 85(1991), 1321-1337; Michael Malbin, *Religion and Politics: The Intentions of the Authors of the First Amendment* (American Enterprise Institute, 1978); and Thomas Curry, *The First Freedom* (Oxford, 1986).

In the famous school prayer cases, *Abington Township v. Schempp* 374 U.S. 203 and *Engel v. Vitale* 370 U.S. 421, the justices admitted that this different historical context required, in their view, a different interpretation of the establishment clause than would have been given by the framers.

30. Raoul Berger, *Government by Judiciary* (Harvard, 1977).

31. *Brown v. Board of Education* 347 U.S. 483; *Brown v. Board of Education* 349 U.S. 294. The same thing may be said of the Court's voting rights cases, e.g. the "one man one vote" rulings, *Baker v. Carr* 369 U.S. 186 and *Reynolds v. Sims* 377 U.S. 533. This does not even begin to cover the range of cases involving abortion, religious establishment, criminal process, free press, pornography, etc. Since the Congress of 1868 did not even consider the incorporation thesis, it could not have seriously considered these sorts of issues.

32. The best liberals have always stressed this point. They have generally argued from current precedents, widely accepted as having advanced justice, to the conclusion that conservatives like Berger, Bork or Wolfe must be wrong because their interpretations do not allow them to support such obviously enlightened decisions. Thus, Dworkin writes approvingly of judges deciding *Brown* and finding that the community will be morally better off if they overrule *Plessy*: "He knows that the congressmen who proposed the Fourteenth Amendment had a different view which they declared in official legislative history...he does not believe that this matters much now. It cannot be evidence of any deep and dominant contemporary opinion, to which he must refer, as one aspect or dimension of interpretation, for reasons of fairness. The old legislative history is no longer an act of the nation personified declaring some contemporary public purpose....The plaintiff school children are being cheated of what their Constitution, properly interpreted, defines as independent and equal standing in the republic," *Laws Empire* 388-389, Perry, op. cit.

33. This crucial distinction between meaning and significance is advanced against Gadamer by E.D. Hirsch, *Validity in Interpretation* (Yale, 1967).

34. One way to see this point is to look at the responses to Raoul Berger's examination of the background and shaping of the Fourteenth Amendment. Many liberals admitted his basic thesis, with some qualifications, and then proceeded to reject Berger's interpretivism, thus rendering his historical studies irrelevant for judicial purposes. Cf. reviews of Walter Murphy, *Yale Law Journal* 87(1978) 1752-1771; J.A. Scott, *Civil Liberties* 5(1979) 403-435 devoted to Berger's book; Michael Perry's judgment is typical, "The fact that Berger's reading of the original understanding of the Fourteenth Amendment is not free from doubt in every particular has a very limited significance for present purposes. For it is nonetheless true that very little Fourteenth Amendment doctrine—including the notion that various provisions of the Bill of Rights...constrain state action by virtue of the Fourteenth Amendment—can be explained by reference to the original understanding of the Fourteenth Amendment," Perry, *Constitution, Courts and Human Rights*, 69.

35. This view might be thought to have some affinity with John Hart Ely's "process" jurisprudence in which the Court is to concern itself primarily with the process of democratic representation and policymaking, and not with the substantive results reached by an otherwise fair process. Ely's instincts are to a certain extent sound. Republican democracy is powerfully concerned with the process of representation and governance and not with results that philosophic or religious teachers would regard as fully just. In this regard Ely is better at showing the errors of decisions he does not like, e.g. the quintessentially substantive case of *Roe*, than demonstrating how his theory works at the margin to support what he does approve of. He obviously wants to include *Brown* in his panoply of great decisions but how he can do so is obscure. Only by concluding that segregation drastically affects representation and thus access can his theory reflect his moral sentiments. But in an age when black politicians are clamoring to preserve "majority black" districts in Congress and black educators are defending schools devoted to the education of black males, the claim that segregation itself is per se devastating to the political representation of minorities may not be so obvious. The fundamental problem seems to be that the most crucial question of "who counts" or who has what rights is not neutral and does affect representation in sometimes profound ways. Put the other way, if the court is concerned with representation then it will have to decide the very sorts of cases involving substantive values that Ely initially concluded were an impermissible expansion of judicial power. See John Hart Ely, *Democracy and Distrust* (Harvard, 1980).

36. One of the most sensitive, broadly conservative treatments of interpretive issues that avoids the usual problems of the conservative position by tying not to skepticism but to the concerns of democratic governance is James Bond, *The Art of Judging* (Transaction Books, 1987).

Chapter 1

The Founders' Liberal Arts

Ralph Lerner
University of Chicago

Is there anything worth saying about the Founders' liberal arts? Or in raising the topic is one merely reviving the hoopla of bicentennial marketing that mercifully seemed finally to have come to an end? After all, it is not written in the stars that *every* good thing must have its connection with the Founders of this country. Although close to half of the members of the Philadelphia Convention had attended college, few of that broader group whom we call the Founders would have passed muster as scholars. Some, like Benjamin Franklin and George Washington, barely had any formal schooling to speak of. John Adams had an unhappy stint as a country schoolmaster and, like other disgruntled liberal arts graduates, gave it up for what he hoped would be a more rewarding profession, the law. A few — Benjamin Rush and, most notably, Thomas Jefferson and James Madison — turned their efforts toward fostering higher education in America but never saw their handiwork rise above the level of merely provincial institutions. A number of them were serious readers and avid book collectors — for study and use, not for furniture — but their total output as authors, as measured by book titles, is remarkably small, even minuscule. All in all, the Founders do not appear to be among the more obvious exemplars of practitioners of the liberal arts.

Yet even if this were a sufficient account, I could hardly be said to have disposed of the question of the Founders' liberal arts. Schooling, after all, is not the same as learning, and in the latter respect the Founders as a group were impressively at home in significant parts of the Western political and legal tradition. Nor is it even obvious that I have been speaking of the liberal arts at all, but rather about the Founders' eligibility to be awarded tenure at your university or mine. And that would truly be missing the point. So let us put all that aside and turn instead to looking into *their* liberal arts.

In one way or another we know — even if we are not familiar with the history of scholarship in the West or with the development of universities from medieval times onward — we know somehow that the liberal arts form part of a tradition, even as they have been formed by a tradition. As little as our parents invented the language they first taught us did they invent or discover the logical categories they used, the picture of the universe and of man's place in it that they conveyed to us, or even the many tales and rhymes with which they amused or astonished us. We are the inheritors of a vast complex tradition, painfully accumulated and refined, adjusted and rejected, half-forgotten and recovered. We cannot escape the fact, the presence, the insistent pressure of this intellectual inheritance. The liberal arts are an inheritance that will not go away.

At the same time, however, we have to recognize how out of step, even awkward, the liberal arts may be at any particular time. Far from being current or trendy, far from fitting in well with whatever it is that most people opine, the liberal arts seem rather to suggest questions and concerns that are quaint at best and perverse at worst. That may strike you as fairly predictable. After all, a tradition is old and could hardly be expected to be up-to-date. But consider this another way. It may, in fact, be paradoxical: A tradition that is old may, precisely because it is old, have the capacity to liberate someone from the ready-made questions and answers, attitudes and assumptions, that are dinned into our ears during every waking hour. In short, the liberal arts may be, at one and the same time, a tradition *and* a means of emancipating oneself from the thoughtless conventions of the day. Thus, one part of what we have inherited may free us for the tyranny of another legacy.

Nor is this the only paradoxical feature of the liberal arts. As an inheritance, as something so to speak given to us, the liberal arts compel us to acknowledge our debts to others. Furthermore, even though we do not and in many cases cannot know the names of our benefactors, our recognition that we owe them much serves to create and strengthen a sense of kinship or friendship with them. The more we feel and know that we have much in common with the past, the more keenly are we aware of the bonds that make us and keep us part of an enlarged community.

But in stressing that we are the recipients of the fruits of others' labors, I do not mean to suggest that we have only to sit back and take it. In fact, as anyone knows who has ever had to study hard, the liberal arts are no free good. We can enjoy them only by making them truly our own, and that unfortunately means only by taking pains, by laboring. If and when we succeed, to whatever extent, we then find ourselves in this surprising situation. Our sense of connection with others is much altered, even reduced. For the good we now possess turns out to be intensely private — *my* good — and the pleasure I feel from having achieved something especially fine is likewise something I can barely convey to another.

In short, the liberal arts send us conflicting and ambiguous messages. They remind us of how much we owe to others and inspire us with feelings of gratitude and respect for goods not of our making. At the same time, they encourage us to adopt a critical and independent-minded stance toward the customary and unexamined assumptions of our age. They train and invite us to turn inward, to think *our* thoughts, prompted by the example of critical and independent-minded predecessors.

These may fairly be regarded as some of the ways in which the arts are liberal, indeed liberating. This way of speaking should remind us that the liberal arts we are discussing now are hardly exhausted by the medievals' trivium and quadrivium: grammar, rhetoric and logic; arithmetic, geometry, astronomy and music. Likewise, I should note that the way I have been using the term "liberal" is quite removed from today's ordinary usage. "Oh," someone says, "he's liberal about things like that." The intended compliment suggests that the one being so characterized is open, nonjudgmental, prepared to live and let live. Liberal in that sense would also be close to "doing one's thing," but not just any old thing. After all, Cotton Mather and those other characters dressed up in Puritan costumes were, in a way, doing their own thing —very single-mindedly, in fact— but by the current usage of "liberal" they would have to be labeled "illiberal."

This vulgarized misunderstanding of the term, I am trying to suggest, misses the point. Those arts that were honored by being designated "liberal" were so singled out not because of their openness or indifference or neutrality. On the contrary, the liberal arts were believed (rightly or wrongly) to be indispensable means for individuals seeking a standard of human excellence. Beyond that, the liberal arts were thought to be of inestimable value for individuals seeking ways of measuring up to that standard of human excellence. That struggle for achievement would be the business of a lifetime, conducted in conjunction with others (as students, colleagues, and friends) and, of course, in solitude. The life devoted to that search and struggle might well be called "free."

I.

Starting, then, with this rough characterization, what can be said of the Founders' liberal arts? I propose to look for evidence, first, in the way they lived their lives, in the way they exhibited their sense of accountability to others and independence of others. Then I shall consider whether the Founders can be regarded as a model for others to follow, indeed whether they themselves had some model human type in mind. Finally, I shall examine their use of constitutions and institutions as means whereby an entire people could be shaped and made fit to govern themselves. In this last connection I shall look more closely at John Adams' deeply considered thoughts on popular education.

Let us begin with the most obvious fact. The Founders are known to us, first and foremost, because they were public men. As instigators of revolution, conductors of the new nation's military and foreign policies, reshapers of local and federal government, constitution makers and lawgivers, holders of high office and public trust: in these and similar respects their life-stories remind us that the Founders were emphatically political men pursuing public careers. Theirs was an age when a sealed letter was a standing provocation to the curious and malicious through whose hands the paper passed. Those priers were rewarded, almost without fail, for even the Founders' private correspondence was preoccupied with public affairs and political dealings. In an age when inns were few and far between (and execrable at that), domestic hospitality was often an extension of their political business and concerns. In a word, the Founders' lives seem suffused with politics and were lived in public view.

But there is another side as well, one equally noteworthy though less often commented upon. Although the Founders may appear to have lived and breathed politics, they often and loudly hankered for home. Early retirement was a favorite theme of theirs. However this may be understood — politics was not yet accepted as a full-time vocation in late eighteenth-century America —the fact of the matter is that they did go home and stay home, in the most famous cases in a country house or on a farm. Their retirement was notorious. Leaving behind the arena of politics (if not politics itself), they repeatedly proclaimed their satisfaction at having at long last been freed of public duties. Private life was a matter of reserve, withdrawal to a closed circle of relatives and intimates. With no long lenses of paparazzi to pry, the Founders could live out their lives as not-so-ordinary citizens under laws applicable to all and consented to by the citizenry at large. They were free men living at home among their kind.

Those life-stories can be viewed as enactments of the Founders' liberality. They did not hesitate to give their all to public purposes. Youth, fortune, health, sometimes life itself, were sacrificed to their ambition to serve in a public cause that would bring their fellows liberty and themselves fame. The models of Plutarch's *Lives* were vivid and present to mind. None of this, however, led to the extinction of the private man. For their model of excellence, with all its distinctive Roman colorings, called as well for a life that knew its own business and cared for it. (Of how many of our current public figures can we even entertain a benign suspicion that there is something solidly individual and private behind the cosmetician's and image-maker's art?) In this respect, then, the core of the pursuit of happiness might seem no larger than domestic tranquillity itself. And what is the measurable diameter of that? From hearth to property line? The width of a congenial dining table surrounded by friends? The distance from reading chair to bookshelf?

Nor were these the only aspects of their liberality. Consider their concern to give an account of their principles and acts not only to their constituents and contemporaries but to us, their successors and descendants. Accountability was a pervasive principle with them; it informed their political structures, their laws, and their lives. In an age that had to conduct most of its business in writing — an age that lacked photocopier, typewriter, even carbon paper — the leading and most active Founders made it their business to take the time to copy out with quill and ink a record of the letters they sent, to keep memoranda of decisive meetings and conversations, to carefully catalogue their incoming mail. The archivist-founder tended to the record of his public life taken as a whole because it was by that totality that he wished to be judged.

At the same time it is important to note that these popular leaders of a democratic revolution were not simply driven by whatever happened to be generally popular. Although they surely differed in their individual psychic makeups, in the relative importance they assigned to immediate popular acclaim, none of them (I believe) was prepared simply to settle for that. Just as they were not clones of one another, still less were they mindless echoes of public sentiment. As popular politicians they necessarily had to take popular feelings and concerns to heart. Some of them were masters at sensing and using those movements in public sentiment. But they were also their own men. The standards of judgment, the notions of fitness and rightness that they brought to bear in the controversies of their age were by no means infallible or beyond reproach. They were, however, their own standards — earned, one might say, through long observation, experience, and study.

In these respects, too, the Founders showed their liberal arts. Working for and with a larger public, they were not swallowed up by it. Having the courage and candor and desire to be judged by others, they did not lose themselves, their inner core of principle and character, in the process. At their best moments those Founders showed the qualities of genuinely free men both in what they were willing to give to others and in what they were insistent on keeping for themselves. To see them whole, we need to see both their public and their private faces.

II.

This rare blend of public commitment and private self-sufficiency might well be admired — and then pushed aside as a rare piece of good fortune with no special relevance for us or our present situation. Or, as beginning students sometimes like to say of things vaguely interesting and strange, "All that is merely academic." That some of the Founders were able to lead such lives may have been their good luck, and ours as well inasmuch as their success generated continuing benefits for us. But can such a human type matter today as a model for us? Can the fostering of such human beings be the goal of an entire political and social system?

Our first, indeed sound, inclination is to doubt that, for a number of reasons. Theirs, after all, is a world beyond our recall. Many features of a rapidly passing old order still figured large in the world of their youth, but not for much longer. Although aristocratic notions and tastes, if not aristocracy itself, were more than relics in eighteenth-century America, today even their memory is lost in mist. Moreover, the excitement and hopes stirred by the leading thinkers of the age energized those colonial youths to work for a saner, more rational regime with a kind of confidence that many today would find naive or quaint. Then, too, it is at least problematic whether the critical elements in the Founders' success could be an object of planning. At bottom, their distinctiveness and distinction may come down to a question of human character. They had special moral tastes, only some of which can be traced to the enlightened Augustan age in which they grew up. They had peculiar individual temperaments; and of course they had singular abilities with which they might go about trying to fulfill their inclinations. All these considerations suggest that theirs was a special case and that they were not likely candidates for routine replication, let alone on a continental scale.

Against this interpretation, however, are some of the explicit and implicit views of the Founders themselves. It is certain — one of the few things that can be so asserted about them — that they did not regard the *proper* peopling of America as something that could be safely left to chance. America may well have been a kind of promised land in the eyes of many, the overflowing cornucopia of a benign providence, but a trust in the promiscuous productions of nature did not run far or deep. Most emphatically was this the case in matters of human upbringing. America, after all, was home to the most vivid and arresting exemplars of what the philosophical anthropologists of the eighteenth century thought of as natural man. Those Indians might be envied for their freedom, admired for their courage, and the like; but for the Founders they were and remained savages. In thinking about the kinds of human beings who would be required if their proposed social and political order were to flourish, the Founders knew that it was not enough to let nature take its course.

Flying to the opposite extreme was equally unsatisfactory. The high civilization or culture of Europe carried its own cautionary lessons. Refinement, beauty, grace, all those aristocratic qualities that can make life easy, had no necessary relation to the conditions that made men free. Think of Versailles with its palace, its gardens, its superb vistas. The staggering statement that it makes to every beholder conveys not only grandeur, ambition, and pride, but a breathtaking engrossing of the wealth and labor of an entire kingdom. The other side of the Sun King's splendor was the misery and oppression of his subjects.

It appeared to come down to this: To do nothing was to coast down the road to barbarism, but to purchase grandeur at any cost was to condemn most of society to a sentence of serfdom. As far as the Founders were concerned, neither outcome was to be endured. At the same time they entertained no illusions that Everyman could become his own Thomas Jefferson or Benjamin Franklin. The liberal arts *they* cultivated and enjoyed could only very roughly and simply be imitated by the bulk of the citizenry. Instead, the Founders offered another way, more profitable and honorable to mankind at large and more conformable to their own large designs. They proposed using nature not for its purposes but theirs. They devised institutions and political arrangements that might shape and foster the traits and habits of mind most needed. In such ways the Founders sought to make it possible for their successors to secure the object of their original design. This is hardly a case of the dead hand of the past constraining us from pursuing our current notions of happiness, for (in truth) parchment barriers — even those handcrafted by the Founders — are only parchment barriers. Rather, the constitutional regime that is their legacy invites its beneficiaries to aspire to be the kind of people who deserve such opportunities. It is this subtle but insistent message that best displays the Founders' liberal arts.

In speaking of the Founders' design I have been content to emphasize the universal reach of their plans, the sense in which all kinds of men and women over the entire world might choose to take heart from those early efforts. After all, the Founders —even those of them who owned men — were by no means believers in *natural* slavery. In principle all peoples were capable of benefitting from their liberal arts because, as Jefferson maintained to his dying day, "the mass of mankind has not been born with saddles on their backs, nor a favored few booted and spurred, ready to ride them legitimately, by the grace of God. These are grounds of hope for others."[1]

None of this, however, persuaded the Founders that they had any abiding duty to make strenuous efforts on other people's behalf. The cause of human liberty and self-government would best be served by promoting and securing that cause at home in America. It seemed undeniable to those Founders that American circumstances and the character of the American people made success more likely here than elsewhere. But even that favorable prospect was only relative to other situations in their age; there was no guarantee. The great cause, as well as their personal stake in it, depended on the Founders' ability to fit people and institutions, habits and beliefs, in a mutually reinforcing system. With the limited time available to them, they could at best only lay the foundations.

Considering the urgency of their self-appointed task, one is inclined to wonder about the use those Founders may have made of the tools at hand. Family structures, religious institutions, the whole complex of existing customs: How serviceable were these to the Founders' purposes? How energetically were they put to use by them? I am hard pressed to reach any simple, even clear, answers. In some respects, it is fair to say, those features of social life may have contributed to the Founders' political difficulties more than they helped to ease them. At any rate, one can readily imagine how family, church, and habit might well be *il*liberal or make new hopes and plans seem wild and futile. For those features of social life work powerfully against rapid change — in part because of their intrinsic parochialism, in part because they take so much of their bearings from the larger social and political setting in which they find themselves.

To the extent, then, that the Founders had very large plans in mind, their reliance on these social forces might have been contingent on their first effecting some far-reaching political changes. As political men with a broadly revolutionary and liberal program, they may have understood this order of causes. Once they had succeeded in altering and redirecting the general setting, the Founders might then have expected family, religion, and custom to work their good effects in shaping the citizens of their new social and political order. Even in the so-called Age of Reason, some revolutionaries understood why these powerful forces could be neither scorned nor scuttled.

III.

All this may strike you as remote from that activity with which we most often and vividly associate the names of the Founders, the process by which they created the Constitution of the United States and helped bring it to life. Consider, if you will, not only what the Constitution speaks of, but that about which it seems to be silent. To begin with, it is obvious to even the hastiest reader that the focus of that document is on structures and procedures. What shall be the form and shape of the new government? What powers shall be assigned, and to whom? How and within what limits shall the business of governance proceed? The overwhelming concern is with means. Apart from the few famous words of the Preamble there is almost total silence about the great ends that are being sought or preserved through this choice of means.

This striking proportion (or disproportion) invites continuing reflection, for it is improbable that this feature of the Constitution is owing to either chance or neglect. To some extent the objectives of the American political union were already clear and widely shared and needed no further elaboration. The memorable pronouncements of the Revolutionary struggle had sketched in bold broad characters what the Americans hoped to keep or gain. But in many interesting respects the great ends of union were implicit as well in the formal structures being proposed by the Constitutional Convention of 1787. Here the silences of the original document are quite audible. Consider the following features. It is clear from its provisions that the Constitution has in view an economy as long and broad as the entire United States of America. Within that vast market there are to be no significant *political* barriers to the free movement of human beings, goods, information, or money. Yet if Americans are to be active participants in a single market, in no sense are they to be adherents of a single creed. The then-common examples and aspirations of an established national church are rejected out of hand for reasons left for us to imagine or surmise. Further, the Constitution locates with tolerable precision who in the new government shall be responsible for determining the nation's foreign and military policies. Yet there is not a word to suggest that anyone is charged with determining the kind of life *worth* defending. Indeed, one is left with an overwhelming sense that a vast new arena has been created out of the core of British North America, an arena in which diversities of almost any kind may live, let live, and ultimately either come to find some firm and lasting common ground — or fail.

Nothing perhaps was more doubtful in 1776, in 1787, in 1812, or in 1861, than whether the Americans were to be a nation. That outcome still lay in the future. For what was at stake was something more than an alliance of convenience and something other than a mechanical reproduction of look-alikes. At issue was the capacity of the new American regime to foster a character authentically national and genuinely worthy. Could this mixture of diverse, divided, and suspicious people be assimilated to some new standard of democratic worthiness? That depended not only on the outcome of wars that lay ahead but on a host of less bloody and less noted triumphs and failures.

It was the rare Washington who from the outset saw a *national* task in trying to form such continental characters on American soil. His early but frustrated efforts to promote a national university pointed others to appropriate means, but the congressional will could not be brought further than to establish an academy at West Point. More commonly — and not so commonly at that — the task of forming a people fit for self-governance was conceived as a challenge for individual states to rise to. It is here that we see some of the Founders exerting all their liberal arts. The efforts of Thomas Jefferson first to reform the College of William and Mary, then to establish a system of publicly supported education at all levels, and finally to create a new university at Charlottesville are well known. James Madison's efforts in these projects as well as his interest in Kentucky's ambitious educational plans replicate his friend's reasons and objectives. For both of these Founders it was axiomatic that every class in society had a stake in the kinds of educational institutions that "give to the human mind its highest improvements, and to every Country its truest and most durable celebrity."[2]

This emphasis upon the way in which a people earns and deserves self-respect is especially marked in the writings of John Adams. It expresses itself in the famous chapter V, section II, which he drafted for the Massachusetts Constitution of 1780, proclaiming the duty of legislators and magistrates "to cherish the interests of literature and the sciences, and all seminaries of them." There is no doubt that by "cherish" Adams meant "pay for." At least as important as the fact that there be a school was that it be seen as a public charge. Thereby, Adams thought, the whole people would gain respect in their own eyes; they would "be taught to reverence themselves, instead of adoring their servants, their generals, admirals, bishops, and statesmen."[3] No more authentic display of popular "power and majesty" could be imagined than the continued existence of free republican government.[4] For that happy effect, President Adams thought, would bear powerful witness to its root cause — a people fit for self-governance. Here, at last, was a genuine object of national pride.

A corollary of all this is that poverty should be no bar to the liberal education of youth. Just as the founding fathers of Massachusetts had required that every town of defined size support a full-time schoolmaster, so too would Adams treat "the preservation of the means of knowledge, among the lowest ranks" as a public utility.[5] Indeed, he did not hesitate to assert that the rich in particular had a special interest in the education of the poor, and "that to a humane and generous mind, no expence for this purpose would be thought extravagant."

Despite this emphatic talk of public support for schools, Adams hardly limited his educational field of vision to those conventional means of instruction. Education would proceed on a broader front than the classroom and lecture hall. I would even go so far as to say that for John Adams (as for Thomas Jefferson) the greater part of a people's education would come not from school but from their active participation in their own governance. By this I mean more than that the people might learn from their mistakes, or that experience might perhaps make them wiser if sadder. Of all this, John Adams said little. Rather, he stressed how a properly founded constitutional system "introduces knowledge among the People, and inspires them with a conscious dignity, becoming Freemen." He envisioned a setting in which the usually divisive strivings of individual emulation and ambition might provoke more civil behavior.[6]

None of this bespeaks faith in some magical transformation of individuals or of the people as a whole. Rather, the thought and expectation refer to the enlarged opportunities ordinary and not-so-ordinary folk would have under republican institutions. The comparative advantage of New England— so obvious to Adams at the Second Continental Congress —turned in no small measure on its system of local government. He was quick to note how that system, "empowering Towns to assemble, choose officers, make Laws, mend roads, and twenty other Things, gives every Man an opportunity of shewing and improving that Education which he received at Colledge or at school, and makes Knowledge and Dexterity at public Business common."[7] In short, political participation in and of itself contributes to an education. The great value of a popularly elected assembly is not only that it "gives free access to the whole nation" and gives voice to all its wants and wishes. Beyond that, it "affords opportunities of exertion to genius, though in obscurity, and gives full scope to all the faculties of man; it opens a passage for every speculation to the legislature, to administration, and to the public; it gives a universal energy to the human character, in every part of the state, such as never can be obtained in a monarchy."[8] Where James Madison held the protection of diverse human faculties to be the first object of government, John Adams held the enlargement and enlivening of those faculties to be the great object of republican education broadly conceived.

This sense of grander objectives, of goods that extend beyond political independence — indeed, beyond politics — is displayed nowhere more clearly than in the correspondence between anxious parents. Abigail Adams, left alone on the farm to provide for their children's education, was all too aware of her own inadequacies relative to her expectations. The lesson she drew was also clear.

From now on, the education of American daughters could no more be neglected than the education of American sons. "If we mean to have Heroes, Statesmen and Philosophers, we should have learned women."[9] John could only agree; and when he in turn was left alone to provide for their sons' education in Holland, he showed that he too had no little plans. He complained of his trouble in trying to find suitable schools for young Charles and John Quincy. "I should not wish to have Children, educated in the common Schools in this Country, where a littleness of Soul is notorious. . . .Their is besides a general Littleness arising from the incessant Contemplation of Stivers and Doits, which pervades the whole People." It was not that Adams held frugality or industry in contempt. He well understood how necessary close attention to expenditures might be in order to maintain one's independence. But the preoccupations of merchants and traders, and the rules by which they governed their behavior, were objects "that I hope none of my Children will ever aim at."[10]

More fitting for the younger Adamses would be those very subjects in which John Adams dared not now indulge. His rambles among the beauties and refinements of Paris and Versailles brought these thoughts vividly to his mind. "The Science of Government it is my Duty to study, more than all other Sciences: the Art of Legislation and Administration and Negotiation, ought to take Place, indeed to exclude in a manner all other Arts —I must study Politicks and War that my sons may have liberty to study Mathematicks and Philosophy. My sons ought to study Mathematicks and Philosophy, Geography, natural History, Naval Architecture, navigation, Commerce and Agriculture, in order to give their Children a right to study Painting, Poetry, Musick, Architecture, Statuary, Tapestry and Porcelaine."[11] Once again, John Adams showed that the establishment of good government, however much the focus of his thoughts and energies, was but the means to a larger and more richly human life.

Notwithstanding the nobility and beauty of this vision, John Adams never let it distract him for long from an immediate concern with governance. His reasons are plain enough to see. Almost everything that might enlarge the soul and lend dignity to man still presupposed a political order; for without some auxiliary system of holding human prejudices, appetites, and passions in check, neither reason nor conscience could prevail. Left to fend for themselves, the most eligible plans for improvement and reformation would be hectored to death by the envious and ambitious. Adams believed that for all the good education might do, it still could not suffice against that brute fact, "the great and important and melancholy Truth . . . that all Men would be Tyrants if they could."[12] Indeed, far from being sufficient to contain political dangers, education might make matters worse. In a defectively organized government— defective because too simple or "unballanced"—the "Influence of general Science would be especially baneful." By raising the level of competence without correspondingly raising the level of character, education would be multiplying the "number of able and ambitious Men, who would only understand the better, how to worry one another with greater Art and dexterity."[13] Nor would the heightened conscientiousness of religious men in such a flawed political setting ease the pain; their earnestness might only intensify their uncivil single-mindedness.

As a result, Adams was impelled to return to his point of departure. By all means promote knowledge and benevolence as much as possible; but by no means count on "seeing them sufficiently general for the security of society." From first to last, he was intent on "seeking institutions which may supply in some degree the defect." To the extent that "knowledge, virtue, and benevolence" increased through education, mankind would be confirmed in belief in the good sense of the republicanism of John Adams. They, like him, would hold to "the opinion of the necessity of preserving and strengthening the dikes against the ocean, its tides and storms." Even a revolutionary people, hot for liberty, needed to be redoubled in their resolve to adhere to "the true principles." That necessary task would proceed by spreading "light" wherever possible and, "at least in the greatest number," by enlisting "prejudice, passion, and private interest . . . on the side of truth."[14] Here, Adams thought, was a continuing field for the education and the educational efforts of the few and the many. Perhaps this comes close enough to expressing the educational thought of the Founders: no one's needs could be ignored, no one's contributions could be spared.

IV.

The relevance of the Founders' thought and liberal arts to our situation today is far from being obvious or clear. They were, let us never forget, reared under a system of government they overthrew or radically revised. Those qualities of mind and pen for which we may admire them most also owed much to modes of thinking and interacting that the Founders' political success has rendered less likely or even unsuitable. Whether their political foresight also took in those kinds of changes, changes that would call for another kind of compensatory education, I cannot say.

More obvious to us and more fit for emulation by us is their keen awareness of the relation between general education and political independence, between the moral tastes (what we today might call the attitudes) of a population and their capacity to be and remain their own masters. Exhortation, indoctrination, and civic rituals might all make some contributions toward creating a public of fellow citizens, but for none of the Founders did those devices hold talismanic powers. At bottom, sound prejudices could support sound reasons, but prejudice and passion were no substitutes for reason. Accordingly, just as self-governance posed the greatest challenge to mankind, so would its success stand as the greatest compliment to the species. It is just shy of astonishing to reflect that those unsentimental Founders, intent on taking men as they are, nonetheless thought they had cause for hope. Their reasons for thinking so are still worth pondering.

Their grounds for hope had little or nothing to do with their adherence to a general philosophy of optimism, or with a belief in a benign human nature, or with a doctrinal assumption that Americans were somehow exempt from the historic failings of their forebears. These thumbnail characterizations of the men of '76 and '87, once beloved by textbook writers and their student readers, have little basis in reality — at least as far as the leading Founders are concerned. Nor was hope for their revolutionary project limited to the Jeffersonians among them, as distinguished from sour Federalists caught in their own net of paranoia and ideology. This is another tribute to the ingenuity of latter-day scholarship, but it too misses what the Founders themselves recognized as their common ground.

They agreed that Americans were no better than other human beings and yet had better opportunities than others had even imagined. Those singular circumstances consisted as much in what was missing from America — what did not require overcoming — as in the positive qualities of men, land, and institutions. Together, they formed an unprecedented opportunity to show what might be possible for nonangelic men without benefit of special revelation. It was not a case of making a whole new beginning, going back as it were to the First Pair. Yet there was a possibility of making a new order of the ages and of doing so in a way that might serve as a model for those less fortunately situated and as an inspiration for those others to do better for themselves.

The education of the Americans was thus both a conservative task and a revolutionary challenge. By better preparing the people at large for their principal business, self-governance, American education would at one and the same time be securing domestic tranquillity and demonstrating that the cause of liberty was a practical ideal. In this respect the Founders were themselves teachers. By showing how considerations of self-interest might be joined to a philanthropic impulse, they hoped to teach their successors a useful lesson. The career of the American people need suffer from neither mean-spirited calculation nor grandiose futility. Learning how to avoid both of those extremes in the conduct of their domestic and foreign affairs would be a necessary lesson for each generation to master for itself.

In creating an institutional environment that would promote and protect that learning, the Founders showed their liberal arts at their best. They worked to establish institutions of education as well as institutions of self-governance. They hoped for leaders with rare qualities as well as for a people capable of learning from their own experiences. Finally, they left us a legacy of aspirations as well as a reminder that we ought not always to settle for the merely customary and familiar. From today's vantage point their work and legacy seem markedly incomplete, for their liberal arts require the continued contribution of our own liberal arts. And that, I believe, was precisely what they had in mind.

Notes

1. Thomas Jefferson to Roger C. Weightman, 24 June 1826.
2. James Madison to W.T. Barry, 4 Aug. 1792.
3. John Adams to John Jebb, 10 Sept. 1785.
4. John Adams, Inaugural Address, 4 Mar. 1797.
5. John Adams, "A Dissertation on the Canon and the Feudal Law," no. 3, 30 Sept. 1765.
6. John Adams, "Thoughts on Government," Apr. 1776.
7. John Adams to Abigail Adams, 29 Oct. 1775.
8. John Adams, Preface to *Defence of the Constitutions of Government of the United States of America*, 1787.
9. Abigail Adams to John Adams, 14 Aug. 1776.
10. John Adams to Abigail Adams, 18 Dec. 1780.
11. John Adams to Abigail Adams, post-12 May 1780.
12. John Adams, "U," nos. 6-7, 29 and post-29 Aug. 1763.
13. John Adams to Benjamin Rush, 19 June 1789.
14. John Adams to Samuel Adams, 18 Oct. 1790.

Chapter 2

Neutral Principles and Some First Amendment Problems

Robert Bork
American Enterprise Institute

A persistently disturbing aspect of constitutional law is its lack of theory, a lack which is manifest not merely in the work of the courts but in the public, professional, and even scholarly discussion of the topic. The result, of course, is that courts are without effective criteria and, therefore we have come to expect that the nature of the Constitution will change, often quite dramatically, as the personnel of the Supreme Court change. In the present state of affairs that expectation is inevitable, but it is nevertheless deplorable.

The remarks that follow do not, of course, offer a general theory of constitutional law. They are more properly viewed as ranging shots, an attempt to establish the necessity for theory and to take the argument of how constitutional doctrine centers upon the implications of Professor Herbert Wechsler's concept of "neutral principles," and to apply those implications to some important and much-debated problems in the interpretation of the First Amendment. The style is informal since these remarks were originally lectures and I have not thought it worthwhile to convert these speculations and arguments into a heavily researched, balanced and thorough presentation, for that would result in a book.

The Supreme Court and the Demand for Principle

The subject of the lengthy and often acrimonious debate about the proper role of the Supreme Court under the Constitution is one that preoccupies many people these days: when is authority legitimate? I find it convenient to discuss that question in the context of the Warren Court and its works simply because the Warren Court posed the issue in acute form. The issue did not disappear along with the era of the Warren Court majorities, however. It arises when any court either exercises or declines to exercise the power to invalidate any act of another branch of government. The Supreme Court is a major power center, and we must ask when its power should be used and when it should be withheld.

Our starting place, inevitably, is Professor Wechsler's argument that the Court must not be merely a "naked power organ," which means that its decisions must be controlled by principle.[1] "A principled decision," according to Wechsler, "is one that rests on reasons with respect to all the issues in a case, reasons that in their generality and their neutrality transcend any immediate result that is involved."[2]

Wechsler chose the term "neutral principles" to capsulate his argument, though he recognizes that the legal principle to be applied is itself never neutral because it embodies a choice of one value rather than another. Wechsler asked for the neutral application of principles, which is a requirement, as Professor Louis L. Jaffe puts it, that the judge "sincerely believe in the principle upon which he purports to rest his decision." "The judge," says Jaffe, "must believe in the validity of the reasons given for the decision at least in the sense that he is prepared to apply them to a later case which he cannot honestly distinguish."[3] He must not, that is, decide lawlessly. But is the demand for neutrality in judges merely another value choice, one that is no more principled than any other? I think not, but to prove it we must rehearse fundamentals. This is familiar terrain but important and still debated.

The requirement that the Court be principled arises from the resolution of the seeming anomaly of judicial supremacy in a democratic society. If the judiciary really is supreme, able to rule when and as it sees fit, the society is not democratic. The anomaly is dissipated, however, by the model of government embodied in the structure of the Constitution, a model upon which popular consent to limited government by the Supreme Court also rests. This model we may for convenience, though perhaps not with total accuracy, call "Madisonian."[4]

A Madisonian system is not completely democratic, if by "democratic" we mean completely majoritarian. It assumes that in wide areas of life majorities are entitled to rule for no better reason than that they are majorities. We need not pause here to examine the philosophical underpinnings of that assumption since it is a "given" in our society; nor need we worry that "majority" is a term of art meaning often no more than the shifting combinations of minorities that add up to temporary majorities in the legislature. That majorities are so constituted is inevitable. In any case, one essential premise of the Madisonian model is majoritarianism. The model has also a counter-majoritarian premise, however, for it assumes there are some areas of life a majority should not control. There are some things a majority should not do to us no matter how democratically it decides to do them. These are areas properly left to individual freedom, and coercion by the majority in these aspects of life is tyranny.

Some see the model as containing an inherent, perhaps an insoluble, dilemma.[5] Majority tyranny occurs if legislation invades the areas properly left to individual freedom. Minority tyranny occurs if the majority is prevented from ruling where its power is legitimate. Yet, quite obviously, neither the majority nor the minority can be trusted to define the freedom of the other. This dilemma is resolved in constitutional theory, and in popular understanding, by the Supreme Court's power to define both majority and minority freedom through the interpretation of the Constitution. Society consents to be ruled undemocratically within defined areas by certain enduring principles believed to be stated in, and placed beyond the reach of majorities by, the Constitution.

But this resolution of the dilemma imposes severe requirements upon the Court. For it follows that the Court's power is legitimate only if it has, and can demonstrate in reasoned opinions that it has, a valid theory, derived from the Constitution, of the respective spheres of majority and minority freedom. If it does not have such a theory but actually follows its own predilections, the Court violates the postulates of the Madisonian model that alone justifies its power. It then necessarily abets the tyranny either of the majority or of the minority.

This argument is central to the issue of legitimate authority because the Supreme Court's power to govern rests upon popular acceptance of this model. Evidence that this is, in fact, the basis of the Court's power is to be gleaned everywhere in our culture. We need not canvass here such things as high school civics texts and newspaper commentary, for the most telling evidence may be found in the *U.S. Reports*. The Supreme Court regularly insists that its results, and most particularly its controversial results, do not spring from the mere will of the justices in the majority but are supported, indeed compelled, by a proper understanding of the *Constitution of the United States*. Value choices are attributed to the Founding Fathers, not to the Court. The way an institution advertises tells you what it thinks its customers demand.

This is, I think, the ultimate reason the Court must be principled. If it does not have and rigorously adhere to a valid and consistent theory of majority and minority freedoms based upon the Constitution, judicial supremacy, given the axioms of our system, is, precisely to that extent, illegitimate. The root of its illegitimacy is that it opens a chasm between the reality of the Court's performance and the constitutional and popular assumptions that give it power.

I do not mean to rest the argument entirely upon the popular understanding of the Court's function. Even if society generally should ultimately perceive what the Court is in fact doing and, having seen, prove content to have major policies determined by the unguided discretion of judges rather than by elected representatives, a principled judge would, I believe, continue to consider himself bound by an obligation to the document and to the structure of government that it prescribes. At least he would be bound so long as any litigant existed who demanded such adherence of him. I do not understand how, on any other theory of judicial obligation, the Court could, as it does now, protect voting rights if a large majority of the relevant constituency were willing to see some groups or individuals deprived of such rights. But even if I am wrong in that, at the very least an honest judge would owe it to the body politic to cease invoking the authority of the Constitution and to make explicit the imposition of his own will, for only then would we know whether the society understood enough of what is taking place to be said to have consented.

Judge J. Skelly Wright, in an argument resting on different premises, has severely criticized the advocates of principle. He defends the value-choosing role of the Warren Court, setting that Court in opposition to something he refers to as the "scholarly tradition," which criticizes that Court for its lack of principle.[6] A perceptive reader, sensitive to nuance, may suspect that the judge is rather out of sympathy with that tradition from such hints as his reference to "self-appointed scholastic mandarins."[7]

The "mandarins" of the academy anger the judge because they engage in "haughty derision of the Court's powers of analysis and reasoning."[8] Yet, curiously enough, Judge Wright makes no attempt to refute the charge but rather seems to adopt the technique of confession and avoidance. He seems to be arguing that a Court engaged in choosing fundamental values for society cannot be expected to produce principled decisions at the same time. Decisions first, principles later. One wonders, however, how the Court or the rest of us are to know that the decisions are correct or what they portend for the future if they are not accompanied by the principles that explain and justify them. And it would not be amiss to point out that quite often the principles required of the Warren Court's decisions never did put in an appearance. But Judge Wright's main point appears to be that value choice is the most important function of the Supreme Court, so that if we must take one or the other, and apparently we must, we should prefer a process of selecting values to one of constructing and articulating principles. His argument, I believe, boils down to a syllogism. I. The Supreme Court should "protect our constitutional rights and liberties." II. The Supreme Court must "make fundamental value choices" in order to "protect our constitutional rights and liberties." III. Therefore, the Supreme Court should "make fundamental value choices."[9]

The argument displays an all too common confusion. If we have constitutional rights and liberties already, rights and liberties specified by the Constitution,[10] the Court need make no fundamental value choices in order to protect them, and it certainly need not have difficulty enunciating principles. If, on the other hand, "constitutional rights and liberties" are not in some real sense specified by the Constitution but are the rights and liberties the Court chooses, on the basis of its own values, to give to us, then the conclusion was contained entirely in the major premise, and the judge's syllogism is no more than an assertion of what it purported to prove.

If I am correct so far, no argument that is both coherent and respectable can be made supporting a Supreme Court that "chooses fundamental values" because a

Court that makes rather than implements value choices cannot be squared with the presuppositions of a democratic society. The man who understands the issues and nevertheless insists upon the rightness of the Warren Court's performance ought also, if he is candid, to admit that he is prepared to sacrifice democratic process to his own moral views. He claims for the Supreme Court an institutionalized role as perpetrator of limited coups d'état.

Such a man occupies an impossible philosophic position. What can he say, for instance, of a Court that does not share his politics or his morality? I can think of nothing except the assertion that he will ignore the Court whenever he can get away with it and overthrow it if he can. In his view the Court has no legitimacy, and there is no reason any of us should obey it. And, this being the case, the advocate of a value-choosing Court must answer another difficult question. Why should the Court, a committee of nine lawyers, be the sole agent of change? The man who prefers results to processes has no reason to say that the Court is more legitimate than any other institution. If the Court will not listen, why not argue the case to some other group, say the Joint Chiefs of Staff, a body with rather better means for implementing its decisions?

We are driven to the conclusion that a legitimate Court must be controlled by principles exterior to the will of the justices. As my colleague Professor Alexander Bickel puts it, "The process of the coherent, analytically warranted, principled declaration of general norms alone justifies the Court's function. . . ."[11] Recognition of the need for principle is only the first step, but once that step is taken much more follows. Logic has a life of its own, and devotion to principle requires that we follow where logic leads.

Professor Bickel identifies Justice Frankfurter as the leading judicial proponent of principle but concedes that even Frankfurter never found a "rigorous general accord between judicial supremacy and democratic theory."[12] Judge Wright responds, "The leading commentators of the scholarly tradition have tried ever since to succeed where the justice failed."[13] As Judge Wright quite accurately suggests, the commentators have so far had no better luck than the Justice.

One reason, I think, is clear. We have not carried the idea of neutrality far enough. We have been talking about neutrality in the *application* of principles. If judges are to avoid imposing their own values upon the rest of us, however, they must be neutral as well in the *definition* and the *derivation* of principles.

It is easy enough to meet the requirement of neutral application by stating a principle so narrowly that no embarrassment need arise in applying it to all cases it subsumes, a tactic often urged by proponents of "judicial restraint." But that solves very little. It certainly does not protect the judge from the intrusion of his own values. The problem may be illustrated by *Griswold v. Connecticut*,[14] in many ways a typical decision of the Warren Court. *Griswold* struck down Connecticut's statute making it a crime, even for married couples, to use contraceptive devices. If we take the principle of the decision to be a statement that government may not interfere with any acts done in private, we need not even ask about the principle's dubious origin for we know at once that the Court will not apply it neutrally. The Court, we may confidently predict, is not going to throw constitutional protection around heroin use or sexual acts with a consenting minor. We can gain the possibility of neutral application by reframing the principle as a statement that government may not prohibit the use of contraceptives by married couples, but that is not enough. The question of neutral definition arises: Why does the principle extend only to married couples? Why, out of all forms of sexual behavior, only to the use of contraceptives? Why, out of all forms of behavior, only to sex? The question of neutral derivation also arises. What justifies any limitation upon legislatures in this area? What is the origin of any principle one may state?

To put the matter another way, if a neutral judge must demonstrate why principle *X* applies to cases *A* and *B* but not to case *C* (which is, I believe, the requirement laid down by Professors Wechsler and Jaffe), he must, by the same token, also explain why the principle is defined as *X* rather than as *X minus*, which could cover *A* but not cases *B* and *C*, or as *X plus*, which would cover all cases, *A*, *B*, and *C*. Similarly, he must explain why *X* is a proper principle of limitation on majority power at all. Why should he not choose *non-X*? If he may not choose lawlessly between cases in applying principle *X*, he may certainly not choose lawlessly in defining *X* or in choosing *X*, for principles are after all only organizations of cases into groups. To choose the principle and define it is to decide the cases.

It follows that the choice of "fundamental values" by the Court cannot be justified. Where constitutional materials do not clearly specify the value to be preferred, there is no principled way to prefer any claimed human value to any other. The judge must stick close to the text and the history, and their fair implications, and not construct new rights. The case just mentioned illustrates the point. The *Griswold* decision has been acclaimed by legal scholars as a major advance in constitutional law, a salutary demonstration of the Court's ability to protect fundamental human values. I regret to have to disagree, and my regret is all the more sincere because I once took the same position and did so in print.[15] In extenuation I can only say that at the time I thought, quite erroneously, that new basic rights could be derived logically by finding and extrapolating a more general principle of individual autonomy underlying the particular guarantees of the Bill of Rights.

The Court's *Griswold* opinion, by Justice Douglas, and the array of concurring opinions, by Justices Goldberg, White and Harlan, all failed to justify the derivation of any principle used to strike down the Connecticut anti-contraceptive statute or to define the scope of the principle. Justice Douglas, to whose opinion I must confine myself, began by pointing out that "specific guarantees in the Bill of Rights have penumbras, formed by emanations from those guarantees that help give them life and substance."16 Nothing is exceptional there. In the case

Justice Douglas cited, *NAACP v. Alabama*,[17] the state was held unable to force disclosure of membership lists because of the chilling effect upon the rights of assembly and political action of the NAACP's members. The penumbra was created solely to preserve a value central to the First Amendment, applied in this case through the Fourteenth Amendment. It had no life of its own as a right independent of the value specified by the First Amendment.

But Justice Douglas then performed a miracle of transubstantiation. He called the First Amendment's penumbra a protection of "privacy" and then asserted that other amendments create "zones of privacy."[18] He had no better reason to use the word "privacy" than that the individual is free within these zones, free to act in public as well as in private. None of these penumbral zones from the First, Third, Fourth, and Fifth Amendments, all of which he cited, along with the Ninth covered the case before him. One more leap was required. Justice Douglas asserted that these various "zones of privacy" created an independent right of privacy,[19] a right not lying within the penumbra of any specific amendment. He did not disclose, however, how a series of specified rights combined to create a new and unspecified right.

The *Griswold* opinion fails every test of neutrality. The derivation of the principle was utterly specious, and so was its definition. In fact, we are left with no idea of what the principle really forbids. Derivation and definition are interrelated here. Justice Douglas called the amendments and their penumbras "zones of privacy," though of course they are not that at all. They protect both private and public behavior and so would more properly be labeled "zones of freedom." If we follow Justice Douglas in his next step, these zones would then add up to an independent right of freedom, which is to say, a general constitutional right to be free of legal coercion, a manifest impossibility in any imaginable society.

Griswold, then, is an unprincipled decision, both in the way in which it derives a new constitutional right and in the way it defines that right, or rather fails to define it. We are left with no idea of the sweep of the right of privacy and hence no notion of the cases to which it may or may not be applied in the future. The truth is that the Court could not reach its result in *Griswold* through principle. The reason is obvious. Every clash between a minority claiming freedom and a majority claiming power to regulate involves a choice between the gratifications of the two groups. When the Constitution has not spoken, the Court will be able to find no scale, other than its own value preferences, upon which to weigh the respective claims to pleasure. Compare the facts of *Griswold* with a hypothetical suit by an electric utility company and one of its customers to void a smoke pollution ordinance as unconstitutional. The cases are identical.

In *Griswold* a husband and wife assert that they wish to have sexual relations without fear of unwanted children. The law impairs their sexual gratifications. The state can assert, and at one stage in that litigation did assert, that the majority finds the use of contraception immoral. Knowledge that it takes place and that the state makes no effort to inhibit it causes the majority anguish, impairs their gratifications.

The electrical company asserts that it wishes to produce electricity at low cost in order to reach a wide market and make profits. Its customer asserts that he wants a lower cost so that prices can be held low. The smoke pollution regulation impairs his and the company's stockholders' economic gratifications. The state can assert not only that the majority prefer clean air to lower prices, but also that the absence of the regulation impairs the majority's physical and aesthetic gratifications.

Neither case is covered specifically or by obvious implication in the Constitution. Unless we can distinguish forms of gratification, the only course for a principled Court is to let the majority have its way in both cases. It is clear that the Court cannot make the necessary distinction. There is no principled way to decide that one man's gratifications are more deserving of respect than another's or that one form of gratification is more worthy than another.[20] Why is sexual gratification more worthy than moral gratification? Why is sexual gratification nobler than economic gratification? There is no way of deciding these matters other than by reference to some system of moral or ethical values that has no objective or intrinsic validity of its own and about which men can and do differ. Where the Constitution does not embody the moral or ethical choice, the judge has no basis other than his own values upon which to set aside the community judgment embodied in the statute. That, by definition, is an inadequate basis for judicial supremacy. The issue of the community's moral and ethical values, the issue of the degree of pain an activity causes, are matters concluded by the passage and enforcement of the laws in question. The judiciary has no role to play other than that of applying the statutes in a fair and impartial manner.

One of my colleagues refers to this conclusion, not without sarcasm, as the "Equal Gratification Clause." The phrase is apt, and I accept it, though not the sarcasm. Equality of human gratifications, where the document does not impose a hierarchy, is an essential part of constitutional doctrine because of the necessity that judges be principled. To be perfectly clear on the subject, I repeat that the principle is not applicable to legislatures. Legislation requires value choice and cannot be principled in the sense under discussion. Courts must accept any value choice the legislature makes unless it clearly runs contrary to a choice made in the framing of the Constitution.

It follows, of course, that broad areas of constitutional law ought to be reformulated. Most obviously, it follows that substantive due process, revived by the *Griswold* case, is and always has been an improper doctrine. Substantive due process requires the Court to say, without guidance from the Constitution, which liberties or gratifications may be infringed by majorities and which may not. This means that *Griswold*'s antecedents were also wrongly decided, e.g., *Meyer v. Nebraska*,[21] which struck down a statute forbidding the teaching of subjects in any language other than English; *Pierce v. Society of Sisters*,[22] which set aside a statute compelling all Oregon school children to attend public schools; *Adkins v. Children's Hospital*,[23] which invalidated a statute of Congress authorizing a board to fix minimum wages for women and children in the District of Columbia; and *Lochner v. New York*,[24] which voided a statute fixing maximum hours of work for bakers. With some of these cases I am in political agreement, and perhaps *Pierce*'s result could be reached on acceptable grounds, but there is no justification for the Court's methods. In *Lochner*, Justice Peckham, defending liberty from what he conceived as a mere meddlesome interference, asked, "[A]re we all . . . at the mercy of legislative majorities?"[25] The correct answer, where the Constitution does not speak, must be "yes."

The argument so far also indicates that most of substantive equal protection is also improper. The modern Court, we need hardly be reminded, used the equal protection clause the way the old Court used the due process clause. The only change was in the values chosen for protection and the frequency with which the Court struck down laws.

The equal protection clause has two legitimate meanings. It can require formal procedural equality, and, because of its historical origins, it does require that government not discriminate along racial lines. But much more than that cannot properly be read into the clause. The bare concept of equality provides no guide for courts. All law discriminates and thereby creates inequality. The Supreme Court has no principled way of saying which nonracial inequalities are impermissible. What it has done, therefore, is to appeal to simplistic notions of "fairness" or to what it regards as "fundamental" interests in order to demand equality in some cases but not in others, thus choosing values and producing a line of cases as improper and as intellectually empty as *Griswold v. Connecticut*. Any casebook lists them, and the differing results cannot be explained on any ground other than the Court's preferences for particular values: *Skinner v. Oklahoma*[26] (a forbidden inequality exists when a state undertakes to sterilize robbers but not embezzlers); *Kotch v. Board of River Port Pilot Commissioners*[27] (no right to equality is infringed when a state grants pilots' licenses only to persons related by blood to existing pilots and denies licenses to persons otherwise as well qualified); *Goesaert v. Cleary*[28] (a state does not deny equality when it refuses to license women as bartenders unless they are the wives or daughters of male owners of licensed liquor establishments); *Railway Express Agency v. New York*[29] (a city may forbid truck owners to sell advertising space on their trucks as a distracting hazard to traffic safety though it permits owners to advertise their own business in that way); *Shapiro v. Thompson*[30] (a state denies equality if it pays welfare only to persons who have resided in the state for one year); *Levy v. Louisiana*[31] (a state may not limit actions for a parent's wrongful death to legitimate children and deny it to illegitimate children). The list could be extended, but the point is that the cases cannot be reconciled on any basis other than the justices' personal beliefs about what interests or gratifications ought to be protected.

Professor Wechsler notes that Justice Frankfurter expressed "disquietude that the line is often very thin between the cases in which the Court felt compelled to abstain from adjudication because of their 'political' nature, and the cases that so frequently arise in applying the concepts of 'liberty' and 'equality'."[32] The line is not very thin; it is nonexistent. There is no principled way in which anyone can define the spheres in which liberty is required and the spheres in which equality is required. These are matters of morality, of judgment, of prudence. They belong, therefore, to the political community. In the fullest sense, these are political questions.

We may now be in a position to discuss certain of the problems of legitimacy raised by Professor Wechsler. Central to his worries was the Supreme Court's decision in *Brown v. Board of Education.*[33] Wechsler said he had great difficulty framing a neutral principle to support the *Brown* decision, though he thoroughly approved of its result on moral and political grounds. It has long been obvious that the case does not rest upon the grounds advanced in Chief Justice Warren's opinion, the specially harmful effects of enforced school segregation upon black children. That much, as Wechsler and others point out, is made plain by the per curiam decisions that followed outlawing segregated public beaches, public golf courses and the like. The principle in operation may be that government may not employ race as a classification. But the genesis of the principle is unclear.

Wechsler states that his problem with the segregation cases is not that:

> History does not confirm that an agreed purpose of the Fourteenth Amendment was to forbid separate schools or that there is important evidence that many thought the contrary; the words are general and leave room for expanding content as time passes and conditions change.[34]

The words are general but surely that would not permit us to escape the framers' intent if it were clear. If the legislative history revealed a consensus about segregation in schooling and all the other relations in life, I do not see how the Court could escape the choices revealed and substitute its own, even though the words are general and conditions have changed. It is the fact that history does not reveal detailed choices concerning such matters that permits, indeed requires, resort to other modes of interpretation.

Wechsler notes that *Brown* has to do with freedom to associate and freedom not to associate, and he thinks that a principle must be found that solves the following dilemma:

> [I]f the freedom of association is denied by segregation, integration forces an association upon those for whom it is unpleasant or repugnant. Is this not the heart of the issue involved, a conflict in human claims of high dimension. . . . Given a situation where the state must practically choose between denying the association to those individuals who wish it or imposing it on those who would avoid it, is there a basis in neutral principles for holding that the Constitution demands that the claims for asso-

ciation should prevail? I should like to think there is, but I confess that I have not yet written the opinion. To write it is for me the challenge of the school-segregation cases.[35]

It is extremely unlikely that Professor Wechsler ever will be able to write that opinion to his own satisfaction. He has framed the issue in insoluble terms by calling it a "conflict between human claims of high dimension," which is to say that it requires a judicial choice between rival gratifications in order to find a fundamental human right. So viewed it is the same case as *Griswold v. Connecticut* and not susceptible of principled resolution.

A resolution that seems to me more plausible is supported rather than troubled by the need for neutrality. A court required to decide *Brown* would perceive two crucial facts about the history of the Fourteenth Amendment. First, the men who put the amendment in the Constitution intended that the Supreme Court should secure against government action some large measure of racial equality. That is certainly the core meaning of the amendment. Second, those same men were not agreed about what the concept of racial equality requires. Many or most of them had not even thought the matter through. Almost certainly, even individuals among them held such views as that blacks were entitled to purchase property from any willing seller but not to attend integrated schools, or that they were entitled to serve on juries but not to intermarry with whites, or that they were entitled to equal physical facilities but that the facilities should be separate, and so on through the endless anomalies and inconsistencies with which moral positions so frequently abound. The Court cannot conceivably know how these long-dead men would have resolved these issues had they considered, debated and voted on each of them. Perhaps it was precisely because they could not resolve them that they took refuge in the majestic and ambiguous formula: the equal protection of the laws.

But one thing the Court does know: it was intended to enforce a core idea of black equality against governmental discrimination. And the Court, because it must be neutral, cannot pick and choose between competing gratifications and, likewise, cannot write the detailed code the framers omitted, requiring equality in this case but not in another. The Court must, for that reason, choose a general principle of equality that applies to all cases. For the same reason, the Court cannot decide that physical equality is important but psychological equality is not. Thus, the no-state-enforced-discrimination rule of *Brown* must overturn and replace the separate-but-equal doctrine of *Plessy v. Ferguson*. The same result might be reached on an alternative ground. If the Court found that it was incapable as an institution of policing the issue of the physical equality of separate facilities, the variables being insufficiently comparable and the cases too many, it might fashion a no-segregation rule as the only feasible means of assuring even physical equality.

In either case, the value choice (or, perhaps more accurately, the value impulse) of the Fourteenth Amendment is fleshed out and made into a legal rule not by moral precept, not by a determination that claims for association prevail over claims for separation as a general matter, still less by consideration of psychological test results, but on purely juridical grounds.

I doubt, however, that it is possible to find neutral principles capable of supporting some of the other decisions that trouble Professor Wechsler. An example is *Shelley v. Kraemer*,[36] which held that the Fourteenth Amendment forbids state court enforcement of a private, racially restrictive covenant. Although the amendment speaks only of denials of equal protection of the laws by the state, Chief Justice Vinson's opinion said that judicial enforcement of a private person's discriminatory choice constituted the requisite state action. The decision was, of course, not neutral in that the Court was most clearly not prepared to apply the principle to cases it could not honestly distinguish. Any dispute between private persons about absolutely any aspect of life can be brought to a court by one of the parties; and, if race is involved, the rule of *Shelley* would require the court to deny the freedom of any individual to discriminate in the conduct of any part of his affairs simply because the contrary result would be state enforcement of discrimination. The principle would apply not merely to the cases hypothesized by Professor Wechsler, i.e. the inability of the state to effectuate a will that draws a racial line or to vindicate the privacy of property against a trespasser excluded because of the homeowner's racial preferences, but to any situation in which the person claiming freedom in any relationship had a racial motivation.

That much is the common objection to *Shelley v. Kraemer*, but the trouble with the decision goes deeper. Professor Louis Henkin has suggested that we view the case as correctly decided, accept the principle that must necessarily underline it if it is respectable law and proceed to apply that principle:

> Generally, the equal protection clause precludes state enforcement of private discrimination. There is, however, a small area of liberty favored by the Constitution even over claims to equality. Rights of liberty and property, of privacy and voluntary association, must be balanced in close cases, against the right not to have the state enforce discrimination against the victim. In the few instances in which the right to discriminate is protected or preferred by the Constitution, the state may enforce it.[37]

This attempt to rehabilitate *Shelley* by applying its principle honestly demonstrates rather clearly why neutrality in the application of principle is not enough. Professor Henkin's proposal fails the test of the neutral derivation of principle. It converts an amendment whose text and history clearly show it to be aimed only at governmental discrimination into a sweeping prohibition of private discrimination. There is no warrant anywhere for that conversion. The judge's power to govern does not become more legitimate if he is constrained to apply his principle to all cases but is free to make up his own principles. Matters are only made worse by Professor Henkin's suggestion that the judge introduce a small number of exceptions for cases where liberty is more important than equality, for now even the possibility of neutrality in the application of principle is lost. The judge cannot find in the Fourteenth Amendment or its history any choices between equality and freedom in private affairs. The judge, if he were to undertake this task, would be choosing, as in *Griswold v. Connecticut*, between competing gratifications without constitutional guidance. Indeed, Professor Henkin's description of the process shows that the task he would assign is legislative:

> The balance may be struck differently at different times, reflecting differences in prevailing philosophy and the continuing movement from laissez-faire government toward welfare and meliorism. The changes in prevailing philosophy themselves may sum up the judgment of judges as to how the conscience of our society weighs the competing needs and claims of liberty and equality in time and context, the adequacy of progress toward equality as a result of social and economic forces, the effect of lack of progress on the life of the Negro and, perhaps, on the image of the United States, and the role of official state forces in advancing or retarding this progress.[38]

In short, after considering everything a legislator might consider, the judge is to write a detailed code of private race relations. Starting with an attempt to justify *Shelley* on grounds of neutral principle, the argument rather curiously arrives at a position in which neutrality in the derivation, definition and application of principle is impossible and the wrong institution is governing society.

The argument thus far claims that, cases of rare discrimination aside, it is always a mistake for the Court to try to construct substantive individual rights under the due process or the equal protection clause. Such rights cannot be constructed without comparing the worth of individual gratifications, and that comparison cannot be principled. Unfortunately, the rhetoric of constitutional adjudication is increasingly a rhetoric about "fundamental" rights that inhere in humans. That focus does more than lead the Court to construct new rights without adequate guidance from constitutional materials. It also distorts the scope and definition of rights that have claim to protection.

There appear to be two proper methods of deriving rights from the Constitution. The first is to take from the document rather specific values that text or history shows the framers actually to have intended and that are capable of being translated into principled rules. We may call these specified rights. The second method derives rights from governmental processes established by the Constitution. These are secondary or derived individual rights. This latter category is extraordinarily important. This method of derivation is essential to the interpretation of the First Amendment, to voting rights, to criminal procedure and to much else.

Secondary or derivative rights are not possessed by the individual because the Constitution has made a value choice about individuals. Neither are they possessed because the Supreme Court thinks them fundamental to all humans. Rather, these rights are located in the individual for the sake of a governmental process that the Constitution outlines and that the Court should preserve. They are given to the individual because his enjoyment of them will lead him to defend them in court and thereby preserve the governmental process from legislative or executive deformation.

The distinction between rights that are inherent and rights that are derived from some other value is one that our society worked out long ago with respect to the economic market place, and precisely the same distinction holds and will prove an aid to clear thought with respect to the political market place. A right is a form of property, and our thinking about the category of constitutional property might usefully follow the progress of thought about economic property. We now regard it as thoroughly old hat, passe and in fact downright tiresome to hear rhetoric about an inherent right to economic freedom or to economic property. We no longer believe that economic rights inhere in the individual because he is an individual. The modern intellectual argues the proper location and definition of property rights according to judgments of utility, i.e. the capacity of such rights to forward some other value. We may, for example, wish to maximize the total wealth of society and define property rights in a way we think will advance that goal by making the economic process run more efficiently. As it is with economic property rights, so it should be with constitutional rights relating to governmental processes.

The derivation of rights from governmental processes is not an easy task, and I do not suggest that a shift in focus will make anything approaching a mechanical jurisprudence possible. I do suggest that, for the reasons already argued, no guidance whatever is available to a court that approaches, say, voting rights or criminal procedures through the concept of substantive equality.

The state legislative reapportionment cases were unsatisfactory precisely because the Court attempted to apply a substantive equal protection approach. Chief Justice Warren's opinions in this series of cases are remarkable for their inability to muster a single respectable supporting argument. The principle of one man, one vote was not neutrally derived: it runs counter to the text of the Fourteenth Amendment, the history surrounding its adoption and ratification and the political practice of Americans from colonial times up to the day the Court invented the new formula.[39] The principle was not neutrally defined: it presumably rests upon some theory of equal weight for all votes, and yet we have no explanation of why it does not call into question other devices that defeat the principle, such as the executive veto, the committee system, the filibuster, the requirement on some issues of two-thirds majorities and the practice of districting. And, as we all know now, the principle, even as stated, was not neutrally applied.[40]

To approach these cases as involving rights derived from the requirements of our form of government is, of course, to say that they involve guarantee clause claims. Justice Frankfurter opposed the Court's consideration of reapportionment precisely on the ground that the "case involves all the elements that have made the Guarantee Clause cases nonjusticiable," and was a "Guarantee Clause claim masquerading under a different label."[41] Of course, his characterization was accurate, but the same could be said of many voting rights cases he was willing to decide. The guarantee clause, along with the provisions and structure of the Constitution and our political history, at least provides some guidance for a Court. The concept of the primary right of the individual in this area provides none. Whether one chooses to use the guarantee of a republican form of government of Article IV, Section 4 as a peg or to proceed directly to considerations of constitutional structure and political practice probably makes little difference. Madison's writing on the republican form of government specified by the guarantee clause suggests that representative democracy may properly take many forms, so long as the forms do not become "aristocratic or monarchical."[42] That is certainly less easily translated into the rigid one person, one vote requirement, which rests on a concept of the right of the individual to equality, than into the requirement expressed by Justice Stewart in *Lucas v. Forty-Fourth General Assembly*[43] that a legislative apportionment need only be rational and "must be such as not to permit the systematic frustration of the will of a majority of the electorate of the State."[44] The latter is a standard derived from the requirements of a democratic process rather than from the rights of individuals. The topic of governmental processes and the rights that may be derived from them is so large that it is best left at this point. It has been raised only as a reminder that there is a legitimate mode of deriving and defining constitutional rights, however difficult intellectually, that is available to replace the present unsatisfactory focus.

At the outset I warned that I did not offer a complete theory of constitutional interpretation. My concern has been to attack a few points that may be regarded as salient in order to clear the way for such a theory. I turn next to a suggestion of what neutrality, the decision of cases according to principle, may mean for certain First Amendment problems.

Some First Amendment Problems: The Search for Theory

The law has settled upon no tenable, internally consistent theory of the scope of the constitutional guarantee of free speech. Nor have many such theories been urged upon the courts by lawyers or academicians. Professor Harry Kalven, Jr., one whose work is informed by a search for theory, has expressed wonder that we should feel the need for theory in the area of free speech when we tolerate inconsistencies in other areas of the law so calmly.[45] He answers himself:

> If my puzzle as to the First Amendment is not a true puzzle, it can only be for the congenial reason that free speech is so close to the heart of democratic organization that if we do not have an appropriate theory for our law here, we feel we really do not understand the society in which we live.[46]

Kalven is certainly correct in assigning the First Amendment a central place in our society, and he is also right in attributing that centrality to the importance of speech to democratic organization. Since I share this common ground with Professor Kalven, I find it interesting that my conclusions differ so widely from his.

I am led by the logic of the requirement that judges be principled to the following suggestions. Constitutional protection should be accorded only to speech that is explicitly political. There is no basis for judicial intervention to protect any other form of expression, be it scientific, literary or that variety of expression we call obscene or pornographic. Moreover, within that category of speech we ordinarily call political, there should be no constitutional obstruction to laws making criminal any speech that advocates forcible overthrow of the government or the violation of the law.

I am, of course, aware that this theory departs drastically from existing Court-made law, from the views of most academic specialists in the field and that it may strike a chill into the hearts of some civil libertarians. But I would insist at the outset that constitutional law, viewed as the set of rules a judge may properly derive from the document and its history, is not an expression of our political sympathies or of our judgments about what expediency and prudence require. When decision making is principled it has nothing to say about the speech we like or the speech we hate; it has a great deal to say about how far democratic discretion can govern without endangering the basis of democratic government. Nothing in my argument goes to the question of what laws should be enacted. I like the freedoms of the individual as well as most, and I would be appalled by many statutes that I am compelled to think would be constitutional if enacted. But I am also persuaded that my generally libertarian commitments have nothing to do with the behavior proper to the Supreme Court.

In framing a theory of free speech the first obstacle is the insistence of many very intelligent people that the "First Amendment is an absolute." Devotees of this position insist, with a literal respect they do not accord other parts of the Constitution, that the framers commanded complete freedom of expression without governmental regulation of any kind. The First Amendment states: "Congress shall make no law . . . abridging the freedom of speech. . . ." Those who take that as an absolute must be reading "speech" to mean any form of verbal communication and "freedom" to mean total absence of governmental restraint.

Any such reading is, of course, impossible. Since it purports to be an absolute position we are entitled to test it with extreme hypotheticals. Is Congress forbidden to prohibit incitement to mutiny aboard a naval vessel engaged in action against an enemy, to prohibit shouted harangues from the visitors' gallery during its own deliberations or to provide any rules for decorum in federal courtrooms? Are the states forbidden, by the incorporation of the First Amendment in the Fourteenth, to punish the shouting of obscenities in the streets?

No one, not the most obsessed absolutist, takes any such position, but if one does not, the absolute position is abandoned, revealed as a play on words. Government cannot function if anyone can say anything anywhere at any time. And so we quickly come to the conclusion that lines must be drawn, differentiations made. Nor does that in any way involve us in a conflict with the wording of First Amendment. Laymen may perhaps be forgiven for thinking that the literal words of the amendment command complete absence of governmental inhibition upon verbal activity, but what can one say of lawyers who believe any such thing? Anyone skilled in reading language should know that the words are not necessarily absolute. "Freedom of speech" may very well be a term referring to a defined or assumed scope of liberty, and it may be this area of liberty that is not to be "abridged."

If we turn to history, we discover that our suspicions about the wording are correct, except that matters are even worse. The framers seem to have had no coherent theory of free speech and appear not to have been overly concerned with the subject. Professor Leonard Levy's work, *Legacy of Suppression*,[47] demonstrates that the men who adopted the First Amendment did not display a strong libertarian stance with respect to speech. Any such position would have been strikingly at odds with the American political tradition. Our forefathers were men accustomed to drawing a line, to us often invisible, between freedom and licentiousness. In colonial times and during and after the Revolution they displayed a determination to punish speech thought dangerous to government, much of it expression that we would think harmless and well within the bounds of legitimate discourse. Jeffersonians, threatened by the Federalist Sedition Act of 1798, undertook the first American elaboration of a libertarian position in an effort to stay out of jail. Professor Walter Berns offers evidence that even then the position was not widely held.[48] When Jefferson came to power it developed that he read the First Amendment only to limit Congress and he believed suppression to be a proper function of the state governments. He appears to have instigated state prosecutions against Federalists for seditious libel. But these later developments do not tell us what the men who adopted the First Amendment intended, and their discussions tell us very little either. The disagreements that certainly existed were not debated and resolved. The First Amendment, like the rest of the Bill of Rights, appears to have been a hastily drafted document upon which little thought was expended. One reason, as Levy shows, is that the Anti-Federalists complained of the absence of a Bill of Rights less because they cared for individual freedoms than as a tactic to defeat the Constitution. The Federalists promised to submit one in order to get the Constitution ratified. The Bill of Rights was then drafted by Federalists, who had opposed it from the beginning; the Anti-Federalists, who were really more interested in preserving the rights of state governments against federal power, had by that time lost interest in the subject.[49]

We are, then, forced to construct our own theory of the constitutional protection of speech. We cannot solve our problems simply by reference to the text or to its history. But we are not without materials for building. The First Amendment indicates that there is something special about speech. We would know that much even without a First Amendment, for the entire structure of the Constitution creates a representative democracy, a form of government that would be meaningless without freedom to discuss government and its policies. Freedom for political speech could and should be inferred even if there were no First Amendment. Further guidance can be gained from the fact that we are looking for a theory fit for enforcement by judges. The principles we seek must, therefore, be neutral in all three meanings of the word: they must be neutrally derived, defined and applied.

The law of free speech we know today grows out of the Supreme Court decisions following World War I, *Schenck v. United States*,[50] *Abrams v. United States*,[51] *Gitlow v. New York*,[52] *Whitney v. California*,[53] not out of this majority position but rather from the opinions, mostly dissents or concurrences that were really dissents, of Justices Holmes and Brandeis. Professor Kalven remarks upon "the almost uncanny power" of these dissents. And it is uncanny, for they have prevailed despite the considerable handicap of being deficient in logic and analysis as well as in history. The great Smith Act cases of the 1950s, *Dennis v. United States*,[54] as modified by *Yates v. United States*,[55] and, more recently, in 1969, *Brandenburg v. Ohio*[56] (voiding the Ohio criminal syndicalism statute), mark the triumph of Holmes and Brandeis. And other cases, culminating perhaps in a modified version of *Roth v. United States*,[57] have pushed the protections of the First Amendment outward from political speech all the way to the fields of literature, entertainment and what can only be called pornography. Because my concern is general theory I shall not attempt a comprehensive survey of the cases nor engage in theological disputation over current doctrinal niceties. I intend to take the position that the law should have been built on Justice Sanford's majority positions in *Gitlow* and *Whitney*. These days such an argument has at least the charm of complete novelty, but I think it has other merits as well.

Before coming to the specific issues in *Gitlow* and *Whitney*, I wish to begin the general discussion of First Amendment theory with consideration of a passage from Justice Brandeis' concurring opinion in the latter case. His *Whitney* concurrence was Brandeis' first attempt to articulate a comprehensive theory of the constitutional protection of speech, and in that attempt he laid down premises which seem to me correct. But those premises seem also to lead to conclusions which Justice Brandeis would have disowned.

As a starting point Brandeis went to fundamentals and attempted to answer the question why speech is protected at all from governmental regulation. If we overlook his highly romanticized version of history and ignore merely rhetorical flourishes, we shall find Brandeis quite provocative.

> Those who won our independence believed that the final end of the state was to make men free to develop their faculties; and that in its government the deliberative forces should prevail over the arbitrary. They valued liberty both as an end and as a means. They believed liberty to be the secret of happiness and courage to be the secret of liberty. The belief that freedom to think as you will and to speak as you think are means indispensable to the discovery and spread of political truth: that without free speech and assembly discussion would be futile; that with them, discussion affords ordinarily adequate protection against, the dissemination of noxious doctrine. . . .

They recognized the risks to which all human institutions are subject. But they knew . . . that it is hazardous to discourage thought, hope and imagination: that hate menaces stable government: that the path of safety lies in the opportunity to discuss freely supposed grievances and proposed remedies: and that the fitting remedy for evil counsels is good ones.[58]

We begin to see why the dissents of Brandeis and Holmes possessed the power to which Professor Kalven referred. They were rhetoricians of extraordinary potency, and their rhetoric retains the power, almost half a century later, to swamp analysis, to persuade, almost to command assent.

But there is structure beneath the rhetoric, and Brandeis is asserting, though he attributes it all to the Founding Fathers, that there are four benefits to be derived from speech. These are:

1. The development of the faculties of the individual;
2. The happiness to be derived from engaging in the activity;
3. The provision of a safety valve for society; and,
4. The discovery and spread of political truth.

We may accept these claims as true and as satisfactorily inclusive. When we come to analyze these benefits, however, we discover that in terms of constitutional law they are very different things.

The first two benefits — development of individual faculties and the achievement of pleasure — are or may be found, for both speaker and hearer, in all varieties of speech, from political discourse to shop talk to salacious literature. But the important point is that these benefits do not distinguish speech from any other human activity. An individual may develop his faculties or derive pleasure from trading on the stock market, following his profession as a river port pilot, working as a bartender, engaging in sexual activity, playing tennis, rigging prices or in any of thousands of other endeavors. Speech with only the first two benefits can be preferred to other activities only by ranking forms of personal gratification. These functions or benefits of speech are, therefore, to the principled judge, indistinguishable from the functions or benefits of all other human activity. He cannot, on neutral grounds, choose to protect speech that has only these functions more than he protects any other claimed freedom.

The third benefit of speech mentioned by Brandeis — its safety valve function — is different from the first two. It relates not to the gratification of the individual, at least not directly, but to the welfare of society. The safety valve function raises only issues of expediency or prudence, and, therefore, raises issues to be determined solely by the legislature or, in some cases, by the executive. The legislature may decide not to repress speech advocating the forcible overthrow of the government in some classes of cases because it thinks repression would cause more trouble than it would prevent. Prosecuting attorneys, who must in any event pick and choose among cases, given their limited resources, may similarly decide that some such speech is trivial or that ignoring it would be wisest. But these decisions, involving only the issue of the expedient course, are indistinguishable from thousands of other managerial judgments governments must make daily, though in the extreme case the decision may involve the safety of the society as surely as a decision whether or not to take a foreign policy stand that risks war. It seems plain that decisions involving only judgments of expediency are for the political branches and not for the judiciary.

This leaves the fourth function of speech — the "discovery and spread of political truth," its ability to deal explicitly, specifically and directly with politics and government, is different from any other form of human activity. But the difference exists only with respect to one kind of speech: explicitly and predominantly political speech. This seems to me the only form of speech that a principled judge can prefer to other claimed freedoms. All other forms of speech raise only issues of human gratification and their protection against legislative regulation involves the judge in making decisions of the sort made in *Griswold v. Connecticut.*

It is here that I begin to part company with Professor Kalven. Kalven argues that no society in which seditious libel, the criticism of public officials, is a crime can call itself free and democratic.[59] I agree, even though the framers of the First Amendment probably had no clear view of that proposition. Yet they indicated a value when they said that speech in some sense was special and when they wrote a Constitution providing for representative democracy, a form of government that is meaningless without open and vigorous debate about officials and their policies. It is for this reason, the relation of speech to democratic organization, that Professor Alexander Meiklejohn seems correct when he says:

> The First Amendment does not protect a "freedom to speak." It protects the freedom of those activities of thought and communication by which we "govern." It is concerned, not with a private right, but with a public power, a governmental responsibility.[60]

But both Kalven and Meiklejohn go further and would extend the protection of the First Amendment beyond speech that is explicitly political. Meiklejohn argues that the amendment protects:

> Forms of thought and expression within the range of human communications from which the voter derives the knowledge, intelligence, sensitivity to human values: the capacity for sane and objective judgment which, so far as possible, a ballot should express.

He lists four such thoughts and expressions:

1. Education, in all its phases. . . .
2. The achievements of philosophy and the sciences. . . .
3. Literature and the arts. . . .
4. Public discussions of public issues. . . .[61]

Kalven, following a similar line, states: "[T]he invitation to follow a dialectic progression from public official to government policy to public policy to matters in the public domain, like art, seems to me to be overwhelming."[62] It is an invitation, I wish to suggest, the principled judge must decline. A dialectic progression I take to be a progression by analogy from one case to the next, an indispensable but perilous method of legal reasoning. The length to which analogy is carried defines the principle, but neutral definition requires that, in terms of the rationale in play, those cases within the principle be more like each other than they are like cases left outside. The dialectical progression must have a principled stopping point. I agree that there is an analogy between criticism of official behavior and the publication of a novel like *Ulysses*, for the latter may form attitudes that ultimately affect politics. But it is an analogy, not an identity. Other human activities and experiences also form personality, teach and create attitudes just as much as does the novel, but no one would on that account, I take it, suggest that the First Amendment strikes down regulations of economic activity, control of entry into a trade, laws about sexual behavior, marriage and the like. Yet these activities, in their capacity to create attitudes that ultimately impinge upon the political process, are more like literature and science than literature and science are like political speech. If the dialectical progression is not to become an analogical stampede, the protection of the First Amendment must be cut off when it reaches the outer limits of political speech.

Two types of problems may be supposed to arise with respect to this solution. The first is the difficulty of drawing a line between political and nonpolitical speech. The second is that such a line will leave unprotected much speech that is essential to the life of a civilized community. Neither of these problems seems to me to raise crippling difficulties.

The category of protected speech should consist of speech concerned with governmental behavior, policy or personnel, whether the governmental unit involved is executive, legislative, judicial or administrative. Explicitly political speech is speech about how we are governed, and the category therefore includes a wide range of evaluation, criticism, electioneering and propaganda. It does not cover scientific, educational, commercial or literary expressions as such. A novel may have impact upon attitudes that affect politics, but it would not for that reason receive judicial protection. This is not anomalous, I have tried to suggest, since the rationale of the First Amendment cannot be the protection of all the kinds of activities that influence political attitudes. Any speech may do that, and we have seen that it is impossible to leave all speech unregulated. Moreover, any conduct may affect political attitudes as much as a novel, and we cannot view the First Amendment as a broad denial of the power of government to regulate conduct. The line drawn must, therefore, lie between the explicitly political and all else. Not too much should be made of the undeniable fact that there will be hard cases. Any theory of the First Amendment that does not accord absolute protection for all verbal expression, which is to say any theory worth discussing will require that a spectrum be cut and the location of the cut will always be, arguably, arbitrary. The question is whether the general location of the cut is justified. The existence of close cases is not a reason to refuse to draw a line and so deny majorities the power to govern in areas where their power is legitimate.

The other objection that the political-nonpolitical distinction will leave much valuable speech without constitutional protection is no more troublesome. The notion that all valuable types of speech must be protected by the First Amendment confuses the constitutionality of laws with their wisdom. Freedom of nonpolitical speech rests, as does freedom for other valuable forms of behavior, upon the enlightenment of society and its elected representatives. That is hardly a terrible fate. At least a society like ours ought not to think it so.

The practical effect of confining constitutional protection to political speech would probably go no further than to introduce regulation or prohibition of pornography. The Court would be freed of the stultifying obligation to apply its self-inflicted criteria: whether "(a) the dominant theme of the material taken as a whole appeals to a prurient interest in sex; (b) the material is patently offensive because it affronts contemporary community standards relating to the description or representation of sexual matters; and (c) the material is utterly without redeeming social value."[63] To take only the last criterion, the determination of "social value" cannot be made in a principled way. Anything some people want has, to that degree, social value, but that cannot be the basis for constitutional protection since it would deny regulation of any human activity. The concept of social value necessarily incorporates a judgment about the net effect upon society. There is always the problem that what some people want some other people do not want, or wish actively to banish. A judgment about social value, whether the judges realize it or not, always involves a comparison of competing values and gratifications as well as competing predictions of the effects of the activity. Determination of "social value" is the same thing as determination of what human interests should be classed as "fundamental" and, therefore, cannot be principled or neutral.

To revert to a previous example, pornography is increasingly seen as a problem of pollution of the moral and aesthetic atmosphere precisely analogous to smoke pollution. A majority of the community may foresee that continued availability of pornography to those who want it will inevitably affect the quality of life for those who do not want it, altering, for example, attitudes toward love and sex, the tone of private and public discourse and view of social institutions such as marriage and the family. Such a majority surely has as much control over the moral and aesthetic environment as it does over the physical, for such matters may even more severely impinge upon their gratifications. That is why, constitutionally, art and pornography are on a par with industry and smoke pollution. As Professor Walter Berns says, "[A] thoughtful judge is likely to ask how an artistic judgment that is wholly idiosyncratic can be capable of supporting an objection to the law. The objection, 'I like it,' is sufficiently rebutted by 'we don't.'"[64]

We must now return to the core of the First Amendment, speech that is explicitly political. I mean by that criticisms of public officials and policies, proposals for the adoption or repeal of legislation or constitutional provisions and speech addressed to the conduct of any governmental unit in the country.

A qualification is required, however. Political speech is not any speech that concerns government and law, for there is a category of such speech that must be excluded. This category consists of speech advocating forcible overthrow or violation of law. The reason becomes clear when we return to Brandeis' discussion of the reasons for according constitutional protection to speech.

The fourth function of speech, the one that defines and sets apart political speech, is the "discovery and spread of political truth." To understand what the Court should protect, therefore, we must define "political truth." There seem to me three possible meanings to that term:

1. An absolute set of truths that exist independently of Constitution or statute.
2. A set of values that are protected by constitutional provision from the reach of legislative majorities.
3. Within that area of life which the majority is permitted to govern in accordance with the Madisonian model of representative government, whatever result the majority reaches and maintains at the moment.

The judge can have nothing to do with any absolute set of truths existing independently and depending upon God or the nature of the universe. If a judge should claim to have access to such a body of truths, to possess a volume of the annotated natural law, we would, quite justifiably, suspect that the source of the revelation was really no more exalted than the judge's viscera. In our system there is no absolute set of truths, to which the term "political truth" can refer.

Values protected by the Constitution are one type of political truth. They are, in fact, the highest type since they are placed beyond the reach of simple legislative majorities. They are primarily truths about the way government must operate, that is, procedural truths. But speech aimed at the discovery and spread of political truth is concerned with more than the desirability of constitutional provisions or the manner in which they should be interpreted.

The third meaning of "political truth" extends the category of protected speech. Truth is what the majority thinks it is at any given moment precisely because the majority is permitted to govern and to redefine its values constantly. "Political truth" in this sense must, therefore, be a term of art, a concept defined entirely from a consideration of the system of government which the judge is commissioned to operate and maintain. It has no unchanging content but refers to the temporary outcomes of the democratic process. Political truth is what the majority decides it wants today. It may be something entirely different tomorrow, as truth is rediscovered and the new concept spread.

Speech advocating forcible overthrow of the government contemplates a group less than a majority seizing control of the monopoly power of the state when it cannot gain its ends through speech and political activity. Speech advocating violent overthrow is thus not "political speech" as that term must be defined by a Madisonian system of government. It is not political speech because it violates constitutional truths about processes and because it is not aimed at a new definition of political truth by a legislative majority. Violent overthrow of government breaks the premises of our system concerning the ways in which truth is defined, and yet those premises are the only reasons for protecting political speech. It follows that there is no constitutional reason to protect speech advocating forcible overthrow.

A similar analysis suggests that advocacy of law violation does not qualify as political speech any more than advocacy of forcible overthrow of the government. Advocacy of law violation is a call to set aside the results that political speech has produced. The process of the "discovery and spread of political truth" is damaged or destroyed if the outcome is defeated by a minority that makes law enforcement, and hence the putting of political truth into practice, impossible or less effective. There should, therefore, be no constitutional protection for any speech advocating the violation of law.

I believe these are the only results that can be reached by a neutral judge who takes his values from the Constitution. If we take Brandeis' description of the benefits and functions of speech as our premise, logic and principle appear to drive us to the conclusion that Sanford rather than Brandeis or Holmes was correct in *Gitlow* and *Whitney.*

Benjamin Gitlow was convicted under New York's criminal anarchy statute which made criminal advocacy of the doctrine that organized government should be overthrown by force, violence or any unlawful means. Gitlow, a member of the left-wing section of the Socialist party, had arranged the printing and distribution of a "Manifesto" deemed to call for violent action and revolution. "There was," Justice Sanford's opinion noted, "no evidence of any effect resulting from the publication and circulation of the Manifesto."[65] Anita Whitney was convicted under California's criminal syndicalism statute, which forbade advocacy of the commission of crime, sabotage, acts of force or violence or terrorism "as a means of accomplishing a change in industrial ownership or control, or effecting any political change." Also made illegal were certain connections with groups advocating such doctrines. Whitney was convicted of assisting in organizing the Communist Labor Party of California, of being a member of it and of assembling with it.[66] The evidence appears to have been meager, but our current concern is doctrinal.

Justice Sanford's opinions for the majorities in *Gitlow* and *Whitney* held essentially that the Court's function in speech cases was the limited but crucial one of determining whether the legislature had defined a category of forbidden speech which might constitutionally be suppressed.[67] The category might be defined by the nature of the speech and need not be limited in other ways. If the category was defined in a permissible way and the defendant's speech or publication fell within the definition, the Court had, it would appear, no other issues to face in order to uphold the conviction. Questions of the fairness of the trial and the sufficiency of the evidence aside, this would appear to be the correct conclusion. The legislatures had struck at speech not aimed at the discovery and spread of political truth but aimed rather at destroying the premises of our political system and the means by which we define political truth. There is no value that judges can independently give such speech in opposition to a legislative determination.

Justice Holmes' dissent in *Gitlow* and Justice Brandeis' concurrence in *Whitney* insisted the Court must also find that, as Brandeis put it, the "speech would produce, or is intended to produce, a clear and imminent danger of some substantive evil which the state constitutionally may seek to prevent."[68] Neither of them explained why the danger must be "clear and imminent" or, as Holmes had put it in *Schenck*, "clear and present"[69] before a particular instance of speech could be punished. Neither of them made any attempt to answer Justice Sanford's argument on the point:

> [T]he immediate danger [created by advocacy of overthrow of the government] is none the less real and substantial, because the effect of a given utterance cannot be accurately foreseen. The state cannot reasonably be required to measure the danger from every such utterance in the nice balance of a jeweler's scale. A single revolutionary spark may kindle a fire that, smoldering for a time, may burst into a sweeping and destructive conflagration. It cannot be said that the state is acting arbitrarily or unreasonably when in the exercise of its judgment as to the measures necessary to protect the public peace and safety, it seeks to extinguish the spark without waiting until it has enkindled the flame or blazed into conflagration. It cannot reasonably be required to defer the adoption of measures for its own peace and safety until the revolutionary utterances lead to actual disturbances of the public peace or imminent and immediate danger of its own destruction; but it may, in the exercise of its judgment, suppress the threatened danger in its incipiency. . . .[70]

To his point that proof of the effect of speech is inherently unavailable and yet its impact may be real and dangerous, Sanford might have added that the legislature is not confined to consideration of a single instance of speech or a single speaker. It fashions a rule to dampen thousands of instances of forcible overthrow advocacy. Cumulatively these may have enormous influence, and yet it may well be impossible to show any effect from any single example. The "clear and present danger" requirement, which has had a long and uneven career in our law, is improper not, as many commentators have thought, because it provides a subjective and an inadequate safeguard against the regulation of speech, but rather because it erects a barrier to legislative rule where none should exist. The speech concerned has no political value within a republican system of government. Whether or not it is prudent to ban advocacy of forcible overthrow and law violation is a different question althogether. Because the judgment is tactical, implicating the safety of the nation, it resembles very closely the judgment that Congress and the President must make about the expediency of waging war, an issue that the Court has wisely thought not fit for judicial determination.

The legislature and the executive might find it wise to permit some rhetoric about law violation and forcible overthrow. I am certain that they would and that they should. Certain of the factors weighted in determining the constitutionality of the Smith Act prosecutions in *Dennis* would, for example, make intelligible statutory, though not constitutional, criteria: the high degree of organization of the Communist party, the rigid discipline of its members and the party's ideological affinity to foreign powers.[71]

Similar objections apply to the other restrictions Brandeis attempted to impose upon government. I will mention but one more of these restrictions. Justice Brandeis argued that:

> Even imminent danger cannot justify resort to prohibition of these functions essential to effective democracy, unless the evil apprehended is relatively serious. . . . Thus, a state might, in the exercise of its police power, make any trespass upon the land of another a crime, regardless of the results or of the intent or purpose of the trespasser. It might, also, punish an attempt, a conspiracy, or an incitement to commit the trespass. But it is hardly conceivable that this court would hold constitutional a statute which punished as felony the more voluntary assembly with a society formed to teach that pedestrians had the moral right to cross unenclosed, unposted, waste lands and to advocate their doing so, even if there was imminent danger that advocacy would lead to a trespass. The fact that speech is likely to result in some violence or in destruction of property is not enough to justify its suppression. There must be the probability of serious injury to the state.[72]

It is difficult to see how a constitutional court could properly draw the distinction proposed. Brandeis offered no analysis to show that advocacy of law violation merited protection by the Court. Worse, the criterion he advanced is the importance, in the judge's eyes, of the law whose violation is urged.

Modern law has followed the general line and the spirit of Brandeis and Holmes rather than of Sanford, and it has become increasingly severe in its limitation of legislative power. *Brandenburg v. Ohio*, a 1969 per curiam decision by the Supreme Court, struck down the Ohio criminal syndicalism statute because it punished advocacy of violence, the opinion stating:

> . . . Whitney [the majority opinion] has been thoroughly discredited by later decisions. . . . These later decisions have fashioned the principle that the constitutional guarantees of free speech and free press do not permit a State to forbid or proscribe advocacy of the use of force or of law violation except where such advocacy is directed to inciting or producing imminent lawless action and is likely to incite or produce such action.[73]

It is certainly true that Justice Sanford's position in *Whitney* and in *Gitlow* has been completely undercut, or rather abandoned, by later cases, but it is not true that his position has been discredited, or even met, on intellectual grounds. Justice Brandeis failed to accomplish that, and later justices have not mounted a theoretical case comparable to Brandeis'.

These remarks are intended to be tentative and exploratory. Yet at this moment I do not see how I can avoid the conclusions stated. The Supreme Court's constitutional role appears to be justified only if the Court applies principles that are neutrally derived, defined and applied. And the requirement of neutrality in turn appears to indicate the results I have sketched here.

Notes

1. H. Wechsler, "Toward Neutral Principles of Constitutional Law," *Principles, Politics, and Fundamental Law* 3, 27 (1961) [hereinafter cited as Wechsler].
2. Ibid.
3. L. Jaffe, *English and American Judges as Lawmakers* 38 (1969).
4. See R. Dahl, *A Preface to Democratic Theory* 4-33 (1956).
5. Ibid., 23-24.
6. J. S.Wright, "Professor Bickel, the Scholarly Tradition, and the Supreme Court," 84 *Harv. L. Rev.* 769 (1971) [hereinafter cited as Wright].
7. Ibid., 777.
8. Ibid., 777-78.
9. This syllogism is implicit in much of Judge Wright's argument. For example, "If it is proper for the Court to make fundamental value choices to protect our constitutional rights and liberties, then it is self-defeating to say that if the Justices cannot come up with a perfectly reasoned and perfectly general opinion *now*, then they should abstain from decision altogether" Id., 779. The first clause is the important one for present purposes; the others merely caricature the position of commentators who ask for principle.
10. A position Judge Wright also seems to take at times. "Constitutional choices are in fact different from ordinary decisions. The reason is simple: the most important value choices have already been made by the framers of the Constitution" Id., 784. One wonders how the judge squares this with his insistence upon the propriety of the judiciary making "fundamental value choices." One also wonders what degree of specificity is required before the framers may realistically be said to have made the "most important value choices." The Warren Court has chosen to expand the Fourteenth Amendment's theme of equality in ways certainly not foreseen by the framers of that provision. A prior Court expanded the amendment's theme of liberty. Are both Courts to be judged innocent of having made the most important value choices on the ground that the framers mentioned both liberty and equality? If so, the framers must be held to have delegated an almost complete power to govern to the Supreme Court, and it is untrue to say that a constitutional decision is any different from an ordinary governmental decision. Judge Wright simply never faces up to the problem he purports to address: how free is the Court to choose values that will override the values chosen by elected representatives?
11. A. Bickel, *The Supreme Court and the Idea of Progress* 96 (1970).

12. Ibid., 34.

13. Wright, *supra* note 6, 775.

14. 381 U.S. 479 (1965).

15. R. Bork, "The Supreme Court Needs a New Philosophy," *Fortune*, Dec., 1968, 170.

16. 381 U.S. at 484.

17. 357 U.S. 449 (1958).

18. 381 U.S. at 484.

19. Ibid., 485, 486.

20. The impossibility is related to that of making interpersonal comparisons of utilities. See L. Robbins, *The Nature and Significance of Economic Science*, ch. 4 (2d ed. 1969); P. Samuelson, *Foundations of Economic Analysis* 243-52 (1965).

21. 262 U.S. 390 (1922).

22. 268 U.S. 510 (1925).

23. 261 U.S. 525 (1923).

24. 198 U.S. 45 (1905).

25. Ibid., 59.

26. 316 U.S. 535 (1942).

27. 330 U.S. 552 (1947).

28. 335 U.S. 464 (1948).

29. 336 U.S. 106 (1949).

30. 394 U.S. 618 (1969).

31. 391 U.S. 68 (1968).

32. Wechsler, *supra* note 1, at 11, citing Frankfurter, "John Marshall and the Judicial Function," 69 *Harv. L. Rev.* 217, 227-28 (1955).

33. 347 U.S. 483 (1954).

34. Wechsler, *supra* note 1, 43.

35. Ibid., 47.

36. 334 U.S. 1 (1948).

37. Henkin, *Shelley v. Kraemer*: "Notes for a Revised Opinion," 110 U. *PA. L. Rev.*

38. Ibid., 494.

39. See the dissents of Justice Frankfurter in *Baker v. Carr*, 369 U.S. 186, 266 (1962); Justice Harlan in *Reynolds v. Sims*, 377 U.S. 533, 589 (1964); and Justice Stewart in *Lucas v. Forty-Fourth Gen. Ass'y*, 377 U.S. 713, 744 (1964).

40. See Fortson v. Morris, 385 U.S. 231 (1966).

41. Baker v. Carr, 369 U.S. 186, 297 (1962).

42. Ibid.

43. *The Federalist* No. 43 (J. Madison).

44. Ibid., 753-54.

45. H. Kalven, *The Negro and the First Amendment* 4-5 (1966) [hereinafter cited as Kalven].

46. Ibid., 6.

47. L. Levy, *Legacy of Suppression* (1960) [hereinafter cited as Levy].

48. W. Berns, "Freedom of the Press and the Alien and Sedition Laws: A Reappraisal," 1970 *Sup. Ct. Rev.* 109.

49. Levy, *supra* note 47, 224-33.

50. 249 U.S. 47 (1919).

51. 250 U.S. 616 (1919).

52. 268 U.S. 642 (1925).
53. 274 U.S. 357 (1927).
54. 341 U.S. 494 (1951).
55. 354 U.S. 298 (1957).
56. 395 U.S. 444 (1969).
57. 354 U.S. 476 (1957).
58. 274 U.S. at 375.
59. Kalen, *supra* note 45, 16.
60. A. Meiklejohn, "The First Amendment Is an Absolute," 1961 *Sup. Ct. Rev.* 245, 255.
61. Ibid., 256-57.
62. Kalven, "The New York Times Case: A Note on "The Central Meaning of the First Amendment ," 1964 *Sup. Ct. Rev.* 191, 221.
63. *A Book Named "John Clelend's Memoirs of a Woman of Pleasure" v. Attorney General*, 383 U.S. 413, 418 (1966).
64. Berns, "Pornography vs. Democracy: The Case for Censorship," *The Pub. Interest*, Winter, 1971, 23.
65. 268 U.S. at 656.
66. 274 U.S. at 372 (Brandeis, Ju., dissenting).
67. 268 U.S., 668; 274 U.S., 362-63.
68. 274 U.S., 373.
69. 249 U.S., 52.
70. 268 U.S., 669.
71. 341 U.S., 511.
72. 274 U.S., 377-78.
73. 395 U.S., 447.

Chapter 3

Tocqueville and the Future of the American Constitution

Harvey C. Mansfield
Harvard University

> "If ever liberty is lost in America, one will have to lay the blame on the omnipotence of the majority which will have driven minorities to despair and forced them to appeal to material force." (Tocqueville, *Democracy in America*, I.II.8)

> "It seems that if despotism came to be established in the democratic nations of our day, it would have different characteristics [from those of violent, arbitrary tyranny]: it would be more widespread and milder, and it would degrade men without tormenting them." (Tocqueville, *Democracy in America*, II.IV.6)

These quite contrary judgments of Tocqueville as to the principal danger to democracy, one taken from the first volume of *Democracy in America* and the other from the second, pose the problem of understanding the future of the American Constitution. Within the five years separating his first volume from the second (1835 to 1840) Tocqueville seems to have changed the object of his anxiety for the future from fear of a people too active to fear of a people too inactive.[1] This change within Tocqueville's books mirrors the change in outlook between the founders of the American constitution and most Americans today: the founders feared an overbearing majority faction (Madison's famous argument in *Federalist* 10 leaps to mind), but today we fear an apathetic or disabled majority that does not claim its rights or cannot exercise them. Now, the founders' remedy against an overactive people was, to describe it most generally, a Constitution that put government at a distance from the people. Our question today must be: is such a Constitution, resting on the assumption of an active people, now obsolete? What should we think of the remedy in our day called "populism," which, contrary to the intention of the founders, attempts to reduce the distance between government and people?

It is not easy to recover the original understanding of the Constitution because the difference between then and now is largely a matter of the spirit with which the Constitution is regarded and of practices related to that spirit; the document and the formal institutions remain largely the same. Nor was the difference properly appreciated by J. Allen Smith and Charles Beard when they maintained 75 years ago, Smith more directly than Beard, that the Constitution was originally undemocratic.[2] Beard in particular initiated an attitude of scholarly skepticism as to the democratic character of the Constitution which has survived the demise of his "economic interpretation." For while later research has overturned Beard's conclusions and displayed some embarrassment with his arguments,[3] most scholars today still accept the premise of his work.[4] Quickly stated, his premise was that measures taken to control the people are antidemocratic. But this is precisely the premise on which popular movements of our day, both right and left, act in regard to the Constitution. They regard the Constitution not as a *form of government* but as a *means of getting what they want.*

Conservatives have a series of constitutional amendments they seem to favor more than the Constitution itself, and the recent advance of "conservative" ideas has not emphasized, sometimes not included, the conservatism or restoration of the Constitution from liberal misinterpretation. Instead, many conservatives are eager merely to get their own back by expelling liberals and replacing them with conservatives who also do not respect the Constitution. These conservatives push for a conservatism no longer considered a constitutional interpretation but rather a set of salutary ideas unconnected to a form of government. Liberals, for their part, have adopted an openly exploitative attitude towards a "living constitution" that is theirs to use, manipulate or ignore as they please. Liberals are fearful that if they leave the Constitution as it is, it will become out-of-date, which means a hindrance to liberals. They seem to have lost any sense that a Constitution should embody principles, procedures and institutions that do not go out-of-date. From both sides, then, the Constitution appears today as an instrument of the people, not as a control on them; it is to be used, not to be lived under; it is to be regarded with a spirit of utilitarian opportunism, not indeed as having a "spirit" of its own by which we must live. The Constitution, we think, is below the people, not above them. Although we sometimes admit — and rarely deny altogether — the need for divine authority, we have forgotten why we need a human authority over the people.

Then what does it mean to consider the Constitution as a form of government? This was the intent of the framers of the Constitution, as set forth most authoritatively in *The Federalist.* There it is explained that the American Constitution establishes a popular government, but of a new kind it is an "experiment." An experiment is needed because almost all previous popular governments outside America had failed (as we learn from *Federalist* 9, 10, and 14). Instead of appealing to classical republican tradition as one might expect in a country of republican governments that had allied to fight and win a war of independence against a monarchy, "Publius" attacks that tradition. He expresses "horror and disgust" at the extremes of tyranny and anarchy which are continually to be found in the history of "the petty Republics of Greece and Italy." Their defect also to be seen in the republican state governments then existing in America was susceptibility to "majority faction," through which measures were decided "by the superior force of an interested and overbearing majority."

Thus Publius presents the Constitution as mainly addressing the problem of majority faction arising from an overconfident and overzealous republican people. This people does not have to be roused from stupid subservience to the false majesty of monarchy, nor does it need to be taught lessons in how to use the government to get what it wants. Its republican ardor and its pursuit of self-interest are unquestioned, but its justice and its devotion to the public good are in doubt, so much so that "enlightened friends to liberty" would have been obliged to abandon the cause of republicanism if the modern "science of politics" had not been able to suggest improvements in republican government (*Federalist* 9).

Two such improvements are singled out and presented as remedies for the general failure of popular government in the celebrated *Federalist* 10.[5] These are the principle of representation, by which government is delegated to a small number elected by the rest, and the idea of an extensive republic, in which the imperial size that had previously been thought fatal to a republic is deliberately embraced as a means of its salvation. If you "extend the sphere" or "enlarge the orbit," you include many more "fit characters" to serve as representatives, who are more likely to be elected from large constituencies; and more important, you take in a greater variety of parties and interests less likely to combine in a majority faction than a homogeneous majority would be. These two remedies together constitute a "Republican remedy for the diseases most incident to Republican Government" because they do not qualify the principle that the people should rule but only specify how it should be done. They are not the devices of mixed government which would not be agreeable to the republicanism of the American people. They are, however, remedies that will distinguish the American republic from a democracy (or a "pure Democracy") in which the people, necessarily a small number, administer the government in person rather than through representatives.

So, political science comes to the rescue of republicanism, first by accepting the principle of republicanism, but second, by also accepting that republican diseases exist and not agreeing that the republican principle by itself produces remedies for them. Political science demonstrates that the qualities of imperial size and remoteness of the government from the people, previously thought to be antirepublican (and still proclaimed so by the Antifederalists), are in fact republican as opposed to democratic. It is noteworthy that in *Federalist* 10 republics are distinguished from democracies but not from their usual enemies, aristocracies and monarchies. In American, republicanism is so strong as to be its own worst enemy when uninstructed by political science. Political science is capable of such instruction, we may note for the attention of political scientists today, not when it is value-free but when its end or guiding "value" is wider than the mere promotion of republicanism or democracy. To adopt such an end may in a sense be undemocratic, since it admits that democracy can go wrong, but since it foresees democracy to cure its ills, it is not antidemocratic.

Thus the American Constitution, according to Publius, is "wholly popular government" because in all its parts it is derived from the people. But it is also a wholly representative government because it never allows the people to rule directly; as opposed to pure democracy, or to the idea of mixed government, the people are not a part of the government but rather the source of all government. The reason for this deliberate withdrawal of government from the people and its implications are not made clear in *Federalist* 10, where it is enough to contend that republicanism has a characteristic problem and the American Constitution a brand-new republican remedy for it. But as Publius proceeds to explain and defend the nature of the Constitution, after proving the need for it (in the first 36 papers), he discloses less arguably republican aspects. In *Federalist* 49 James Madison as Publius advises against a proposal by his friend Thomas Jefferson for an appeal to a convention of the people whenever breaches of the Constitution might occur. Publius objects that government that has its origin in the people cannot recur to the people if it is to maintain its authority over the people. Although — indeed, *because* — the Constitution must originate in the people, it must be elevated over the people if they are to respect it. Popular government needs not merely legitimacy or credibility, as we would say today to emphasize its closeness to the people, but especially "veneration" and "a reverence for the laws." To recur to the people on the occasion of a breach of the Constitution would invite a partisan quarrel followed by a partisan decision. It would encourage the will or the passion of the people to predominate. But, Publius says, it is the *reason* of the public alone that ought to control and regulate the government. The passions ought to be controlled and regulated *by* the government. Popular government cannot dispense with the necessity of keeping reason paramount over the passions, and to do this, it cannot dispense with a seemingly irrational "veneration" for the Constitution which makes it possible for the government to keep reason paramount. The framers of the Constitution were neither so foolishly optimistic as to think that a republican people was rational because of its republicanism nor so foolishly sophisticated as to think that its irrationality does not matter.

In the new Constitution, then, were two other innovations besides representation and extensive size. Although we take them for granted today, they were not proclaimed as innovations in the *Federalist* because they were generally thought to be unrepublican or undemocratic. These are a strong executive and judicial review. In considering them, the *Federalist* maintains that each is a way of enabling the reason of the people to prevail over their passions. A strong, energetic executive is needed for sound administration of the government and for developing long-term plans to direct it. The people are not merely to be *led*, as we would say now; they are to be *directed*. "Leader" in the *Federalist* is a pejorative term usually reserved for demagogues who try to ride to power on popular passions.[6] Similarly, judicial review of laws and executive actions that might be breaches of the Constitution is justified because judges will not have "too great a disposition to consult popularity" (*Federalist* 78). Instead, they will consult "the intention of the people" as it is revealed in the Constitution and the laws. The people's intention is more settled, thus presumably more reasonable, than their will or "momentary inclination." Judges must have "firmness and independence" to help ensure that popular government is exercised not by popular will alone but through the rule of law.

Even the branch of government closest to the people, the legislative, is presented as effective insofar as it does not merely reflect popular will. In explaining the Senate, Publius takes a stand against the instability of most republican government and offers this notoriously aristocratic institution as a remedy against the "impulse of sudden and violent passions" to which republican assemblies without a senate are likely to yield. Unstable government, it is pointed out, gives an unreasonable advantage to "the sagacious, the enterprising and the moneyed few"; so an institution of the few is enlisted to hinder the few who prosper unreasonably from the instability of a legislature too republican. And in discussing the popular branch itself, Publius is at pains to refute the opinion that the greater the number of representatives, the safer is government from oligarchy; for in a crowd, the few will prevail either by oratory or by secret machination. Publius, moreover, emphasizes the knowledge and experience necessary for representatives, qualities which lift them above the people they represent. Once again, we are impressed, on the one hand, that nonrepublican qualities and devices are made instrumental to republicanism, but on the other, that republican government needs such things. When Publius comes to explain the separation of powers to a fellow-founder, he says, in a famous sentence: "You must first enable the government to control the governed; and in the next place, oblige it to control itself" (*Federalist* 51). Clearly the separate institutions of constitutional government, which oblige the government to control itself, also, by being separated from the people, enable the government to control the people. Control the people! What statesman today could speak so frankly of the first necessity of popular government? But what observer today would find the American people sufficiently spirited to need control?

In considering the Constitution as a form of government we have not yet mentioned *rights*; yet surely the Constitution was intended to secure rights. To see how it was intended to do this, one must revert to a distinction well known to the founders that is forgotten, or is not stressed, in current discussion — that between natural and civil rights. Natural rights are the rights on which civil society is founded; civil rights are the ones it secures. Natural rights belong to natural man, who is understood as having a fixed nature worthy of certain rights; these would be the rights to life, liberty and the pursuit of happiness, according to the Declaration of Independence. They are the rights for the sake of which we establish a Constitution. But the rights actually secured under this Constitution are civil rights, such as those in the Bill of Rights. They are more specific, but therefore also more limited than natural rights. The hallmark of civil rights is that you cannot be deprived of them. Civil society secures rights precisely by *depriving* those who violate them of their rights, providing of course that this deprivation occurs by due process of law. You cannot be deprived of your natural rights, but you cannot secure them by yourself without a government either; the "state of nature" in constitutional theory describes a situation where rights are unlimited but very insecure. So it makes sense to deprive yourself of the exercise of natural rights in order to establish a Constitution that will secure civil rights.

The move from natural to civil rights is accomplished by consent and protected by the right of consent, which means the right of consent to government. The right of consent is derived from the rights to life, liberty and the pursuit of happiness because those rights cannot be effective without government yet would not be rights unless each person could consent on his own. (If someone else consents for you, then your right depends on him.) The right of consent, therefore, is both natural and civil, and between natural and civil rights; natural insofar as it is prior to civil rights; civil insofar as consent establishes conventional, limited civil rights (including the right to vote, which is the civil version of the right of consent). Consent is the crucial right that joins rights to government and makes it clear that although rights are *secured* by government, they are *created* by government and do not exist merely at the *convenience* of government. When we consider today whether governments maintain the "human rights" of their peoples, we should be concerned with the right of consent above all others, because governments that create rights without seeking consent can as easily take them away.

At the same time, we should be aware on our own account that rights must be understood as being accompanied by a form of government. That form secures rights by governing under law so that the rule of the majority is the rule of a *constitutional* majority as opposed to a *factious* majority. The form and the working of this government are set down in the body of the Constitution rather than in the Bill of Rights. Hamilton was correct to say that the Constitution itself is a Bill of Rights (*Federalist* 84) even if he was wrong to deny the need for a Bill of Rights. The due process of law mentioned above refers most obviously to procedural rights in trials, to the right of habeas corpus and to protections against *ex post facto* laws and bills of attainder. But ultimately due process of law depends on the rule of law that results from the rule of a constitutional majority through our form of government, for no right of due process could withstand a determined majority faction. Since all civil rights depend on the people's right of consent, all civil rights depend on the form of government through which they exercise their consent.

This dependence of rights on our form of government is not denied but forgotten today. We speak constantly of rights and frequently invent new rights that a free or civilized people cannot live without. We also calculate policies to guarantee these rights. But we take for granted the Constitution that secures rights and forms the government that makes policies. We regard the Constitution as instrumental to the policies that are instrumental to our rights. As our instrument, the Constitution is not above us; it is not to be honored, revered, or looked up to. Accordingly, it is not today the object of scholarly study, either in political science or law. Political scientists deplore "systemic" faults in political parties and in the constitutional institutions, but they do not look at the whole Constitution; they never see it as a whole because they are always trying to look underneath or behind it. Legal scholarship on constitutional history hardly exists today, and legal publicists use the Constitution to supply an aura for rights without really believing in its power to do so, often while denying that power. The philosophy professors who elaborately and solemnly discuss rights are oblivious of the Constitution; if it were brought to their attention, they would regard it as an accident not deserving consideration in their arguments.

This general disregard for the Constitution in the political elite and in intellectual and scholarly establishments can perhaps be explained best by examining the new understanding of rights which has succeeded that of the founders. Today rights are not distinguished as natural and civil because men are understood fundamentally as changing, historical beings rather than natural beings with a fixed definition. When rights are defined historically, they are in practice impossible to distinguish from wants (even "needs" come to mean "felt needs"). These wants alternate in status between posited rights whose positing is not necessary but merely asserted (the deontological view) and preferences capable of being "traded off" for one another (the utilitarian view). Their status alternates because in practice proponents find the first view too absolute and the second too relative. They have abandoned the distinction between natural and civil rights by which the absoluteness and the relativity of rights are reconciled through the right of consent, and they have substituted for it two partisan views that cannot be reconciled and hence must be alternated.

When rights are defined as wants, government is set the impossible task of guaranteeing those wants that happen to be defined as rights in our time, or in our decade. It cannot justify limiting rights or providing what is practicable in present circumstances since in the absence of any distinction, every civil right is demanded with the full force of a natural right: justice *now!* And who does the demanding? When rights are wants, those who have the wants are no longer required to claim their rights, to fight for them, and to defend them once gained. Elite groups can make the necessary claims on behalf of those who want, who are regarded as too weak actually to enjoy the rights they have had in a formal sense until now. For in the constitutional understanding of rights, a right is a license or permission to be exercised on one's own; and some people by choice or circumstance will always excel others in the exercise of rights, being better speakers of free speech or better enterprisers under free enterprise. But in the new post-constitutional understanding, any discrepancy between the formal possession of a right and its actual exercise cannot be tolerated: you do not have a right or a choice unless it is an equal right or choice. If you show by your inactivity that you are too weak to exercise your rights, the government, prompted by elite groups, will step in to guarantee those rights, in effect exercising them better than you do. Guaranteeing rights now means guaranteeing their exercise, not the possibility or free choice of their exercise. To do this, government does not by right have to seek your consent or the consent of your fellow-citizens because you may feel too weak to consent and your fellow-citizens may be overlooking your wants when they consent.

In the post-constitutional understanding, progress in the attainment of rights consists in exposing and correcting the formal and consensual character of rights hitherto; it consists in denying previous progress towards rights. Indeed, when rights are defined historically, no standard exists by which to judge progress except today's wants, which will be superseded by tomorrow's. A critique of rights because of their unequal exercise implies a definition of rights by their exercise alone. But such "rights" do not have to be exercised by those who are said to have them; they do not require consent and cannot result in progress.

Since these new rights are guaranteed to each individual, and individuals do not have to claim them, individuals do not have to take responsibility for their exercise. In this view you have a right to fair housing, for example, not merely a right to seek housing on your own under fair terms specified by the government. And as your rights do not necessitate that you take responsibility for their exercise, they do not result from any contribution you make or might make to the community, if they were secured to you. Your rights do not flow from strengths — your talents and capacities — but rather from weaknesses: your handicaps and needs. Indeed, you do not "deserve" your rights.[7] Since in the latest conception rights are not rights unless they are equal in exercise or in result, you have rights especially when you do not deserve them, and they must be asserted especially against those who might deserve them and thus exercise them better than yourself. Instead of examining the weak to find their latent strength and then calling forth that strength by securing a right to use it, we seek out weakness itself and finding it mute (since no one boasts of his or her weakness in order to claim rights), we file a suit on its behalf. To be weak is to be "disadvantaged"; we may claim a tort against society to require society to make you whole without any effort of your own. Compassion takes over from justice, even usurping its name; and society discovers its victims but forgets to make them citizens.

In the new version, we have seen, rights are no longer "civil" as distinguished from and related to natural rights. They are human rights, and as such have no necessary relationship to civil society, the Constitution, or the common good. Your right is not qualified by any requirement to contribute to society by improving, maintaining or defending it. You do not even have to obey its laws; so it has now become more correct to speak of prisoners' rights than of citizens' rights. "Human" rights so understood have both the absoluteness of natural rights and the specificity of civil rights without the insecurity of the former or the limitedness of the latter. They are unembarrassed, unrelenting claims on the public treasury, private compassion, nature and God to be made whole according to an increasingly costly, if not lofty definition of what it means to be a whole human being. In our day they are known as "entitlements," originally a technical term for claims on a budget that must be paid out regardless of how many claim them. When rights in general are taken as entitlements, even the sky is not the limit, and your rights culminate, not in the right of consent, but in your right to feel dissatisfied. To sum up entitlements: they have no reference to the common good; they result from no actual or potential contribution by the entitled; they do not have to be individually, much less responsibly, exercised; and they deny past progress in rights while producing a static society of defensive special interests.

These new "entitlements" are guaranteed by a government no longer seen as constitutional. Although the American people of course continue to vote, voting is understood more as the registering of wants than as consent to a government under the Constitution, thus over the people. As an instrument to get the people what they want government comes more and more to be regarded as a *bureaucracy* and not merely in one subordinate part but as a whole. Judged by this instrumental standard, American government proves to be inefficient; precisely the constitutional safeguards make it seem too remote to serve the people faithfully and expeditiously. When judged as a bureaucracy, for some reason, these faults, unlike other human faults, have no hidden compensations: for bureaucracy is large but petty, meddlesome but unconcerned, stupid but complex, flight but insistent, and forgetful but inflexible. Politicians from both parties have in recent times run electoral campaigns successfully against government by equating government with bureaucracy. They and we regard government as unreason with the outward look of reason, as if government were meant to be a rational or efficient instrument of the people which somehow in practice never works properly. That our government was intended through its constitutional processes to *add* reason to the will of the people, so as to produce the reasoned "intention" of the people as opposed to their "momentary inclinations" (*Federalist* 78) is now all but forgotten. What the founders praised as constitutional government we now condemn, from both left and right, as "bureaucracy."

"Bureaucracy" as it appears in its accusatory usage is an instrument that fails as an instrument because it always tries to be more than an instrument. It should confine itself to rationally effecting the will of the people, but the reason it brings to this task has an ambition of its own that refuses to be so confined. "Bureaucracy" is unresponsive to the people because it claims to know better than they what is good for them; it tries to correct or "refine" (Publius' word) their will. "Bureaucracy," like reason itself, is heavy, cold and remote. It is too formal and too paternal, like an old-fashioned father who shows his love by making rules. It now seems hardly conceivable that a people, knowing the fallibility of its reason when judging in one's own cause and when ignorant of the circumstances of others, might actually choose — not a father but a constitutional government — over itself.

In our view today the main problem facing government becomes government itself. Nothing the government has to do is more important or even more urgent than overcoming its own bureaucratic nature. To do this, it is thought that government cannot turn to reason, and try to make the reason of the American people control their passions as the framers did. Too much reliance on reason in the sense of either unhurried deliberation or bureaucratic formalism is precisely the problem rather than the solution. The solution, we seem to believe, has to be a new resort to passion so that government can recover its lost connection to the American people.

The passion in question is usually compassion, sometimes anger; both are included in the vogue word "care." Thus government, it is supposed, can overcome its unfeeling bureaucratic nature by showing that it cares. Showing compassion or anger makes a direct and informal contact with the people which is quite different from the formal connections between government and people established in our constitutional system. It is as if all government can and should behave to the people in the manner of a passerby who sees an accident in the street and rushes to see if he can be of any assistance. Our politicians, when running for office, promise to act not like the deliberative legislator or responsible bureaucrat but like the compassionate passerby.

The institutions closest to the people in our society are believed to be the media; so to get closer to the people, government tries to resemble the media, which relentlessly demand and provide direct contact between the people and their government. The media are not, of course, "institutions" in the sense of associations formally established by consent of the people. They are networks for informing and entertaining the people that constitute the indispensable "medium" between people and government in which the right of consent takes effect. They seem to be nothing in themselves, and often say that they merely report what goes on. In truth, they *do* nothing on their own; they act in the manner of a compassionate passerby who sees an accident in the street and rushes to see if someone else can be of any assistance. But the media greatly affect how we regard government. With unfailing emphasis and unremitting insinuation they require the government to be "responsive" and "sensitive" to the people, control them, because they find enough morality and wisdom in what the people want or feel.

In order to be responsive and sensitive, government is forced to be "charismatic." "Charisma" is a term to designate irregular authority taken from Max Weber's sociology and now moralized and democratized in current usage. "Charisma" now means popularity that is deserved, yet for no apparent reason. "Charisma" resembles "leadership" — the term used pejoratively by Publius that Woodrow Wilson brought into favor as praise — but it is more irrational and it is unconnected to progress. Charisma is an explicable, unpredictable gift for knowing what the people want or think right before they know, and it attaches to the person, not the office. All officers in the regular constitutional departments must now reckon with charisma: the president must have it, as must legislators who seek to be president; senators and congressman must deliberate in the shadow of charisma, aware that undramatic sober prudence is not appreciated; even judges are not immune from charisma's temptations, which many of them regard as innocent. Although each of the branches of government retains the flavor of its constitutional essence, our praise for "charisma" is a sign that we no longer consider popularity to be an evil, or *the* evil, of popular government.

It would take too long to show how the workings of the constitutional branches today reflect the spirit of charismatic popularity that has originated in our ideas and been spread by the media. But one can mention such well-known features of our politics as our presidential primaries, media-based campaigns, and populistic programs in the executive; loss of leadership, subcommittee proliferation, constituency servicing, and an uncontrolled budget in the Congress; and the complex of intrusions upon the legislature, executive, and state governments known as "judicial activism." And besides the influence of the media and their own workings, government must contend with a plethora of surveys, many originating from the government, which imply that people ought to have what they want, and right away.

Yet somehow the new requirements of exposure do not make government more honest, the new demands for compassion do not make it care, and the new techniques for measuring popularity do not make it more popular. The reason is that our capacity to fool ourselves easily surpasses every advance in technology or social science. The more popular government tries to be, the more unpopular it becomes, because popularity is not a standard any government can live by — even, or especially, a popular government. No government can govern without imposing duties and asking for sacrifices, but duty and sacrifice must be called forth by a higher ideal than popularity.

When government seeks popularity, it seeks more than consent. With the right of consent, the people call government to account and give it scope to govern within the limits of the Constitution and constrained by the need to maintain a constitutional majority. To do this, the people put aside their desire to rule directly but retain, through elections, their right of independent judgment. But when government seeks to do what is popular, it must claim to know what people will consent to in advance of elections. Popularity as determined by surveys becomes a substitute for consent in elections, and we face the paradox of a popular government seeking popularity under which many people do not bother to vote. The right of consent to government becomes the right — in the new sense of entitlement — to have the government do popular things.

Our government's eagerness for popularity might make one believe that it is trying to please a people that knows what it wants and is determined to have it. But as we have seen, the American people, no longer so ready to exercise their rights, have been made anxious over their entitlements. And because both people and government are so large, each individual has so small a share in popularity that he has to consider it an outside force to which he must conform rather than a means of self-government. The sovereign people have yielded to a sovereignty of popularity in which "the people" is like — or is — a weak ruler open to the suggestion and manipulation of dubious advisers, both venal and partisan. Bringing government closer to the people by forcing it to seek popularity was weakened both our government and our people. We seem to have arrived at the "individualism" which Tocqueville feared might become the fate of a democratic people.[8]

In contrast to this gloomy picture, it might be said, is the recent assertion Americans have made, through taxpayers' revolts and by electing President Reagan, to "get the government off our backs." Does not this perky act imply a people not yet lost in dependency? Perhaps it does, but one cannot yet be sure that it signifies more than a desire to be rid of responsibility for oneself and for others. The government's guarantee of entitlements can seem more oppressive to some at some times, for example when one is young and unemployed, but the mere act of throwing off that weight, however exhilarating for the moment, does not signify an ability to live without entitlements. With some age or after ill-success in an "opportunity" the desire for entitlements may return.

Thus the libertarian impulse that is gaining power in our time may turn out to be nothing more than an alternative mode of Tocqueville's "individualism." One mode would be collectivist, as individuals let government run their lives; the other would be individualist, when individuals refuse to pay for this. In both modes people are inactive, either allowing the government to exercise their rights or not understanding the exercise of rights as a responsibility to do something worthwhile — especially, to *govern* oneself. Libertarianism does not admit that the *self* must govern itself in order that self-government may thrive. It is content to let people have what they want, so long as they do not want government, and it suspects, with some reason, that any call to greater responsibility is nothing but the prelude to another expensive and foolish entitlement program. In fact, however, entitlements make people irresponsible, whether they pay or receive. If they pay, they become patrons of a society of clients without realizing the harm they do; if they receive, they envy those who pay — but not for paying. Those who both pay for entitlements and receive them do not get their money's worth, as with Social Security in America today. It is not possible to protect liberty by disconnecting it from responsibility, and thus from government. For nothing prevents the irresponsible from demanding more government, not even previous experience since who says I must be responsible for my costs or for my memory?

Libertarianism needs to become reacquainted with constitutionalism and to stop flirting with the populism that undermines constitutional government. The way back to limited government cannot be found by denying or minimizing the need for government or by setting off government against liberty. Rather, limited government is free *government*, in which a people is free because it governs itself freely. Tocqueville reminds us that free government requires both an active people and government to control it. As against the entitlements of our day, he praises the active, voluntary spirit of Americans; but in contrast to those who disassociate liberty from government, he recommends and provides in his books both the art and the science of association[9] by which free people are made competent to do what they can and warned against attempting what they cannot. A people cannot be active unless it knows how to associate; but such association requires as its precondition a Constitution that allows and encourages it, the mother association which gives birth to free, responsible associations throughout a free society but does not try to rule their activities. So long as they live in the spirit of this Constitution, the American people will not give up their rights in exchange for guarantees from government because they will want to continue governing themselves.

Notes

1. Alexis de Tocqueville, *Democracy in America*, George Lawrence trans. (New York: Doubleday, 1969), II.IV.6.: 690.

2. Charles A. Beard, *An Economic Interpretation of the Constitution of the United States* (New York: Macmillan, 1913), ch. 6; J. Allen Smith, *The Spirit of American Government* (New York: Macmillan, 1907), ch. 3; Richard Hofstadter, *The Progressive Historians* (New York: Knopf, 1968): 247.

3. Robert E. Brown, *Charles Beard and the Constitution* (Princeton, N.J.: Princeton University Press, 1956); Forrest McDonald, *We The People; the Economic Origins of the Constitution* (Chicago: Ill.: University of Chicago Press, 1958); Lee Benson, *Turner and Beard* (Glencoe, Ill.: The Free Press, 1960).

4. Gordon S. Wood, for example, while ignoring Beard, does finally seem to say in his own name that the Constitution is not consistent with the democratic principles of 1776; *Creation of the American Republic 1776-1787* (Chapel Hill, N.C.: University of North Carolina Press, 1969): 394n, 524, 562, 606. Martin Diamond, "Democracy and *The Federalist*," *American Political Science Review*, Vol. 53 (1959): 52-68.

5. *Federalist* 10 has never been better analyzed than in David Epstein's recent book, *The Political Theory of The Federalist* (Chicago, Ill.; University of Chicago Press, 1984), ch. 3.

6. See the excellent *Federalist Concordance*, edited by Thomas S. Engeman,

Edward J. Erler and Thomas B. Hofeller (Middletown, Conn.: Wesleyan University Press, 1980).

7. ". . . what [persons and groups] are entitled to is not proportional to nor dependent upon their intrinsic worth." John Rawls, *A Theory of Justice* (Cambridge, Mass.: Harvard University Press, 1971): 311.

8. Tocqueville, *Democracy in America*, II.II.3-5. "Individualism is a calm and considered feeling which disposes each citizen to isolate himself from the mass of his fellows and withdraw into the circle of family and friends; with this little society formed to this taste, he gladly leaves the greater society to look after itself. . .individualism. . .is due more to inadequate understanding than to perversity of heart."

9. Tocqueville calls the science of association the "mother science" (II.II.5) and then, referring back to this statement, calls the art of association the "mother art" (II.II.7).

Chapter 4

Foreign Policy and the Rule of Law

Roger Barrus
Hampden-Sydney College

The Bush Administration in recent months has been the target of criticism for what appears as "drift" in foreign affairs. The Administration, its critics claim, lacks a sense of direction in foreign policy: it has no clear conception of the ends to be pursued in foreign affairs, the present dangers and opportunities for American interests, and the means necessary for achieving the ends of policy amidst the dangers and opportunities of present circumstances. These criticisms, which have come from both the left and right, have been motivated at least in part by the growing opinion, or perhaps feeling, that while the world is undergoing social change, the United States rather than directing the forces of change is merely being carried along in their currents. Potentially world-historical changes are occurring in the East, with the disintegration of the Soviet empire; in the West, with the movement towards economic union in Europe and the continued development of Japan as an economic superpower; and in the South, with the rise of drug cartels, allied with terrorist political organizations, that threaten democratic political regimes in Latin America. It is indeed possible to question whether, at this critical juncture in world history, the United States has any kind of coherent foreign policy. This is not, however, merely a failure of the Bush Administration.

That the problem did not begin with Bush's election in 1988 can be demonstrated by a cursory review of some of the more bizarre goings-on in U.S. foreign policy during the Reagan years. In the Middle East, U.S. policy was buried in the rubble of the carbombed Beirut Marine barracks. The Administration, after lengthy negotiations made necessary by the War Powers Resolution, had committed U.S. troops to the multilateral peacekeeping force in Lebanon. The political divisions reflected in the negotiations invited attack on U.S. troops, by forces in Lebanon that had no interest in the success of peacekeeping efforts. When the attack came, the Administration, with the tenuous political consensus on policy in Lebanon shattered, had no choice but to beat an ignominious retreat. In Central America, U.S. policy was in virtual disarray. What might loosely be called "policy" towards Nicaragua featured on-again, off-again appropriations by Congress for the Contras, the anti-Sandinistas resistance; widely publicized covert operations by the CIA, including direction of the mining of harbors; efforts by Congress, through the Boland Amendments, to prevent the President from assisting the Contras through the exercise of his constitutional executive powers; and the personal intervention of House Speaker Jim Wright in diplomacy in Central America. This policy disarray culminated in the Iran-Contra scandal, in which it was revealed that White House officials, acting with or without the approval of President Reagan, through exceedingly shady intermediaries had sold American arms to the Islamic fundamentalist regime in Iran, and diverted proceeds from the sales to the Nicaraguan resistance. Finally, in the all-important area of military relations with the Soviet Union, U.S. policy was torn by intense debates within the government — amounting almost to internal arms control negotiations — over U.S. strategy in arms control negotiations with the Soviets. This included the insistence, by Senator Sam Nunn, chairman of the Senate Armed Services Committee, on a narrow or restrictive interpretation of the testing provisions of the ABM Treaty, and the threat by Senator Nunn and Senate Majority Leader Robert Byrd to hold up ratification of the INF Treaty unless the Reagan Administration would certify that its explanations of provisions of the treaty were permanently binding.

The perceived policy drift of the Bush Administration is merely one manifestation of a more fundamental problem in the conduct of American foreign relations, and that is the intense conflict that has been going on since the late 1960s and early 1970s over control of the making and implementing of foreign policy. The drift of the cautious Bush Administration is merely the obverse of the frequent disarray of the more ideological and assertive Reagan Administration: both are consequences of the ongoing confrontation between the executive and legislative branches of the federal government for control of foreign policy. This conflict, which is the root not only of the foreign policy problems of the Bush and Reagan Administrations but also of the equivalent problems of the Carter, Ford and Nixon Administrations, has many causes. The Constitution, of course, by allocating to both the executive and legislative branches crucial elements of the foreign affairs power, preordains a certain degree of conflict. It is, as Edwin Corwin puts it, "an invitation to struggle for the privilege of directing American foreign policy."[1] The struggle built into the Constitution has intensified, however, in the past two decades, the result of the collapse of post-World War II "bipartisanship" in foreign affairs brought about by the frustrations and failures of the Vietnam War. It has been further exacerbated by the situation of divided control of government that has generally prevailed since the end of the 1960s. In that period, the Republicans have occupied the White House for all but four years, and the Democrats, except for a six-year period of Republican control of the Senate, have been in control of Congress.

More is at work in the conflict over control of foreign policy, however, than mere turf battles between branches of government and political parties. It concerns, at bottom, the degree to which the conduct of foreign affairs can be "legalized," subject to the rule of law. The deepest cause of the ongoing conflict has been the effort by Congress to fix in law the purposes and especially the practices of U.S. foreign policy. Congress over the past two decades has repeatedly attempted, with at most the grudging acquiescence of Presidents, to establish by law not only the ends that would be pursued, but also the means by which those ends would be pursued, in foreign relations. It has sought to elevate the conduct of foreign affairs from the variable and contingent to the realm of the universal and permanent. This was the understandable result of the widespread perception, stemming from the Vietnam experience, that the presidency was dangerously "out of control" in the making and executing of foreign policy. The attempt to legalize foreign policy has lifted the ongoing conflict over the control of foreign affairs beyond even what might be expected out of the confrontation of Republican Presidents and Democratic Congresses. It provides the moral and political justification for the legislative branch's demands on the executive for an ever-expanding role in the conduct of foreign relations. Opposition to the legalization of foreign policy is the principle behind the resistance to such demands, in the name of "flexibility," by every President from Nixon to Reagan, including Democrat Jimmy Carter. Congress has clearly made headway in its effort to subject the making and executing of foreign policy to the rule of law. The problem with this undertaking — reflected in the drift and disarray so characteristic of American foreign policy during the past two decades — is that it ignores or abstracts from the inherent limits of the rule of law, limits that pertain most directly to the conduct of foreign affairs.

I.

The Boland Amendments — there were five very different and even conflicting versions passed between 1982 and 1986 — are only recent examples of Congress' ongoing effort to bring the rule of law to foreign policy. They are certainly not the first. Earlier attempts include the Clark Amendment (1976), which prohibited all U.S. aid to forces involved in the civil war in Angola, and the Jackson-Vanik Amendment (1974), which tied the extension of Most Favored Nation tariff status to the Soviet Union a crucial element in the Nixon

Administration's policy of detente — to liberalization by the Soviet Union of its immigration policies, particularly with respect to Jewish "refuseniks." Nor are the Boland Amendments the most audacious of Congress' attempts at legalization. That, undoubtedly, is the War Powers Resolution (1973), passed by Congress over the veto of President Nixon, who objected to it as "unconstitutional and dangerous to the best interests of our Nation."[2] The problems inherent in the legalization of foreign policy are perhaps best reflected in the implementation, over the past decade and a half, of the Wars Powers Resolution.[3]

The general purpose of the War Powers Resolution is to define, and hence limit, the authority of the President as commander-in-chief of the armed forces to commit U.S. forces in military conflict. It attempts to legalize what is perhaps the most important element of the executive power exercised by the President. This is done in order to "fulfill the intent of the Framers of the Constitution of the United States and insure that the collective judgment of both the Congress and the President will apply to the introduction of United States Armed Forces into hostilities." The constitutional authority of the President as commander-in-Chief to introduce U.S. forces into combat, or into situations threatening combat involvement, can be exercised, according to the resolution, "only pursuant to (1) a declaration of war, (2) specific statutory authorization, or (3) a national emergency created by attack upon the United States, its territories or possessions, or its armed forces." The resolution requires the President to consult with Congress, if at all possible, before any commitment of troops. It further requires him to report to Congress within 48 hours of any commitment of troops not authorized by a declaration of war, setting forth the reason for the action, the authority under which the action was taken, and "the estimated scope and duration" of the action. In such cases, the President must withdraw the forces committed at any time he is directed by Congress, or at the end of 60 days, unless he receives from Congress a declaration of war, statutory authorization, or an extension of the 60-day limit. This latter provision effectively establishes not only a one-house legislative veto on presidential action, but a legislative veto that can be exercised passively or silently, that is, by the refusal or even failure of either the Senate or the House to act in accordance with its legislative responsibilities.

Presidents, while careful to state their objections to the War Powers Resolution, have generally acceded, albeit often begrudgingly, to its reporting and authorization requirements. Its implementation has created, however, a host of problems for the conduct of U.S. foreign relations. The War Powers Resolution has undermined the foreign policy making process. It slows down policy making. The legislative process in American government is slow, often excruciatingly slow. This can be dangerous in foreign affairs, in which events can move very rapidly. For example, when in 1975 the military collapse of South Vietnam appeared imminent, President Ford went before a joint session of Congress to request that it "clarify immediately its restrictions on the use of U.S. military forces in Southeast Asia for the limited purpose of protecting American lives by insuring their evacuation." He asked for some word within nine days. Eighteen days after his address, with Congress struggling to complete legislative action, and with rocket attacks starting on Saigon, he ordered an immediate evacuation by Marine helicopters. In two days, 1,373 Americans, 5,595 Vietnamese, and 85 other persons were evacuated. Two days after the completion of the evacuation, Congress finished its work on President Ford's original request — with the House rejecting a conference committee report that would have authorized the evacuation.[4] Congress' inertia in legislation is the result of its decentralized legislative process. This turn is the result of the system of separation of power and checks and balances in American government. The decentralized legislative process gives strategically placed individuals in Congress, including many far from the responsibilities of leadership, the opportunity to slow or even stop legislation. This means that the War Powers Resolution presents to such individuals, in circumstances of grave risk or provocation, the opportunity to derail foreign policy.

The War Powers Resolution has further damaged American foreign policy by diverting the attention of Presidents and members of Congress from the substance of policy to its legal forms, that is, from concern for the proper ends and available means, and the prudent adjustment of means and ends, to concern for the observance of the forms required by the law. Ever since the passage of the resolution, debate over the use of American military forces, in whatever danger of involvement in actual conflict, has concentrated on the applicability of its provisions, for example whether the President should have consulted with Congress before committing troops, or whether the President required the authorization of Congress to continue his commitment of troops, or when the 60-day clock on the President's commitment of troops began to tick. This largely has come to replace real argument over the substance of Presidents' policies in the use of military forces. It certainly is easier for members of Congress to argue the legal requirements of the War Powers resolution than the fine points of American foreign policy. In this way, the Resolution encourages members of Congress, and indirectly Presidents, to evade their political, as opposed to their merely legal, responsibilities in the conduct of foreign relations. This evasion of responsibility was most momentous in the debate over President Reagan's commitment of U.S. troops to the multilateral peacekeeping force in Lebanon in the fall of 1983. Debate in Congress concentrated on Reagan's compliance with the requirements of the law, rather than on the prudence of his introduction of essentially unarmed U.S. troops into the chaotic military and political situation in Beirut, in which, because of the U.S. alliance with Israel, they could not really be accepted as disinterested peacekeepers, and thus would inevitably become targets for Israel's enemies. In this case, ignoring the substance in favor of the forms of policy contributed to catastrophe, in the bombing of the Beirut Marine barracks and the deaths of 241 American servicemen, and the virtually total disintegration of American policy in the Middle East. In addition, since legislation is generally the result of bargaining and compromise — between the President and Congress — between the two houses of Congress, among key members of Congress — the War Powers Resolution, by legalizing the conduct of military affairs, has exacerbated the tendencies built into the American system of divided government power towards policy incoherence in foreign relations. For example, it has complicated the problems of articulation and interpretation of foreign policy. The operation of the War Powers Resolution makes it always unclear who speaks for the United States in international relations: the President? the Congress? perhaps ultimately the Courts?

The most pronounced effect of the War Powers Resolution, however, has been to poison the relationship between the executive and legislative branches of the federal government in the conduct of foreign affairs. Its effect in practice has been the direct opposite of its declared intention of encouraging cooperation between the two political branches. This poisoning is in part the result of "criminalizing" policy differences, that is, treating differences over policy as matters of upholding or breaking the law. Congressional criticisms of President Reagan over the 1983 invasion of Grenada, for example, were at least as stringent for his alleged disregard of the law in ordering the invasion, as for the possible problems that he had created by his decision for American security and political interests in Latin America, Western Europe, and the Soviet Union. "We are dealing," charged Democratic Senator Gary Hart, "with an Administration that is not inclined to obey the law." Republican Senator Lowell Weicker accused Reagan of "flouting the law" in Grenada.[5] Members of the House of Representatives went further and called for Reagan's impeachment. This poisoning of relations is even more the result of the creation by the War Powers Resolution of controversies over the constitutional authority of the President and Congress in foreign affairs that are, for all practical purposes, irresolvable. While no President has ever conceded the constitutionality of the resolution, in particular its requirement that troops be withdrawn from combat or combat-situations within 60 days unless there is specific congressional authorization for their continuation, neither has any President sought to directly challenge it legally before the courts of the United States. This is in spite of the fact that the Supreme Court, in *INS v. Chadha* (1983), has declared the legislative veto to be unconstitutional. The reason for this reticence to act is that to challenge the law the President would have to openly break it, in some instance in which he deemed it necessary to commit U.S. military forces into conflict or into a situation in which conflict was likely, and the last thing that any President would choose to do when taking such a serious step would be to divide both the government and the people by boldly refusing to obey the laws passed by Congress. This would be the height of folly, tantamount to fighting a war on two fronts. Such an act, because of the danger it would present to the unity of the nation in a time of crisis, would be profoundly contrary to the President's sworn duty to "preserve, protect, and defend the Constitution of the United States."

Efforts by Congress to legalize the conduct of foreign relations, exemplified by the War Powers Resolution, by the problems they create, invite Presidents, who are charged in the Constitution — indirectly by its assignment of "the executive Power," and directly, by the oath of office it prescribes — with special responsibilities in foreign affairs, to surreptitiously get around or evade the law. They in effect encourage lawlessness in high places. This problem — that the imprudent extension of the rule of law in foreign affairs would inevitably lead to official lawlessness — was well understood by the Framers of the Constitution. Madison, in *Federalist* 41, defending the *indefinite power* granted to Congress "of raising *troops*, as well as providing fleets; and of maintaining both in *peace*, as well as in *war*," argues that only if the Constitution "could chain the ambition or set bounds to the exertions of all other nations" could it "prudently chain the discretion of its own government, and set bounds to the exertions for its own safety." "It is in vain," he claims, "to oppose constitutional barriers to the impulse of self-preservation." Indeed, "It is worse than in vain; because it plants in the Constitution itself necessary usurpations of power, every precedent of which is a germ of unnecessary and multiplied repetitions."[6] What Madison says about constitutionally established limitations applies with almost equal force to legislatively established limitations. The Iran-Contra scandal, the result of efforts by the Reagan Administration to get around legal limits fixed by Congress in the War Powers Resolution, the Boland Amendments, and other provision of the law, is a case study in the consequences of the legalization of foreign policy.

II.

The question of how far foreign policy can be legalized, or subsumed under the rule of law, raises the question of the function of the Constitution, the foundation of the legal regime in the American political community, in defining the powers of the federal government in foreign affairs. The Constitution, of course, delegates certain specific powers to the branches of the federal government, in particular, the executive and legislative, in international relations. In addition, it specifically prohibits to the states the exercise of certain other powers. These together make up the powers that the Constitution, either expressly or implicitly, designates as belonging to the federal government in foreign relations. There is nothing in the Constitution to indicate, however, that these powers are to be understood as comprising the totality of the power at the disposition of the federal government, as the instrument and the representative of the nation, in the conduct of foreign relations. The Constitution is silent about the connection between the various foreign affairs *powers*, and the comprehensive foreign affairs *power*, of the federal government. It certainly does not limit the latter to the former. Nor does it openly acknowledge the latter to transcend the former. The Constitution's ambiguity on the connection between the designated foreign affairs powers and the comprehensive foreign affairs power is studied: it reflects not some absentmindedness on the part of the Constitution's Framers, but rather a deep understanding of the problematic relationship between foreign affairs and the rule of law.

The Constitution concentrates the foreign affairs power in the federal government, and distributes elements of that power between the President and Congress. By prohibiting states from entering into treaties, or, unless authorized by Congress, from levying import and export duties, or maintaining armies and navies, it effectively reserves the conduct of diplomatic relations, foreign commerce, and war to the federal government. Broadly understood, these are the components that together make up the foreign affairs power. The Constitution then goes on to make both the President and Congress share in the foreign affairs power that it reserves to the federal government. Congress is specifically authorized to levy tariffs, regulate foreign commerce, establish rules for immigration and naturalization, define and punish crimes against international law, raise and equip armies and navies, and declare war. More generally, it is authorized to appropriate all funds required for the operation of the national government, and to make all "necessary and proper" laws for carrying into effect the powers granted to it, to any other department or officer of the federal government, or to the U.S. government. The Constitution designates the President as the commander-in-chief of the military forces of the United States. It also authorizes him to receive ambassadors and other public ministers from foreign states and, with the advice and consent of the Senate, to appoint ambassadors and other diplomatic officers to represent the United States, and to make treaties. More generally, it requires the President to "take Care that the Laws be faithfully executed" and, in the oath of office, to "preserve, protect, and defend the Constitution of the United States."

It is possible, and perhaps even natural, to assume that the foreign affairs powers enumerated in the Constitution, with appropriate interpretation and construction, define the foreign affairs power of the federal government. They are the parts out of which the whole is compounded. On this assumption, based on the conventional understanding of the Constitution as the ultimate source of political authority in the United States, defining and limiting government power, and distributing that power among government institutions, the foreign affairs power is essentially within the Constitution or the legal regime established by the Constitution. It is within the "rule of law." There are serious problems, however, with this assumption. It is questionable whether the enumerated powers, even as interpreted and constructed, really add up to all the powers actually exercised by the federal government and its officers in the conduct of foreign relations. There never has been, for example, a fully satisfactory explanation of the constitutional foundations for Executive Agreements, agreements concluded by the President with foreign governments that for all practical purposes have the legal effect of treaties, but which are not submitted to the Senate for ratification. Further, what is here assumed about the foreign affairs power and the Constitution does not really correspond to the way that powers in international relations are asserted and exercised in political practice, and articulated in legal and political theory. Those Presidents recognized as strong, for example, do not seek out hitherto unnoticed powers tucked away in the provisions of the Constitution and then act; rather, they settle on a course of action and then seek justification in the words of the document. They act as Jefferson did in the Louisiana Purchase: fulfilling what they understand as the responsibilities of their office, even in the absence of a clear constitutional mandate.

Most importantly, the assumption that the foreign affairs powers enumerated in the Constitution ultimately define the comprehensive foreign affairs power of the federal government, by implying that there are inherent and absolute limits to government authority, is dangerous to the economic, political, and even security interests of the United States. The understanding that the Constitution somehow, even tacitly, fixes the outer limits of federal power implies that there are things that the federal government simply could not do, regardless of the threat or provocation, to defend the interests, including the very survival, of the American political community. This line of argument leads to the logically absurd conclusion that the Constitution, established to preserve and perfect the Union, in circumstances of extreme danger could prohibit the federal government from taking actions indispensably necessary for the Union's survival. Such irrational legalism is quite alien to the sober realism that suffuses the Constitution. It is explicitly rejected by the Framers. "The authorities essential to the common defense," according to Hamilton in *Federalist* 23, "ought to exist without limitation, *because it is impossible to foresee or define the extent and variety of national exigencies, and the correspondent extent and variety of means which may be necessary to satisfy them.*" "The circumstances that endanger the safety of nations," he argues, "are infinite, and for this reason no constitutional shackles can wisely be imposed on the power to which care of it is committed." Hamilton bases his argument on the self-evident truth that "the *means* ought to be proportioned to the *end*."[7] The assumption that the foreign affairs power of the federal government is defined by the foreign affairs powers enumerated in the Constitution is finally and decisively refuted by its opposition to this self-evident truth.

This leads to what might at first appear to be the bizarre conclusion that the foreign affairs power exercised by the federal government and its officers does not derive from the Constitution. This is the case, however, if it is assumed that the foreign affairs power is inherent in the sovereignty of the United States. It belongs to the United States by virtue of its existence as an independent political community. The Union, on this line of argument, not the Constitution, is the ultimate source of political authority. The Constitution is the creature, not the creator, of the Union. The foreign affairs power, because it is inherent in the Union, precedes the Constitution, which was established to preserve and perfect the Union. The Constitution, by which the American people give themselves a form as a political community, since they can not give themselves a form unless they are free from outside domination, presupposes the working of the foreign affairs power. The federal government, on this assumption, enjoys all the powers that belong to any independent state, including the rights to conduct diplomatic relations, engage in foreign commerce, and make war. These powers, along with all powers necessary to implement them, would belong to the national government, even if the Constitution had not so much as mentioned the matter of international relations. This assumption implies that the foreign affairs power of the federal government is essentially outside the Constitution, or the legal regime established by the Constitution. It is ultimately outside the rule of law.

The Supreme Court, in at least one important case, has affirmed the extraconstitutionality of the foreign affairs power. This was in *United States v. Curtiss-Wright Export Corp.* (1936) Curtiss-Wright had been indicted for conspiring to sell weapons to Bolivia, which was involved in a war with Paraguay, in spite of a presidential proclamation prohibiting such sales. The proclamation was issued pursuant to a Joint Resolution of Congress, authorizing the President to ban weapons sales to the two countries, should he find that this would contribute to the reestablishment of peace between them. Curtiss-Wright argued in U.S. district court that the indictment should be dismissed, on the ground that the Joint Resolution on which the presidential proclamation was based violated the Constitution by delegating legislative power to the executive. The court found for Curtiss-Wright, and the United States appealed to the Supreme Court. The Supreme Court reversed the decision of the lower court, holding that the Joint Resolution had in no way violated the constitutional separation of powers. The basis for the Court's decision was the argument that, since the foreign affairs power exercised by the federal government does not arise from the Constitution, as does the government's power in internal affairs, its exercise is not subject to constitutional restrictions, for example relating to the separation of powers. "The broad statement that the federal government can exercise no powers except those specifically enumerated in the Constitution, and such implied powers as are necessary and proper to carry into effect the enumerated powers is categorically true," according to Justice Sutherland writing for the Court, "only in respect to our internal affairs." "In that field," he claims, "the primary purpose of the Constitution was to carve from the general mass of legislative powers *then possessed by the states* such portions as it was thought desirable to vest in the federal government." The states, however, never had power in international relations. When the American colonies, acting as "a unit in foreign powers," declared their independence from Great Britain, "the powers of external sovereignty did not depend upon the affirmative grants of the Constitution."[8]

On this line of argument, the foreign affairs powers enumerated in the Constitution have nothing to do with defining the comprehensive foreign affairs power of the federal government. They in no way set the limits of what government can do in international relations. Rather, the enumerated powers establish a legal framework within which the officers of the federal government — principally the President and the members of Congress — can assert against one another the right to exercise powers incorporated in the undefined or residual foreign affairs power. The enumerated powers are "levers" in the hands of the President and Congress for moving the undefined foreign affairs power. The Constitution's establishment of a unitary executive, and the generality of the powers which it delegates to the executive, give the President some advantage over Congress, which is institutionally segmented and endowed with more or less specific powers, in the assertion of elements of the foreign affairs power. The powers delegated to the President allow, and even encourage, him to take the initiative in foreign policy. At the same time, the foreign affairs powers enumerated in the Constitution establish a set of standards and a political system by which the officers of the federal government can be judged, and if necessary punished politically, for their stewardship over the extraconstitutional foreign affairs power. Judgment by the American people is ultimately rendered through the ballot box. It is reflected, more subtly but more continuously, in the political relations between the executive and legislative branches. Public support for the President's foreign policy makes Congress more deferential in the ongoing struggle over the undefined foreign affairs power; public opposition to the President's policy allows Congress to assert itself more forcefully. The visibility of the President, a consequence of the unity of the executive office in the Constitution, makes him more subject to the judgment of the American public than the members of Congress. The Constitution establishes, then, a rough equivalence between authority and responsibility in the conduct of foreign relations, in spite of its ambiguity concerning the nature or possible limits of the foreign affairs power.

The Constitution, rather than defining and distributing a foreign affairs power for the federal government, through its delegations to the executive and legislature, sets in motion a foreign affairs power that is inherent in the American political community and is exercised on its behalf by the federal government. Silence on the relationship between the enumerated foreign affairs powers and the comprehensive foreign affairs power is the means adopted in the Constitution for reconciling the rule of law and the conduct of foreign relations. Or perhaps it should be said that silence on this matter is the closest the Constitution comes to a reconciliation between the two. In any event, through its silence the Constitution preserves the conduct of foreign relations from the demands of the rule of law, while preserving the rule of law from the demands of the conduct of foreign relations. If it identified the comprehensive power with the enumerated powers, it would, by in principle fixing the conduct of foreign affairs in law, leave no room for initiative and innovation, regardless of the threats or opportunities that might be presented in international relations. If, however, it openly acknowledged the comprehensive power to transcend the enumerated powers, it would, by in effect officially recognizing a necessity transcending the requirements of the law, undermine the authority of the legal regime that it establishes.

The Constitution in its silence avoids both difficulties, by obscuring the necessity in foreign affairs that transcends the rule of law, while leaving to officers of the federal government, in particular the President, the freedom along with the political responsibility to act in foreign affairs in accordance with that necessity.

III.

The argument that the foreign affairs power of the federal government should not and indeed cannot be legally defined leads to the conclusion that there are inherent or absolute limits to the rule of law. This conclusion is diametrically opposed to what is perhaps the most profound impulse of American political thought and practice, the will to universalize the rule of law. This is the highest aspiration of the American political community. It represents the fulfillment of what is understood in the liberal tradition of political thought, by which the American political community takes its bearings, as human freedom. Human beings realize their freedom through self-legislation, laying down the law for themselves and living in accordance with that law. Ignored, however, in the practical and theoretical zeal for the extension of the rule of law is what liberal political thought has to say about limits. These limits represent the natural pales of human freedom, the metes and bounds set by nature to the freedom of man. Both the purpose and the limits of the rule of law are visible in the teaching of liberal political philosophy concerning the origins of political power, the doctrine of what Hobbes and Locke call the "state of nature." The limits to the legalization of foreign policy are, from the point of view of the liberal political philosophers, merely one manifestation of the limits to the rule of law, and to human freedom, fixed by nature.

The state of nature doctrine is derived from what Jefferson, following a hint from Locke, calls the "self-evident truth" that all human beings are created equal.[9] Because all human beings are equal, they possess certain rights against one another, preeminently the right to life, and following that, the right to what is necessary to life. Equality means that there are no natural duties that men owe to one another, or at least that whatever duties they bear towards their fellow men are derivative or secondary. Because there are no natural duties binding men together, they are by nature asocial. Equality further means that there are no relations of superiority and inferiority, by either natural or divine right, among human beings. Men in the order of nature know nothing of ruling or being ruled. They are by nature apolitical. The natural condition for man — what Locke calls the state of nature — is, then, pre-political and even pre-social. Granted the self-evident truth of human equality, the only foundation for society and government is consent. Human beings will consent to put themselves under unnatural, and hence in a way alienating and oppressive, social organization and political rule — ultimately under the rule of law — in order to escape the evils of the state of nature. According to Hobbes, the state of nature is full of horrors, and the life of man in it "solitary, poor, nasty, brutish, and short."[10] According to Locke, it is laden with "inconveniences," deriving from the problem of executing the "law of nature" that governs the state of nature. The law of nature is that "Everyone, as he is *bound to preserve himself*, and not to quit his station wilfully, ought he, as much as he can, *to preserve the rest of mankind*, and may not unless it be to do Justice to an offender, take away, or impair the life, or what tends to Preservation of the Life, Liberty, Health, Limb or Goods of another."[11] Obligations under Locke's formulation of the law of nature are derivative from the right of nature, which is self-preservation. The problem of the state of nature is that each individual in it must judge for himself of violations of the law of nature, and execute penalties for violations of the law. As Locke points out, human beings are likely to be partial judges in their own cases, that is, too quick to take offense and too severe in punishing offenders when their own interests are involved. It is, according to Locke, precisely to establish an impartial judge and executioner of the law that human beings consent to form civil society and put themselves under the authority of government.

The state of nature, for Locke, is in principle a "State of perfect Freedom," in which men are free to "order their Actions, and dispose of their Possessions, and Persons as they think fit, within the bounds of the Law of Nature, without asking leave, or depending upon the Will of any other Man."[12] Each individual in the state of nature has a kind of natural "legislative authority," his own will, to direct him in his actions.[13] This natural legislative authority constitutes man's natural freedom. The freedom of the state of nature is, however, an empty thing. This is because, all being equally "Kings," and the majority being "no strict Observers of Equity and Justice," the "property" — the life, liberty and estate — of all is "very unsafe, very insecure."[14] The radical contingency of man's existence in the state of nature renders utterly nugatory his natural legislative authority. He may will the achievement of some purpose, but he has no way of insuring the fulfillment of his will. It is indicative that Locke, while referring to the exercise of the executive and judicial powers in the state of nature, says nothing about the exercise of the legislative authority. It exists only in principle, as legislative authority. This is the result of the defective exercise of the executive and judicial powers by individuals in the state of nature. There is no real legislative authority — and hence no real freedom — in the state of nature because men in the natural condition cannot foresee the actions of their fellows. They cannot count on their fellows acting rationally in judging and executing the law of nature. They must then be ready to adjust their actions in accordance with the actions of others. Human beings in the natural condition are inevitably subject to the will of others. They are prevented by the situation of the state of nature from legislating for themselves, that is, from setting their own courses of action, and then following the courses they have set. While the legislative power, as the consummation of man's freedom, is logically prior to the executive and judicial powers, the judicial and especially the executive powers are practically and temporally prior to the legislative power.

It is to make actual their natural freedom, or their natural legislative authority, that human begins form themselves into civil society. They accomplish this by in effect correcting the deficiencies in the exercise of the powers that actually are brought into play in the state of nature, the executive and judicial powers. Each individual, in moving into society, consents to give up the power, belonging to him by nature, "not only to preserve his Property, that is, his Life, Liberty, and Estate, against the Injuries and Attempts of other Men; but to judge of, and punish the breaches of [the Law of Nature] in others, as he is persuaded the Offense deserves, even with Death it self." This power he relinquishes "into the hands of the Community in all cases that exclude him not from appealing for Protection to the Law established by it." By this act, the community is made the "Umpire," to settle "by standing Rules, indifferent, and the same to all Parties," disputes that might arise among its members. This power is exercised "by Men having Authority from the Community."[15] The community, artificially established, can be entrusted with the powers of judgment and execution because, having no purpose beyond that leading to its formation, and reflecting the common interest of all its individual members, it has no particular interest of its own to pervert its actions and decisions. It is inherently impartial, and thus inherently rational. The inherent impartiality and rationality of government power limits its exercise by those individuals in whose hands it is placed. It is possible for human beings in civil society, because they can foresee the actions of government, to more or less foresee one another's actions. They are therefore able to legislate for themselves, that is, to lay down for themselves rules to govern their lives. The highest expression of this artificially acquired power of legislation is the exercise of legislative power by and for the political community, in ordaining the standing rules that will govern it and its members. The "*Freedom of Men under Government*," what for Locke is the only real freedom for human beings, is "to have a standing Rule to live by, common to every one of that Society, and made by the Legislative Power erected in it; A Liberty to follow my own Will in all things, where the Rule prescribes not; and not to be subject to the inconstant, uncertain, unknown Arbitrary Will of another Man."[16]

Human freedom, according to Locke, is actualized in the rule of law. The rule of law, is essentially limited or circumscribed. It is limited by the state of nature: possible only within the political order of civil society, it has no place outside civil society, in the state of nature. The state of nature continues among human beings unless they consent together to give up their right to execute the law of nature, and establish a public authority to govern them. This means that the state of nature continues, even after the creation of civil society, in the relations among independent political communities. It continues among states in the international system. Those who have no "common establish'd Law and Judicature to appeal to, with Authority to decide Controversies between them" are in the state of nature, and this certainly applies to states in international relations.[17] As a matter of fact, Locke, following Hobbes, uses the relations among states to prove the real existence of the state of nature. "Since all *Princes* and Rulers of *Independent* Governments all through the World, are in a State of Nature," Locke argues, "'tis plain the World never was, nor ever will be, without Numbers of Men in that State."[18] There are, then, limits to how far the legislative power of any political community can extend. It can go no further than where the foundations of the rule of law have been laid, and that is only in domestic or internal politics. Outside the arena of domestic politics, there is no real exercise of the legislative power, because of the continuation of the state of nature. State and international affairs are governed by the law of nature, which subordinates their obligations to other states to their right of self-preservation, and are compelled to judge for themselves, with inevitable partiality, of violations of the law of nature by other states. Incapable of really foreseeing the actions of other states, they must be ready to act in accordance with what is done to them. No matter how strong they might be, they are not really free to act according to their own will. The underlying reality of international relations is unaffected by the agreements, for example for trade or mutual defense, that states might make with one another: "'tis not every Compact that puts an end to the State of Nature between Men," according to Locke, "but only this one of agreeing together mutually to enter into one Community, and make one Body Politick."[19]

Governments must operate both in an environment of law and in an environment of lawlessness. They are both under and above the rule of law. This dualism is reflected in Locke's analysis of the parts of government. Locke divides government into "legislative," "executive," and "federative" powers. The legislative power, which has the "right *to direct*" by legal enactment "how *the Force of the Commonwealth* shall be imploy'd for preserving the Community and the Members of it," and the executive power, which is to see that laws once made "have a constant and lasting force," are essential elements in the regime of the rule of law.[20] The federative power, however, which leads the political community as a whole in its relations with other political communities, is necessarily outside the rule of law. Indicatively, Locke calls this power "*natural*, because it is that which answers to the Power every Man naturally had before he entered into Society."[21] The federative power "is much less capable to be directed by antecedent, standing, positive Laws, than the *Executive*." This is because "the *Laws* that concern Subjects one amongst the other, being to direct their actions, may well enough *precede* them. But what is to be done in references to *Foreigners*, depending much upon their actions, and the variation of designs and interests, must be *left* in great part *to* the *Prudence* of those who have this Power committed to them, to be managed by the best of their Skill, for the advantage of the Commonwealth."[22] The federative power is responsible for establishing and defending the space within which the legislative and executive powers may operate, or in which the regime of the rule of law may bear away. Locke argues that, for practical reasons, the federative power must be joined with the executive power. He thus lays the foundation for the office of the "chief executive" in liberal government, which combines "executive" and "federative" functions. This office, the best example of which is the American presidency, is profoundly ambiguous with respect to the rule of law. The President is simultaneously subject to the rule of law and responsible for establishing the necessary conditions for the operation of the rule of law in a lawless world. The legal and political ambiguity of the office of the presidency is the clearest possible manifestation of the natural limits on the rule of law.

Conclusion

The requirement that the government of the United States operate in both an environment of law and an environment of lawlessness — in both "civil society" and the "state of nature" — engenders profound moral tensions in American political practice. These tensions are most pronounced in the conduct of foreign affairs. They cannot be relieved, however, as some in government, in particular in Congress, have attempted, by indefinitely expanding the domain of the rule of law into the arena of foreign policy. Indeed, the indefinite expansion of the rule of law into foreign policy might be the greatest danger in contemporary American politics to the rule of law in the United States. It compels government officers, in extreme circumstances, to find ways to get around the forms of the rule of law. Inviting continued attempts by political leaders, particularly in the executive branch, to circumvent the requirements of the law, it induces criminality in high places. Most importantly, in a still dangerous world, it might so hamper the exercise of the foreign affairs power by those legally entrusted with that responsibility by the American people as to threaten the economic prosperity, the political influence, the freedom of action, and even the very existence of the United States, and with that the legislative power of the American people. Resolution of the moral tensions in American politics — to the extent that they can be resolved — requires restraint on the powerful and noble passion for the rule of law. This in turn presupposes a deep understanding of the natural limits on the rule of law.

Notes

1. Edwin S. Corwin, *The President: Office and Powers*, 4th ed. (New York: New York University Press, 1957): 171.
2. United States Department of State *Bulletin*, Nov. 26, 1973.
3. Public Law (93-148; 87 Stat. 555; 50 U.S.C. 1541-1548).
4. See Robert F. Turner, *The War Powers Resolution: Its Implementation in Theory and Practice* (Philadelphia: Foreign Policy Research Institute, 1983): 51-52, 56-59.
5. *New York Times*, October 28, 1993, I:1. 1; *New York Times*, October 29, 1983, I: 12. 3.
6. Alexander Hamilton, James Madison, and John Jay, *The Federalist Papers*,

intro. by Clinton Rossiter (New York: New American Library, 1961), 41: 256-257.

7. Ibid., 23, 153.

8. *United States v. Curtiss-Wright Export Corp.* 299 U.S. 304.

9. See John Locke, *Two Treatises of Government*, ed. by Peter Laslett (New York: Mentor Books, 1965) II: 2. 4 (p. 309).

10. Thomas Hobbes, *Leviathan*, ed. by C.B. Macpherson (Baltimore: Penguin Books, 1968), I: 13: 186.

11. Locke, *Two Treatises* II: 2. 6: 311.

12. Ibid., II: 2. 4: 309.

13. Ibid., II: 4. 22: 324.

14. Ibid., II: 9. 123: 395.

15. Ibid., II: 7. 87: 367.

16. Ibid., II: 4. 23: 325.

17. Ibid., II: 7. 87: 367.

18. Ibid., II: 2. 14: 317. See II: 12. 145: 411.

19. Ibid., II: 2. 14: 317.

20. Ibid., II: 12. 143, 144: 409-410.

21. Ibid., II: 12. 145: 410.

22. Ibid., II: 12. 147: 411-412.

Chapter 5

Religious Liberty in the Welfare State

Richard Epstein
University of Chicago

I. The Great Divide of 1937

To what extent can our conception of religious liberty survive or even flourish after the advent of the welfare state? This question, which I hope to address here, is in some sense inescapable. The rise of the welfare state is characterized by a high level of government action in all phases of economic and social life. It is therefore a simple consequence of the law of large numbers that some fraction of this legislation will pose a challenge, if not a threat, to the autonomy of religious institutions. The issue, moreover, raises special doctrinal and analytical difficulties because we operate today under a regime of constitutional dualism that is the legacy of the constitutional upheavals of the New Deal.

In this context I want to analyze two aspects of that dualism: economic liberties and, somewhat more briefly, public finance. On the first front the Supreme Court today draws a sharp systematic distinction between ordinary economic liberties and preferred freedoms.[1] By conventional wisdom economic liberties include the right to own and dispose of all forms of property, and to control the disposition of one's labor in the marketplace. Under the earlier constitutional regimes, these received a fairly high measure of protection. As a first approximation, the central role of the government was to ensure that property is protected against encroachment by trespass or other common law wrongs, and to guarantee that contracts were enforced by the terms on which they are made.[2]

There were of course some exceptions to the general rule well recognized before the 1937 watershed. The restrictions on freedom of contract imposed by the antitrust laws were sustained against all constitutional challenge, as they should be today.[3] More doubtfully, various restrictions on land use, from both zoning to rent control laws, were also accepted, at least on a qualified basis under the earlier conceptions of the police power.[4]

Even if the pre-1937 cases on economic liberties did not represent some idealized version of (either) heaven or hell, two distinct limitations on government power did have important economic consequences before they were overrun in the New Deal revolution — limitations with important implications for the place of religious liberty in the United States. First, there were powerful restrictions on the scope of the congressional commerce power prior to 1937. Commerce meant commerce, not agriculture or manufacture, and certainly not every productive activity known to mankind. Some things were within the scope of the commerce power, but unremarkably other things also fell outside of it. Before 1937 regulation of local employment practices were all in the province of the states, save for those employments (e.g., railroad workers) who were engaged in interstate commerce.[5] *Lochner v. New York* was Lochner v. *New York* and not Lochner v. *United States*.[6]

Second, there were certain substantive areas in which the Congress or the state could not regulate. Pre-1937 constitutional law had developed a distinction between "labor" and "health statutes" in the area of employment. Health (including safety) legislation was uniformly held acceptable against employer challenges, even where it was explicitly in derogation of freedom of contract. The distinction between health and labor statutes was drawn conscientiously and fairly. Training coupling statutes,[7] mine regulations, and worker's compensation all fell on the safety side of the line.[8] A modest safety justification was all that was needed to sustain a statute that restricted certain kinds of dangerous employments.[9]

In contrast "labor" statutes were beyond the pale of either Congress or the states to enact. This labor category included two types of regulation critical to understanding the role of religion in the welfare state: collective bargaining statutes were not a justified infringement of the freedom of contract, be it for the unwilling employer who demanded a "yellow dog" contract, or for the employee who wanted to stay out of union orbit.[10] Likewise antidiscrimination laws, if they had been passed, would have fallen, I suspect, to the same challenges as forbidden statutes. Before 1937 the law was something of a hodgepodge because the distinctions it drew did not conform to any consistent theory of the relationship between private ordering and government power.

Even if every doctrinal nuance was not philosophically coherent, one conclusion did remain: There were cases in the employment context where government power could be restricted because of infringements on economic liberties. The last vestiges of those limitations were removed in 1937, with the New Deal victories consolidated in the next five years or so. Congress now had plenary power: individual rights to resist regulation within the economic sphere, including labor markets, was essentially a dead letter. Viewed from a distance, the common law rules of freedom of contract in employment were overrun in two distinct stages. Health risks (which could be assumed at common law) were taken out of the realm of private contract in the first two decades of the twentieth century. Price, wage and bargaining terms followed twenty years later.[11]

Redistribution and public finance yield a similar picture on the question of the government powers to collect and spend tax revenues. Again it should not be supposed that all forms of redistribution of wealth were out of bounds before the 1937 revolution.[12] On this issue too there is something of the same clouded picture found with economic liberties. Thus progressive taxation was explicitly endorsed, and cases before 1900 routinely approved of using public funds to provide welfare for the poor and needy. Nonetheless all forms of redistribution were not viewed with equal favor. The law of special assessments limited the occasions in which one group of individuals could tax other persons for the cost of certain local, but public, improvements from which the first group derived the lion's share of the gain. In these cases the Court did insist, usually under the due process clause, that some measure of benefit be provided for the persons subjected to the tax. While the calculation of benefit was far from an exact science, the Supreme Court did not adopt an "anything goes" posture to the overall problem of local abuse.[13] By 1937, however, the benefit requirement had been eroded away until it became clear that the receipt of government protection became a sufficient benefit to justify virtually any redistributive tax.[14] The partial restraints against redistribution previously in place were thus removed.

I have criticized these 1937 developments elsewhere, and do not want to refight that battle here. What I do hope to do is to assess the impact that the 1937 revolution has had on cases which involve the intersection of religious liberty and government power. My theme is a simple one. The 1937 revolution did not, and could not, completely close the question of how to reconcile state power with individual rights for either economic liberties or public finance. Some relatively small, but theoretically important area of tension remains. Today the constitutional battleground between state power and the common law conceptions of property and liberty has shifted to new arenas. But ironically the modern dialogue over church and state takes the same substantive form as the earlier debate over state and market. While the turf has changed, the vocabulary used, the principles applied, and the enormous size of the stakes have not.[15] The principles of liberty and property that animated the resistance to the state police power before 1937 have found a new voice after 1937. The concerns with redistribution through taxation have also found expression in the religion cases as well — for even if most forms of redistribution are tolerated, redistribution from, and especially to, religious organizations has come under increased judicial scrutiny. The pattern of deference found in economic affairs does not carry over to religious affairs, however murky the boundary is between the two domains. Once scrutiny becomes strict, the protection of liberty and the control of redistribution become central parts of the constitutional enterprise.

The subject of this paper is, then, the fate of religious liberty, a delicate matter in a world in which comprehensive economic regulation is the norm. I shall only be able to address a few instructive illustrations here, but the points I think can be easily generalized to other cases. In general I shall concentrate my energies on employment questions, placing to one side a wide number of areas that also cry out for further analysis, of which education is perhaps the most notable. The next section of this paper looks at labor regulation in connection. The last, a shorter section, deals with public finance.

II. Religious and Contractual Liberty

Let us begin with collective bargaining. The analysis here may seem to be narrow and technical, but in truth it takes us far afield. In the first section I shall discuss the switch from unanimous consent to majority rule, which is the distinctive feature of collective bargaining, and show its inconsistency with the idea of religious freedom. The second section examines the scope of religious freedom, and finds that there is no external test which demarcates it from the world of secular affairs. The third section then shows that justification of religious liberty depends upon the same theories that were once used to defend economic liberties more generally. The fourth section deals with the tension between a broad conception of religious liberty and an equally broad conception of the establishment clause. The fifth section explores the judicial response to the tension between collective bargaining and the labor statutes as revealed in the important if inconclusive case of the *Catholic Bishops v. National Labor Relations Board.*[16]

1. *From unanimous consent to majority rule.* Let us begin with collective bargaining. One major consequence of the 1937 revolution was to legitimate the institution of collective bargaining.[17] The scheme of labor relations has two basic features, both of which are troubling to persons who believe in freedom of contract. First, labor negotiations are not conducted in accordance with the principle of unanimous consent required for complex transactions in free markets. Collective bargaining displaces unanimous consent by the majority rule of workers within a bargaining unit. The state by administrative order first chooses the contours of the unit, whose members then decide whether to have union representation or not. The minority is bound by the choice of the majority; it cannot make direct contracts with the employer, but must be satisfied with a duty of fair representation imposed on the union that represents it. The employer for its part is under a duty to bargain with the union representative. The duty is said to be one in "good faith," where that phrase conveys the clear message that the duty to bargain is not just another name for the duty to agree. (The vagueness of the good faith phrase is not a verbal problem. Any other term will have the same

difficulties when at will contracts are abandoned.) Yet when all is said and done, there are some limits to the amount of employer intransigence allowed, for in the end the ordinary option of just saying "no" and walking away is not available to the unionized firm. All matters about work conditions and wages and the like may be on the table, whether the employer likes it or not.[18]

The system of state limitations on contract necessarily carries with it state-imposed limitations on property. The hallmark of property at common law was the right to exclude others from the use or possession of a thing subject to your ownership. In essence the common law set its face against collective ownership by government fiat. Instead its rules of first possession were individualistic in orientation. Joint ownership was created only by unanimous consent. But the advent of the labor statutes meant the end of exclusivity in the domain of property as well. What sense does it make to say that the employer must bargain with workers in good faith, but then has the absolute right to exclude them from the workplace? If one has to relinquish the autonomy over contract, then absolute control of possession necessarily must be relinquished as well. The point manifests itself both before and after agreement. The laws of trespass cannot be used to keep union representatives from the employer's premises during any organization campaign or election. Once there is a duty to bargain, then the employer cannot in good faith insist upon a contract that allows him to keep workers out of the workplace altogether. The labor statutes go far beyond the common law rules that relax the owner's claims of exclusive possession only in case of extreme necessity.[19]

What happens when collective bargaining is carried over into the area of religious institutions? Initially it should be clear that it is manifestly impermissible to impose a collective governance solution on religious organizations. Thus suppose that Congress passed a law which provided that all religious persons within a given territorial region were to be governed by a single religious board whose officers were chosen by majority vote. The trustees would of course have fiduciary duties toward any minority, and on special application some groups could demand smaller, separate religious units, much the way in which craft unions may seek to organize separately from larger plant unions. It is inconceivable that Catholics, Jews and Protestants could be required to work together under government aegis, or even that different denominations of Jews or of Protestants should be required to iron out their differences with their coreligionists. The principle of freedom of association is implicit in the protection of the free exercise of religion. This principle requires that unanimous consent be obtained for membership in a religious organization. Freedom of association is thus a species of freedom of contract, which cannot be undone by any asserted state interest. Religious liberty is utterly inconsistent with a mandatory collective of any sort.

The intellectual difficulties only increase when religious organizations engage in transactions with their members or indeed with the rest of the world.

Religious principles and interests reach at least some of these questions, for while doctrine and dogma are essential to religion, they do not define or limit its scope. If freedom of contract is not a constitutional norm generally, how does it apply to contracts that religious institutions have, both in their religious matters (dues and official appointments) and in their inevitable contacts with the rest of the world, including their contracts of employment? The dominant question therefore is how to parcel out the turf of the religious institution between two radically disjoint constitutional regimes, one which looks with favor on any government regulation of employment and labor matters — an autonomy that is fully protected only if religious organizations have the freedom of contract routinely denied ordinary firms and individuals. The conflict here is inescapable: freedom might be no longer a general constitutional principle that applies across the board. But so long as there is a clause that protects the free exercise of religion, freedom must have its bite in a narrower sphere whose boundary lines are far from distinct. Someone must parcel out the turf between state and church.

2. *The scope of religion.* One possible way to minimize these difficulties is to give a very narrow conception as to what falls within the sphere of religious activities. In principle it could apply to the choice of doctrine and religious practices. But that view is utterly inconsistent with the views that religious people take of their own affairs. For them religion involves a far broader code of conduct.[20] Here we have one of those jurisdictional puzzles that plagued the relations between church and state throughout English history, long before anyone thought of a constitution: who decides the boundary? If the religious institutions determine the scope of their own sphere of influence, then very little of consequence to them will be kept out. But if the state decides the scope of the religious immunity, then pressures are set up to make the scope of religious freedom a good deal narrower. In a formal, and important, sense the Constitution gives the supreme power to the secular branch, but what it giveth, it also taketh away, for the Constitution itself contains explicit respect to religious freedom that the state is bound to uphold.

The general view taken by the courts is that "sincere" religious beliefs are protected from state cross-examination for their soundness. It is hard to decide whether this principle is motivated by a respect for religion, or for a commendable sense of self-preservation, but the point hardly matters: each reason is sufficient and both together are overpowering. By this one proposition the Court has kept itself at a distance from a set of religious controversies that neither it nor anyone else can authoritatively resolve for believers and nonbelievers alike.

Yet how far does this deference extend? Let us put aside the question of abuse, which might arise with ad hoc religions that have as their major doctrinal points exemption from taxation and military service. It is nonetheless a commonplace of established religions that their codes of conduct govern church members engaged in ordinary worldly transactions who are subject to heavy religious rules. Religion conceived by its practitioners is a total and complete code of human conduct which covers ordinary contracts of sale and employment along with religious rituals.[21]

The imperialist impulse of religious practice places great stress on any preordained boundary line between state and religion. It is a conflict that is only exacerbated by the welfare state. In the earlier age when liberty and contract were protected, these conflicts between the religious and the secular could arise because the rules of the state might well forbid what the principles of religion command. The most obvious illustration might be a (hypothetical) religious rule that required the sacrifice of a human being (outside the faith) in order to propitiate the gods. A more chilling and realistic example is the recent (and effective) death threat by the Ayatollah against Salman Rushdie for blasphemous texts that our Constitution at least protects. In principle, the enforcement of the ordinary criminal law against murder necessarily requires the violation of the free exercise of a religious belief. But the ultimate question is whether the state's prohibition violates the "free exercise of religion" as found in the Constitution.

So it is back to first principles. Freedom in this context is a term that limits as well as empowers. In the religious context, "freedom" must be taken to mean not absolute license, but rather the same kind of freedom used to demarcate the relationships between ordinary individuals. Indeed, there can be protection of religious freedom only by those courts that are wholly indifferent to the internal beliefs of all the religions that they protect. Conviction of the rightness of beliefs is critical for those who join one faith or another. But it is wholly irrelevant in any political order whose first task is to see how people of fundamentally different beliefs can live with each other.

Within this framework, then freedom is not total license to do what one wants, wholly without regard to the consequences that it has upon others. Rather it is to do what one wants within a parameter of rights (property and liberty again) without having to *justify* the choices so made to any other individual. But the parameter of rights is one that has to be good for all persons across the board. The theory has to allow for the compatibility of "like" individual freedom for all individuals simultaneously, and generally seeks that set of mutually consistent rights that maximize, at a best guess, some conception of overall welfare, utility or happiness. There are enormous complications in deciding how to move from a set of social concerns to a set of individual rights, which I bypass in this context, for all theories agree that a prohibition against force and fraud is consistent with the liberty of the individuals whose conduct is thereby restrained. Sacrifice of strangers is clearly an application of the former, and we should have to prohibit it if only to accept the freedom of other individuals.

The use of freedom here is no different, I believe, from the use of freedom with respect to speech where the practice of fraud and defamation may be controlled because while they are undoubtedly forms of speech, they are not forms of freedom, given the correlative duties that exist across persons. It is also, moreover, the same conception of freedom, with the normal baggage of correlative duties, that derives from the conceptions of liberty and property that are today rejected in the economic sphere: slander of title after all is a matter of both speech and of property. But with these limitations on force and fraud foremost in mind, then there is a way for the state to limit religious actions which does not require an examination of religious principles as such. Rather, it undertakes an alternative strategy of importing into religious disputes principles that have been developed elsewhere, and with other ends in mind. There is a virtue in this carryover, because it helps assure us that these conceptions of liberty and freedom are applied to religion without any evident bias for or against religion.

The conclusions here are not always to the liking of religious people whose own codes can be authoritarian as well. Thus in my view the state prohibition against polygamy is as incorrect as the state toleration of sacrifice. Polygamy takes place only with the consent of the men and women involved in the marriage, and as such can be regulated by the ordinary office of contract if so desired. The customary marriage vows in most religions speak about "forsaking all others" and these should be interpreted in both the religious and civil law to bar polygamy by men who take such oaths. But the Mormon oaths were different, and the question is whether the offense at practices of the multitude can justify the limitations on those practices by the few. Decisions that "invent" state interest opposed to polygamy work in the same authoritarian tradition that holds that the dominant political forces know what is right for others better than they know for themselves. The insistence that these contracts are so repugnant to ordinary sensibilities could only have been the result of social coercion or duress that is wholly incompatible with the idea of freedom: exceptions to the basic rule of consent have to be proved, and proved clearly. They cannot presume. Our base line remains that religious liberty ends where force and fraud have been clearly shown to have begun. That line is not approached, let alone crossed in the polygamy cases.[22]

3. *Subjective preferences and religious sincerity.* It should be evident that in constitutional discourse the demarcation between state and church relies upon the same conceptions of property and liberty that once animated the constitutional distinction between state and market. The connection is even closer because the line between church and state depends upon the same conception of value that once separated state from market. As noted earlier, the element of sincerity with respect to religion is the implicit acknowledgment that the state will not inquire into the conception of the good (or the divine) that motivates religious practice and belief. That attitude is also consistent with the general view of property rights and liberty in economic affairs. Recall that Thomas Hobbes, when groping to his (now standard economic) theory of private contract in the *Leviathan*, stressed that the value that any individual attached to that thing was solely a function of the "appetite" and desire he had. Apart from desire, there was not objective measure of value which explained whether an exchange was fair. Within this system, the essential role of consent was to ensure that both parties were better off by their own lights, because otherwise as rational persons, they would not enter into the trade.

The theory of property rights, with its emphasis upon the separate domains of conduct, thus responds to the subjectivity of value. It says, once we know that there is no collective conception of the good, then we should choose that arrangement of rights that allows each person the maximum scope to develop his own conception of the good. What system? Answer: personal liberty and property rights, as ordinarily understood. In practice we can only achieve some incomplete realization of the goal, rendered necessary by the fact of scarcity. The insistence of separate domains prevents the acceptance of individual conceptions of the good which require killing or subjugating persons with different practices or beliefs. Within this system the use of state force is sharply rationed. It is permissible to impose some forced exchanges to raise the taxes to police the boundaries between persons, and (as becomes relevant later) to overcome the intractable holdout problems that can exist in certain common pool settings. But even when coercion is used, its permissible justifications are only two. The first is to prevent coercion by others, which if exercised makes it impossible for them to have any preferences at all. The second is to secure social arrangements that cannot be brought about by consent, but only where the persons coerced are made better off by the use of government force than they would have been without it. These rules are designed to preserve and advance individual conceptions of value. Not only do they minimize the number of collective decisions that have to be made, but they also try to make them in ways that do not prefer one conception of good life to the other, with the single caveat on the use of external force.

This conception fits in very nicely with the separation between state and religion. Again the correct strategy is to choose that delineation of rights that minimizes collective determinations of the good, or of truth. By taking this line, we do not have to decide the merits of religious beliefs, only their sincerity. Using conceptions of liberty and property again minimized conflicts between state and church, even when there is little constitutional protection against general economic regulation of the rights of disposition of property. No other theory can do this job as well. The religious and economic freedoms may occupy separate (but overlapping) domains. But they respond to the same underlying theory of entitlement.

4. *The establishment complication.* Thus far I have shown how the claim of free exercise of religion depends on the adoption of the very conceptions of liberty and property uniformly rejected in connection with economic liberties today. If therefore the free exercise clause is given a faithful rendition, then the Constitution speaks with a clear and powerful voice. Religious organizations can choose with whom to deal on all matters of concern with them. There is, however, another side of the coin which makes the overall constitutional analysis more complex than thus far appears. In addition to the free exercise clause, there is also the establishment clause: Congress shall make no law with respect to the establishment of religion. Historically, the clause has as its most obvious consequence the prohibition of an established church, such as the Church of

England. But as with most general pronouncements it is very difficult to find any principled way to confine it to the very situation that may have been its inspiration. Making a church established is usually the road whereby it receives privileges and benefits that are denied to other religious institutions. It is therefore fair to ask in this context whether the state could drop the formal title of "established church" while still providing financial or other benefits to one church and its members, while denying similar benefit to other religious institutions. The prospect of abuse against purpose seems too great for anyone to tolerate happily these evasions, so that the establishment requirement applies to "partial establishments" much the way the takings clause applies to "partial takings." At a minimum therefore, the bottom line is that the state cannot provide for any church a set of benefits, preferences or privileges that it does not extend on equal terms (and, perhaps, with equal value) to other religions. The prohibition of an established church imports a prohibition against the use of special subsidy or benefit for some religious organizations that are denied to all. There is an inescapable "equal protection dimension" to the establishment clause, just as there is with the eminent domain clause, with its own test of disproportionate impact.[23]

Now in fact the religion clauses have not been limited to cases of preferences and privileges among religions. That view, if accepted, carries with it the implication that it is permissible to have a world of nonreligious people subsidize the world of religious people. The position is inconsistent with the narrow justifications for government coercion set out above, for when the state subsidizes religion, coercion is not used either to restrain force or to provide benefits to the party taxed that could not be achieved through voluntary transactions. Redistribution necessarily presupposes that some set of needs and values are better than others, and thus puts the state in the business of deciding the worth of preferences and beliefs in ways that are inconsistent with the theory of subjective value still used in the religious arena.

Forcing the nonreligious to subsidize the religious thus injects the possibility of one-way transfers across separate factions or political groups. In political terms there is dynamite in such a rule given the systematic forms of redistribution that take place. It is here therefore that the concerns with economic liberties and redistribution, of such concern in the takings area, apply with great force to the religion area.

For those of us who think that the takings (or due process) clause works against these systematic forms of redistribution, then the question of whether the establishment clause prohibits them is conveniently sidestepped. The prohibition against general redistributive taxes takes the pressure off the establishment clause. Independently of the religion question, the takings argument poses a powerful barrier against all forms of redistribution, including that between religious and nonreligious persons. This barrier still has some considerable power even in a world where the welfare function is regarded as wholly legitimate. In line with the pre-1937 distinctions, it is possible to make transfers from rich to poor, from young to old, or old to young, on the strength of criteria that have nothing to do with religion. To be sure, there may in consequence be some redistribution along religious lines, but that may (have to) be tolerated as an "incidental" effect (so we are driven to say) so long as the motive is not religious but secular — to help the poor, not religions with a disproportionate number of poor members. But even so the transfers between religious groups would not fall within the welfare exception, so what we now call the establishment clause prohibition would have arisen as a matter of course under the takings clause.

Nonetheless, with the weak prohibitions against all forms of secular redistribution — farmers can rip off city dwellers, but city renters can get rent subsidies paid by farmers — the stress on the establishment clause is made greater by the general New Deal approach to redistribution. The point here is a precise parallel to the greater pressure placed upon the free exercise clause by the decline in constitutional protection for economic liberties. The nonreligious barriers no longer buffer the religion clauses from a powerful pounding. Today the antiredistributive impulses, properly in my view, have taken wider form than the restrictive view of the establishment clause rhetoric would otherwise have it. What should have been a straightforward implication of the eminent domain argument receives new life as an extension of the establishment clause argument. There can be no redistribution of preference, benefit or favor from nonreligious to religious groups as well. Thus the principle of liberty from the free exercise clause is matched by the principle of nonredistribution from the takings clause.[24]

Within the context of labor relations these two clauses are in powerful tension with each other. While I have given the free exercise argument for the autonomy of religious groups from, say, the collective bargaining statutes, there is an establishment clause argument the other way. Religious institutions are (as the argument from religious liberty concedes) total institutions that express themselves in a wide range of activities, such as care for the elderly and in education for the young, indeed for people of all ages. Now suppose that we have a rule which requires all nonreligious organizations in these areas to abide by collective bargaining. As these groups are in competition with the religious organizations, there is, so the argument goes, a fatal preference and imbalance — if the legal rules permit the religious organizations to escape the heavy costs associated with dealing with labor unions, even for persons of different religious groups or no groups at all. The point is even more pressing when we note that many religious organizations regard service (including service at a cost) as an imperative not only for persons not of their own religious faith but for all persons of need. The Catholic schools in Chicago educate a large number of Protestants, mainly black. So why doesn't this statutory preference create a clear (partial) establishment of religion which offends the establishment clause of the Constitution?

There is in my view no really good answer to this question, if the establishment clause is taken in isolation from the free exercise clause. The former mandates a prohibition on redistribution which arises whenever there is a differential treatment. The latter mandates the adoption of a principle of individual liberty that is rejected in ordinary economic affairs. If we start with the liberty as baseline, then we cannot require these organizations to surrender their autonomy with respect to their workforce (at least over some domains). If we start with parity between religious and nonreligious organizations, then we cannot allow the religious organizations to escape legal constraints that are thought to be necessary for all employment relationships. This tension between the two clauses has been identified before and it is inescapable.

5. *The Catholic Bishops.* The Supreme Court was well aware of the serious tensions involved. In *Catholic Bishops vs. National Labor Relations Board* ,[25] the question was whether the NLRB could hold union elections for the lay teachers that taught at several Catholic parochial schools. The NLRB had taken the position that it would not intervene in those schools whose mission was completely religious, but thought that the labor statutes should apply to those schools which were associated with religious organizations, but which nonetheless had a significant secular component to their activities. In a word, Catholic seminaries were outside the board's jurisdiction, but parochial schools were within it. The Supreme Court by a five to four vote engaged in a tour de force of statutory "construction" which allowed it to avoid the thorny constitutional issues that lurked around the corner. While the language of the NLRB contains a comprehensive definition of who is an employer, complete with eight stated exemptions from coverage, the Court's majority took the position that the statute should not be construed to reach religious schools because there was no explicit textual effort to cover that case. Its position was that the constitutional questions were so acute that it would require Congress to lay down the gauntlet before the Court would attack those issues head on. The dissent of Justice Brennan did not assay the constitutional questions head on, but it forcefully attacked the Court for using dubious stratagems of statutory construction for refusing to deal with the issues that were raised.

There is, however, at least a word to be said for prudence. The status quo ante has proved politically stable even if it is intellectually unsatisfying. There is therefore some practical wisdom to avoiding trouble where it is not wanted and by forcing Congress to lay down the gauntlet after the constitutional issues have been *expressly* brought to its attention. Nonetheless the issues will not go away as easily as all this because the tension is so manifest across the board. How then should it be resolved?

In this context, I believe that the standard mode of American constitutional analysis are not equal to the task. Essentially what is normally done is to require the individual citizen first to demonstrate some prima facie violation of a constitutional right, and then to impose upon the government the duty to justify its action by meeting some standard of review. This last task is complicated by virtue of the fact that our 1937 legacy requires very different standards of review for religious and economic legislation, the latter clearly being subjected to a low standard of "rational basis" review and the former to higher standard of review, which in the religion cases at least, doesn't seem to quite reach the lofty level of strict scrutiny.

No matter how the apple is sliced, it requires a good deal of "balancing" of the liberty infringed against the justification offered. Unfortunately there is no powerful consensus about the strength of either interest. Thus with respect to liberty, a threshold question is whether the same level of protection is accorded to the internal affairs of a religious organization as is accorded to its dealing with outsiders. But even here further distinctions may be required if the "outsiders" are coreligionists, or individuals that perform functions that are sensitive to the religious activities. It is not easy to draw clean lines between the unionization of clergy, kitchen help (with Kosher food, for example), lay and religious teachers, janitors and clerical staff.

Likewise there is massive uncertainty over the power of the state interest. Initially, there can be enormous disagreements whether labor statutes are merely tolerated under the rational basis test or positively welcomed as a form of union democracy that brings American labor law out of the dark ages for the common law into the welcome light of modern jurisprudence. The Court, which can studiously avoid examining the merits of the labor statute where its own constitutionality is at stake, cannot hide behind the rational basis test when the state interest under the labor statutes are in competition with the religious liberties of the organizations that they regulate. Someone has to decide. How?

Even after the strength of the overall labor statute is assessed, there is still a question of whether how strongly it applies to various classifications of workers who might be unionized. It might be thought that teachers are better able to do without a union because they are educated and relatively well to do. Janitorial staff may be a different matter. Nonetheless, outside the religious context, there is scarcely any distinction between the rights of these various groups of employees under the labor statute. Beyond the prohibition against the organization of management as such, all workers are treated alike. So again the competition between labor statutes and religious liberties forces courts to make far closer assessments of the labor statutes than they do in ordinary economic contexts, without giving them the tools to do so.

When the two interests are placed side by side, the possibilities are legion. One can rate the religious interest as high, and the labor regulations as low, or the reverse. It is possible to split the difference and use different gradations for various classes of workers. But these are outcomes driven only by the necessity to decide; they are not dictated by the logical or normative power of the decision principle. The inconsistency between the free enterprise clause and the establishment clause, given collective bargaining, is a logical inconsistency that cannot be evaded or remedied by "balancing." The only way to escape the problem is to knock out the labor statutes altogether, which (while I would do it) is only an idle pipe dream today. Then the clauses can be read in harmony without ad hoc balancing. Religious organizations receive no preference over their secular rivals, as both can hire and fire at will. Religious autonomy is preserved for exactly the same reason. The religious liberty and the equal treatment required by the establishment clause are both preserved. They cannot be preserved in the welfare state.

6. *The antidiscrimination statutes.* While the Court in *Catholic Bishops* could finesse the religion clauses by artful statutory construction, that escape was not available to it in *Corporation of the Presiding Bishop v. Amos* (107 S.Ct. 2862). That case involved the tension between the religion clauses and the antidiscrimination norm embodied in Title VII of the Civil Rights Act of 1964. In principle the antidiscrimination norm is as imperial as the collective bargaining norm. There is no employment relationship which is necessarily excluded from its application. Nonetheless Congress tried to defuse the tension between the free exercise clause and Title VII by including in Title VII an express provision, section 702, which allows religious organizations to discriminate in favor of their own members with respect to employment for any "religious corporation, association, educational institution or society" (42 U.S.C. § 2000e-1). Nonetheless this statutory maneuver exposed the statute to an establishment clause challenge, which in this instance was brought by a building engineer who was discharged from his work in a school gymnasium run by the Mormons because he was no longer qualified for a "temple recommend," that is, participation within the church's religious activities. If the church had not been a religious organization, its decision to fire would have been a per se violation of Title VII. So the exemption therefore gave the religious organization a preference over similar nonreligious organizations, both within and beyond the charitable field. In a world prior to 1937, antidiscrimination statutes probably would have been struck down generally as an impermissible restriction of labor markets, so the tension would not have arisen. But in the modern environment, the conflict cannot be escaped, at least in principle.

The Court, however, wriggled out of difficulties in *Amos* by allowing the exemption to stand under the weaker "rational basis" test, reserving for the moment at least a stricter scrutiny for distinctions that exist among religious organizations in accordance with their belief. Nonetheless the use of rational basis leaves open the harder question of whether the free exercise clause blocks the application of the antidiscrimination laws to religious organizations if Congress chose to extend them that far. Indeed, the problem is in a sense at hand right now, for the exemption provided in section 2000e-1 does not extend to discrimination done by religious organizations on the ground of race or sex. In principle therefore it seems as though the Catholic Church and the Orthodox Jews are in violation of the Title VII because they refuse to ordain women as priests and rabbis respectively. If the Court adheres a rational basis approach to this free exercise claim, then the result is the mirror image of that reached in *Amos*. The state's judgment prevails either way, because the relative strengths of the interests on both sides of the line are such that it is impossible to articulate any judicial test that delineates the boundary of appropriate state action.

Yet the rational basis test is no more appropriate here than it is in any area of constitutional adjudication. The specific protection of religious liberty and the specific prohibition of an establishment of religion both have to be respected as firm constitutional injunctions, not as mushy presumptions, easily overridden by changing congressional fad and fancy. As with the collective bargaining statutes, logical consistency between them is possible only in a world without antidiscrimination laws for private businesses. At that point religious organizations have perfect liberty, but no advantage over ordinary secular institutions.

Nonetheless the prospects for this constitutional revolution are remote at least. Again in the face of explicit contradiction the only illusion of escape is afforded by balancing. Here Title VII takes the first step along that road when it distinguishes religious organizations from the ordinary commercial businesses that they control and excludes only the former from the operation of Title VII. Doubtless the commercial regulation will be accepted as the free exercise claim ebbs, given that the religious organizations themselves have no religious reason to discriminate against outsiders. But as the law moves closer to the religious core, the same tensions that manifested themselves with the collective bargaining statutes surface here. The closer one gets to the religious core, the weaker the case for the antidiscrimination statutes.

Beyond that, the analysis becomes murkier. As with the labor statutes, the takings and due process challenges to the antidiscrimination laws were easily hurdled under the rational basis test, so that the Court did not have to commit itself to saying just how important Title VII was to the structure of American life. But while the labor statutes have remained in that constitutional nether world, it is clear that the antidiscrimination laws have not, for the Court has held in related contexts that a compelling state interest exists for the elimination of all forms of discrimination from our national life, and has thus overrun the claims, for example, of private clubs to discriminate against women (or, for that matter, men), and has shown a regrettable willingness to deny charitable deductions to religious organizations that impose restrictions on interracial dating as well. So the bet here is that Title VII will be sustained in the race, sex, and age cases until one gets to religious personnel or liturgy.

Nonetheless I should honor the free exercise claim across the board for religious institutions, on the ground that the common law baselines offer the only feasible way to understand the scope of organized religious activities. The level of intrusion into religious affairs is just too massive if Title VII, complete with its disparate impact tests, are applied without regard to the ends that they serve. The Catholic Church and the Orthodox Jews have built in sex-classifications that go to the distribution of power throughout their organizations. There is today enormous internal unrest and opposition and thoughtful critics have condemned the status quo as sexist, archaic, and the product of false consciousness, male patriarchy or worse. But it is one thing for a religious institution to yield through internal change in order to keep the consent and the loyalty of the governed. It is quite another for outsiders to impose their own external standards of right and wrong on these bodies. The claim of freedom is the right to decide what is right and wrong for oneself. It rests upon the idea that there is no collective conception of the good to which all persons must follow. The antidiscrimination norm fares no better on this account than any other principle which challenges freedom of association. Where religious organizations use force and deception against outsiders, they interfere with outsiders' rights to organize their own internal affairs. But the decision of one religious organization to practice discrimination for whatever reason only opens the avenue for rival churches to gain the support of disaffected members. The concern is with freedom, and the opposite of freedom is tyranny, which is best avoided by keeping the antidiscrimination laws at a safe distance from religious organizations.

The establishment clause claim on the other side is far weaker. It goes to the matter of competitive imbalance. But how much weight can be attached to that issue in a world in which competitive equilibria are regarded as generally irrelevant in economic affairs? The great assumption of the post-New Deal cases, is that competitive principles do not work in labor cases. It is for that reason that we have the complex cartel structures of labor unions; the minimum wage on other work restrictions in (the irony is in the title) the Fair Labor Standards Act. It is for that reason that we have Title VII. The use of these statutes creates incredible imbalances and distortions that cause substantial welfare losses in ordinary markets. The redeployment of resources toward capital, the relocation of plants, the shifting of labor to off-shore markets are all predictable and necessary economic consequences of the current economic order. But they are ignored because of the belief that centralized control of these matters does not offend the Constitution. Given this background it is odd to regard a condition of competitive balance between religious and nonreligious employers. It seems far safer to avoid the endless entanglements and ad hoc judgments to adopt a simple, but uneasy rule which allows Title VII (of race, sex and age, as well as religion) to apply with full vigor against the commercial businesses owned and controlled by religious organizations and to ban it wholly from the religious side of the organization. There is of course no perfect fit between the competing interests, but there is at least a known and stable accommodation that is consistent with the definition and mission that religious organizations hold for themselves. In the days of big government, this is far more important.

7. *Protection of religious workers.* With both collective bargaining and Title VII, the question posed for the religion clauses is how far the government can go to remove the ordinary protections of contractual freedom from religious organizations. Nonetheless it should not be supposed that every exercise of government power works to strip religious organizations and persons of their ordinary

common law contract rights. In some cases statutes seek to give religious workers advantages that are not held by ordinary individuals. Consistent with our basic analysis, these should generally be struck down. The free exercise of religion is subject to the normal constraint against the use of force on outsiders.

One case that illustrates these issues is the *Estate of Thornton v. Caldor Inc.*, 472 U.S. 703 (1985). There the issue involved the constitutionality of a statute which allowed workers to both keep their jobs and not work on their chosen Sabbath, regardless of the employer's preferences in the area. The statute was passed after the Sunday closing laws (themselves of most doubtful constitutionality) were repealed in Connecticut. The motivation behind the statute was inseparable from the prior state of affairs. When the Sunday closing laws were in effect no employee could ever be told that he had to work against his will on the Sabbath (Sunday). That protection would have been lost when the Sunday laws were repealed, save for the Connecticut statute which restored the status quo ante on this narrow point, and, in conformity with sound establishment clause thinking, which extended to other individuals with other Sabbaths.

At first blush, the statute seems to support the free exercise of religion, at least if the only question is whether religious observance is advanced in virtue of the statute's protection. Nonetheless the court struck down the statute on the grounds that it was a violation of the establishment clause, because it advanced religion over other organizations. I believe that this decision was sound, given the account of religious liberty delineated above. In *Thornton* the religious individual wants to have an exemption from the ordinary principles of freedom of contract that (in the world before 1937) governed economic affairs. In that context what is sought is an explicit subsidy for religion to be funded by individuals who have no particular religious beliefs. The inescapable effect of the rules is to place religious individuals at a systematic competitive advantage over their nonreligious rivals.

So long, however, as the conception of religious liberties today is the same as the earlier conception of economic liberty, then the state has gone beyond its powers. There is no risk of force and fraud that has to be controlled. This is not a case, like *Sherbert v. Verner,* where the question is whether religious persons, unwilling to work on the Sabbath, are nonetheless entitled to receive state unemployment benefits. For while in *Sherbert* the state may have put the worker to a choice between her religious beliefs and unemployment benefits, here the state has not put the individual to any choice at all between his religion and his occupation. The employer has in the exercise of its ordinary private rights. It is a matter of straight private evaluation for the worker as to whether the religious set of claims tugs stronger at the heartstrings than the economic. In practice one expects that some form of accommodation will be reached between workers and employers on issues of this sort: good employees are hard to find. But one cannot speak about the issue categorically independent of the facts. If the employer runs at outlet store that does most of its business on Sundays, which was the case in

Thornton, then the absence of a manager on that day is critical to its operations, and the accommodation would fail. So the worker looks elsewhere for a job which gives Sundays off. In my judgment it sets a very dangerous precedent to say that the power of the religious claim is so strong that it could never trump the employer's economic claim that is placed in opposition to it.

My colleague Michael McConnell has suggested that *Thornton* was wrongly decided because the only cost that was imposed upon the employer was economic, and that for this issue, the employer could protect itself in the legislature if the cost got too high. After all it is somewhat odd that while employers are subject to a barrage of economic regulations far more intrusive than this one, only against religious claims is the employer entitled to ordinary economic liberties.

While I follow McConnell on most points, I must part company with him here. The size of the dollars has little to do with the principles involved, which are the elimination of both religious penalty and religious subsidy. Behind those two injunctions lies the fundamental proposition that values are subjective and manifested in trade. There is in my view no violation of the free exercise clause if the employer is allowed not to hire a worker for any reason, including his religious practices. What the worker wants is subsidy, not freedom. Yet without the free exercise clause, then there is no counterweight to the establishment clause argument that the state has subsidized religious practices. This conclusion would, I take it, be well nigh inescapable if the state offered to pay out of public funds a small sum to the employer to defray the additional costs that it had to bear in virtue of keeping the religious worker on its payroll. The mandated benefit under the Connecticut statute has the unhappy economic feature of imposing a hidden and selective tax on certain employers when the state will not pay the tab itself. But this second vice of the Connecticut statute hardly cancels out the first. If a public subsidy of religious workers is not acceptable under the establishment clause, then a public mandate of a private subsidy is not acceptable either.

This entire problem would not arise if freedom of contract had remained a powerful constitutional principle in economic affairs. But once it is displaced in those areas, it keeps its vitality with regard to interference with business contracts on religious grounds. Unlike the collective bargaining cases and the antidiscrimination cases, *Thornton* is one situation where we can have our cake and eat it too. Striking down the statute offends no claim for religious freedom, and it avoids any possible conflict with the establishment clause. Thornton's problem was that he was caught in the transition between the older regime of the Sunday closing laws and the new regime of open markets. Once the new regime is on the books, however, it is best to allow matters to sort themselves in the marketplace without allowing the hand of state intervention to preserve some small vestige of some untenable statute quo ante.

III.

The three cases analyzed in the previous section were concerned with the possible effect of state regulation on what might be termed the economic liberties of religious organizations and individuals. The question of government control asserts itself as well in the distribution of public benefits to workers. Given what was said before, there were good reasons to think that these fundamentally redistributive programs were not constitutionally tenable before the constitutional revolution of the New Deal. Nonetheless some of the major structural reforms of the New Deal era did involve both unemployment benefits and Social Security payments. Both of these areas have generated important constitutional collision between the state power to redistribute wealth and the claims for religious liberty. As I have already addressed this issue extensively in another context I shall keep my remarks to a minimum here.

1. *Unemployment benefits.* One area of government action has been the provision of unemployment benefits to workers laid off through no fault of their own. The system of unemployment benefits often operates in a way that systematically redistributes wealth across the covered employees, because there is little effort to calibrate the premium charged to the benefits received. In the post-1937 era these difficulties are merely economic and do not rise to constitutional dignity. But the claims are more insistent when there is an asserted exclusion of workers from their unemployment benefits for religious reasons. In *Sherbert v. Verner* the problem came to a head when a Seventh Day Adventist was denied unemployment benefits because she refused to take available work on her Sabbath. As with so many religion cases there is both an establishment clause and a free exercise dimension that work in contradiction to each other. The establishment clause claim is one that says it is not permissible to allow her into the program because then she will receive coverage for one event (not working on her Sabbath) that is denied to nonreligious persons. The free exercise claim cuts in the opposite direction because it says that she should not be "forced" to choose between her religion and unemployment benefits.

I think that the key to this resolution depends on one question: which rule reduces the level of redistribution between religious and nonreligious claimants? Thus if the workers could be broken into two groups, religious and nonreligious, then both the establishment clause and the free exercise clause are respected if there is no systematic redistribution from either. If therefore religious workers have lower unemployment records generally, then they are not being subsidized if they can collect claims when they refuse to work on their own Sabbath. They have in essence funded the claims themselves. There may well be a cross-subsidy within members of the religious class, but that is a straight economic issue, for which under modern law there is no constitutional concern. Stated otherwise, if all Seventh Day Adventists put their unemployment premiums into a separate fund, could the fund cover all those workers' regular claims, with enough left over to handle the claims of those who refused to work on the

Sabbath for religious means? If the answer to that question is yes, then they must be included in the program. If it is no, then they should be excluded, unless (as is surely possible) an extra premium is collected to cover the additional risk. The talk in the cases about "fines" and coercion is therefore somewhat misplaced because we do not deal with private aggression against public practices. Instead we are dealing with public aggression against private practices. We are dealing with the law of "forced exchanges" that is (or should have been) developed with eminent domain cases. With public finance, the principle of noninterference is no longer sufficient. It must be replaced with the weaker principle that tolerates some interference so long as religious and nonreligious people share equally in the gains or (since there is no takings protection) losses of collective government programs.

2. *Social Security payments*. The constraint against redistribution shows the weakness of what I regard to be the most unsound of the Court's recent religion clause cases. In *United States v. Lee*, 455 U.S. 252 (1982), the Court held that the Amish could be required to contribute to the Social Security system even though it was against their sincere religious beliefs to either contribute to or receive payment for any government agency for the support of their own needy or poor. There are four possible permutations of contributions and benefits. The Amish can be kept out of the fund entirely. They could be required to make contributions but not receive benefits. But they could be required to make contributions and required to receive benefits. They could not be required to make contributions but to receive benefits. Within the analysis given above, the normative principles require us to reconcile autonomy with redistribution. Clearly the Amish could not be allowed to receive benefits if they did not to make contributions. Religious beliefs are not sufficient to ground a religious subsidy. And the Amish would not take the benefits under any circumstance, thinking that two sins are worse than one.

Conclusion

I want here to close with another line of argument that is more controversial, but I think fairly drawn from the cases. What we have seen so far is a system wherein all the tensions have arisen because of the rejection of property and contract ideas in employment markets generally. But if we are really prepared to think about issues from the point of view of first principle, then maybe the proper reorientation comes with deference given to economic liberties. Thus there is one way in which we could avoid all establishment clause and all free exercise conflicts. Repeal the labor laws and the antidiscrimination statutes generally. At that point we are back to the common law baseline and can easily insist that religious organizations honor their contracts just as they have to respect the laws of trespass and murder. The point here is that the common law rules are a set of rules good for all seasons, and for all comers. The regulatory rules are not. Their fatal vice is that they abandon the strategy of defining separate zones of authority in which all persons can move at will, and substitute in their place complex regimes of joint ownership in which all has to be done at cause. It is possible to develop theories of justification in a common law world, e.g. self defense, but these principles are a lot more difficult to articulate than might be thought at first instance. What is not possible is to develop a theory of justification, a theory of constitutionally "compelling state interests" that can limit the scope of state power on a for cause basis after it has been expanded so mightily in other ways. The point here is that in a second best world we have to try, and we will stumble. In a first best world most of these conflicts disappear. We have not in short been able to find a powerful theory that preserves religious liberty in the welfare state. Let us hope that the fragile political accommodation that we have reached will hold.

Notes

1. See generally, B. Siegan, *Economic Liberties and the Constitution* (1980).

2. *Addyston Pipe & Steel Co. v. United States*, 175 U.S. 211 (1899). For my views, see Epstein, "The Proper Scope of the Commerce Clause," 73 *Va. L. Rev.* 1387, 1436 n. 156 (1987).

3. See, e.g., *Block v. Hirsh*; *Euclid v. Ambler Realty Co.*, 272 U.S. 365 (1926).

4. See, e.g., *United States v. E.C. Knight Co.*, 156 U.S. 1 (1895).

5. *Carter v. Carter Coal Co.*, 298 U.S. 238 (1936).

6. 198 U.S. 45 (1905).

7. See, e.g., *Southern Railway v. United States*, 222 U.S. 20 (1911); Second Employers' Liability Cases, 223 U.S. 1 (1912).

8. *New York Central Railroad v. White*, 243 U.S. (1917) (workers' compensation); Plymouth Coal Corp.

9. Often two modes, see *Powell v. Pennsylvania*, 289 U.S. 188.

10. See *Adair v. United States*, 208 U.S. (1908); *Coppage v. Kansas*, 236 U.S. 1 (1915).

11. See, e.g., Epstein, "The Mistakes of 1937," *George Mason L. Rev.* (198).

12. See, e.g., Bell's Gap, etc.

13. For discussion, see Diamond, *J. Legal Stud.* (1983).

14. See *Carmichael v. Southern Railroad*, etc.

15. See, e.g., Epstein, *Takings: Private Property and the Power of Eminent Domain*, (1985) for the long version, and Epstein, "Judicial Review: Reckoning on Two Types of Error," 4 *Cato J.* (1986).

16. 440 U.S. 490 (1979).

17. 29 U.S.C. §§ 151-169. I have given a more extensive criticism of these statutes in Epstein, "A Common Law for Labor Relations: A Critique of the New Deal Labor Legislation," 92 *Yale L.J.* 1357 (1983).

18. *Beth Israel Hospital v. NLRB*, 43 U.S. 248 (1978); *Republic Aviation Corp. v. NLRB*, 324 U.S. 793 (1945).

19. See, e.g., *Vincent v. Lake Erie Transp. Co.*, 109 Minn. 456, 124 N.W. 210 (1910).

20. Indeed, the Assize Utrum, which asks whether certain matters belonged to the clergy or the secular courts, raises this point in very powerful fashion.

21. See, the discussion of the point raised in Freed & Polsby, Bob Jones, 1983 *Sup. Ct. Rev.* 1, which I think overstates the difficulty, especially for the established religions whose practices and beliefs long antedate the New Deal Revolution.

22. *Reynolds v. United States*, 99 U.S. 145 (1878).

23. See *Armstrong v. United States*, 364 U.S. 40, 49 (1960). R. Epstein, *Takings*, ch. 14 (1985).

24. I explore these tensions in Epstein, "Foreword: Unconstitutional Conditions, State Power and the Limits of Consent," 102 *Harv. L. Rev.* 4, 79-104.

25. 440 U.S. 490 (1979).

Chapter 6

Moral Rights and the Constitution

Joel Feinberg
University of Arizona

My purpose in this essay is to defend the concept of a moral right from various kinds of attacks that have been made on it by philosophical and legal writers. But first I shall present a variety of examples, some perhaps more plausible than others, of moral rights, and some explanation, designed to fit these examples, of what I shall mean by "a moral right." In the final section, I will consider briefly how skepticism about moral rights in the present sense infects certain theories of constitutional interpretation.

1. *Moral Rights.* Women manifestly have the right to vote in the United States. But there was a time, of course, when women did not have the right to vote in the United States, and even now women do not have the right to vote in Kuwait and some other countries. These appear to be empirical judgments supported by factual evidence. On the other hand, we are inclined to say that even in the United States of 1890, and even in Kuwait at present, women *really* had the right to vote, but that right was wrongfully withheld from them by their legislators and constitution-makers. This second kind of judgment, which by now is familiar to us, is one that raises philosophical problems. The existence of rights in this category is said to be prior to and independent of their enactment by legislatures, or their declarations, explicit or implicit, by constitution-makers. We need not and cannot confirm them, as in the first class of rights, by gathering empirical facts as evidence of their actual acknowledgment or enforcement in the political

societies in question, because their existence is not said to depend in any way upon their recognition in those societies, but has some independent source that can establish them even where they are not generally valued or even wanted. In positing the existence of rights in this second class, we do not act as impartial social scientists describing the facts of actual practice for better or worse; rather we jump into the moral arena, and take a stand ourselves. All adult human beings, we might say, have a right to participate in the political decisions that govern their affairs, and of course, this holds for women too. Even where women as a class do not have a *legal* right to vote, they clearly have a moral right, derived from their humanity and the moral principle or equality, to vote along with men. The philosophical problem is to explain what such moral rights are and "where they come from," how we can recognize them and resolve disagreements about their existence, and what practical consequence, if any, follows from their possession, especially when they are not given legal protection.

When we assert our own rights or the rights of others, very often the rights we affirm are of the sort I am calling "moral rights." An abundance of examples will illustrate how ordinary and familiar this category of rights is. In addition to the Kuwaiti's women's right to vote, one can mention the right to breathe clean air claimed by enemies of tobacco smoking prior to any legal rules that might be adopted to protect it; the right of a married couple to use contraceptives in the privacy of their own bedroom, first affirmed by the Supreme Court in *Griswold v. Connecticut*[1] decades after the practice had become both prevalent and illegal; the right of legally competent couples voluntarily to get married even though the man and woman are of different races, a right first vindicated by the Supreme Court in *Loving v. Virginia*[2] in 1967; the right to organize into trade unions, claimed by British agricultural laborers long before legal recognition was first forthcoming;[3] the right to picket peacefully which, until this century, was honored mainly in the breach; the right to know one's own medical prognosis ("Tell me the truth, Doctor, I have a right to know!"); the child's right to a voice in family decisions, which is not and could not be a *legal* right;[4] and similarly, a student's right to be graded without prejudice; a terminal patient's right (whatever legal rules or hospital codes may say about the matter) to the termination of treatment designed simply to keep him alive as long as possible; a young girl's right, even among peoples whose traditional practice requires it of everyone, not to have a ceremonial clitorectomy imposed on her as a precondition of the wedding ceremony;[5] the Indian widow's right, even before 1829 when the practice of suttee was banned throughout British India, *not* to immolate herself on her husband's funeral pyre;[6] the right to the free exercise of one's religion which was systematically violated, for example, by the legal authorities of Iran in the case of the Baha'i religion, whose temples were destroyed and leaders executed; and finally the right to freedom from arbitrary arrest and incarceration, as in the standard Gestapo practice of raiding the homes of Jews and dissidents at 4:00 in the morning, pounding peremptorily on the door, and then carting away the terrified residents who were often never heard from again. Surely if we have any rights at all, we have rights not to be treated like that!

These examples are designed to show that moral rights are not some esoteric construction of otherworldly philosophers, but common parts of the conceptual apparatus of most if not all of us when we come to make moral and political judgments. One of the best definitions of moral rights in the present sense comes ironically from a philosopher who is an avowed skeptic about their existence. Raymond Frey defines a moral right as "a right which is not created by or the product of community legislation or social practice, which persists even in the face of contrary legislation or practice, and which prescribes the boundary beyond which neither individuals nor the community may go in pursuit of their overall ends."[7]

Several further distinctions must now be made in order to clarify this definition. First of all, obviously, the categories of moral and legal rights overlap, so that a given moral right can also be a legal right if a rule calling for its recognition and enforcement has been duly enacted into law. The right of women to vote, long a moral right, has since 1920 also been in this country a legal right. Secondly, a distinction must be drawn between moral rights in the sense I have been assigning to that term and moral rights in a much weaker sense, namely the rights conferred on people by the rules of the conventional "morality" or the "moral code" as we say of their communities. These are the rights that Frey's definition attributes to "social practice" in contrast to moral rights which, coming from some objective and universal principles of morality, exist as independently of social practice as they do of legislative enactment. Conventional morality varies from group to group; we speak of bourgeois morality, "socialist morality," "Nazi morality" (which was an immoral morality indeed), Catholic morality, Eskimo morality, Hottentot morality, and the morality of the ancient Spartans or Babylonians. These various systems of norms for the most part contain many proscriptions and injunctions in common, but they also differ in some striking ways. Infanticide, for example, was permissible in Spartan and Hottentot morality; it is a dreadful sin in Catholic morality. In contrast, what we may call "true morality" is thought to be immune to such fluctuations, being at least to some degree "part of the nature of things," critical, rational, and correct. True morality, so understood, provides the standards and principles by which to judge the actual institutions of any given society, *including* its conventional morality the rules and principles actually established in that society, for better or worse. Rights conferred by the universal true morality may also be a part of the conventional moralities of many societies, as the rights not to be murdered or to have what was promised to one are for example. Furthermore, a moral right in the objective sense may be conferred by a given code of conventional morality and a system of positive law *both*, in which case it is a true moral right, a conventional moral right, and a legal right, all at once; or it may be unrecognized by both a country's conventional morality and its legal system, in which case it remains a true moral right anyway. This latter point is well illustrated, I think, by the Gestapo arrest, the right to the free exercise of religion in Iran, the right of Indian widows not to immolate themselves, and the right of the daughters of the Cairo garbage collectors not to be subjected to clitorectomies before marriage. Arguably, in each of these cases, critical morality confers a genuine moral right that is unrecognized, indeed explicitly denied both by the conventional morality of the group and by its legal system, insofar as it has one.

Thirdly, there is a distinction between those moral rights that are *exercisable* even prior to legal recognition and those which cannot be exercised before being enacted into law. There is no way, for example, in which women can exercise their moral right to vote in a country where that right has not been given legal recognition, whereas one can exercise the moral right to picket peacefully before legal recognition, at least until the police arrive to haul one away. Better examples of exercisable moral rights are the rights to practice one's religion (secretly) and to commit suicide in order to hurry a death that would otherwise be painful. This distinction is of no deep theoretical importance but a fourth distinction, related to it, may be of greater interest. Women campaigning for the right to vote may say "We demand our rights." This suggests that what they want is to be given rights — legal rights — which they do not yet have, since in the example the only rights they have in respect to voting are moral rights, which being nonexercisable are not in themselves operative "voting rights." What good is it then to have nonexercisable moral rights? Are the women in the example merely demanding recognition of rights they already have when they demand their rights, like the followers of Martin Luther King who assumed that they already had certain constitutional rights whose benefits were being wrongfully withheld from them? King's followers were not asking for new rights but for enforcement of actual legal rights they were confident they already had. But in the women's case, valid laws on the books and "in force" explicitly denied them what they were after. The women's demand for their rights should be interpreted as a demand for new legal rights which they did not at the time have. When they said that they "want their rights" they meant to put in a claim, based on their actual possession of a moral right, to be given the new legal right. What they were asserting is that they have a right to have a right, a moral right against the state to be given a new legal right. The moral right functions as the basis of their entitlement to the legal right analogous to the way in which a title establishes a claim to property. Without the moral right, the women could still *demand* the new legal right and fight for it effectively, but they could not make claim to it as rightfully theirs, and push that claim against the consciences of legislators. What the women want is not simply something that would be good to have, but something *that they have coming anyway as their due*, and this is an idea that the language of rights with its tone of urgency and righteousness is uniquely suited to convey.

A final word about terminology. Sometimes the term "natural right" means nothing more than "moral right" as we have defined it. In eighteenth-century terminology in particular, the natural was contrasted with the artificial, what is "there" to be discovered, quite apart from human design or construction, as opposed to that which owes its existence to human invention and design. If that is all we mean by "natural," then the terms "natural right" and "moral right" are perfectly interchangeable. Natural rights are part of the nature of things to be discovered by human reason, whereas conventional and institutional rights, including legal ones, are the products of human draftsmanship and general compliance and acceptance. But sometimes the term "natural right" means more than critical moral right. In this further sense, a natural right is a moral right derived from "the nature of man," conferred on human beings as parts of their original constitutions, like their biological organs, bones, and muscles. And like their biological counterparts, natural rights are conferred by natural laws — the laws of our being. Here the ideas of scientific laws reporting invariant regularities in experience and jural laws of the sort made by human legislatures, only here discovered not made, intermesh and blend together to the great confusion of some thinkers who would otherwise be sympathetic to the generic idea of a natural, i.e. moral, right. That is why I prefer the language of "moral rights" over the language of "natural rights" even when the terms are synonyms.[8] Finally, we should distinguish between moral rights that some human beings have because of their special properties, offices, or relations to others — the special rights of children and the aged, of women, of students, of criminal defendants, of promises, and of citizens, and the more abstract rights said to belong to all human beings as such, simply by virtue of their humanity. The former group can be called special rights and the latter are commonly called "human rights." Both are equally moral rights — or natural rights in the generic sense, and both are frequently included in conventional moral codes and systems of jural law.

2. *Doubts about the Existence of Moral Rights.* There was a time some forty years ago or more when treatises and textbooks in moral philosophy were overwhelmingly concerned with our duties and what we ought generally to do (these were usually taken as equivalent). Typically, moral rights were addressed, in an appendix[9] or a late chapter,[10] as a kind of afterthought. Unlike duties, which were recognized as commonplace and foundational in the moral life, rights were suspect, and often thought to be mysterious or queer. The commonly heard question was "Where do they come from?" (We know where legal and other conventional rights "come from.") It never seemed to occur to anyone, however, to find moral *duties* perplexing or to wonder where they "come from." This difference is especially puzzling when one remembers how logically connected statements of rights often are to statements of duties. There are, to be sure, more consistent skeptics who have equally severe doubts about moral rights and moral duties, and indeed about all allegedly objective moral rules and principles. That kind of consistent skepticism poses a serious challenge to the theory of moral rights, if only because its doubts apply to rights and duties both. The more selective skep-

ticism, which singles out moral rights, may be somewhat easier to cope with.

More commonly the token chapters on rights were dismissive in another way. Instead of being queer or exotic, moral rights were thought to be commonplace, derivative, and trivial. To be sure, they are logically correlative with duties, but duties were the fundamental notion, and rights were merely an alternative way of speaking of duties.[11] In theory, the moralist can say everything he needs to say in the language of duties (perhaps supplemented by talk of "values"); statements of rights are mere convenient shorthand ways of talking about duties and their logical consequences. Professor Frey is a recent representative of this mode of dismissiveness. Rights talk, on his view, is not merely derivative and secondary; it is in principle and in fact totally *superfluous*. "As far as I can see, not even a practical advantage is gained by positing some moral right based upon agreed moral principles, since I, as a moral man implementing and following my principles, will behave the way you want me to even without [your having] the right."[12] Rights, in short, add nothing; they are dispensable entities with no further function than to confuse philosophers. If we list all the duties people have, then we need no further list of rights, for the universal discharge of duties would fully satisfy anything that might be claimed as a right.

The quick answer to Frey is that what one person's rights add to another person's duties is some measure of control by the right-holder over those duties.[13] He can release the other from his duty if he pleases, for example, thus exercising a kind of "moral power"[14] analogous to legal powers to bind or release. Moreover, the right-holder's right often provides the whole grounding for the other party's duty; it is for his sake that the other has his duty. If *B* has a right that *A* do (or omit doing) *X* for him, then *B* can *claim X* from *A* as his due. He is, morally speaking, in a position to say to *A*, "You owe me *X* as my due...." Moreover, if *A* violates *B*'s valid claim, *B* can voice a grievance against *A*, now being in a position to charge that "You wronged me...." If the wrongful act or omission of *A*'s were a mere dereliction of his own duty instead of being also an infringement of *B*'s right, then *B* would have no personal grievance, and *A* could reply to his complaint by saying: "What business is it of yours whether I perform my duties? That is a matter between me and my conscience, or between me and God. It is no proper concern of yours, so stay out of it." At the very least this reply is a misreading of the moral situation, and if it were correct, then *B*, having no claim, no grievance, no proper business or concern, no representation in the grounds of *A*'s duty, and no control over the content of that duty, would have less dignity in the eyes of others, and, if he himself believed Frey's superfluity thesis, less respect for himself as a maker of moral claims against others, as a person whose own basic interests matter.

Frey does not claim that rights claims are gibberish, communicating no sense. He generally concedes that rights talk is a somewhat confused way of focusing attention on the interests of the party or parties said to have the right, and of asserting the moral wrongness of harming those interests. These functions, he admits, can be forensically useful, provided no one is tempted to believe that there actually are such entities as moral rights.

Frey's most interesting suggestion for preserving the intuitive meaningfulness of rights-talk puts him in an old tradition that goes back at least to Bentham. One can get rid of the mysterious element in rights-talk, he suggests, by interpreting it as a confused indirect way of referring to *legal* rights, which, being plain matters of fact, are not themselves mysterious. I call this approach the "There ought to be a law" theory of moral rights, for it holds that the sentence "*A* has a moral right to do (have or be) *X*" is to be understood, insofar as it makes any sense at all, to be saying "*A ought* to have a *legal* right to *X*." Thus Maurice Cranston, speaking of the "human rights" declared by the United Nations writes: "The intention . . . was to specify something that everybody *ought* to have. In other words they were moral rights."[15]

It may be a plausible interpretation of the U.N. Declaration of Human Rights that the rights it ascribes are proposed targets for legislation merely, in no sense existent and "in force" everywhere now. It is, however, wholly unconvincing to say that the fitness to be legal rights explains what we mean by the expression "moral rights," for this account cannot be reconciled with some familiar uses of the language of moral rights. It cannot explain what is meant, for example, by talk of persons *exercising* their moral rights before those rights were legally recognized, as in the case of demonstrators arrested for illegal picketing or sitting in a segregated section of a bus, or religious worshipers conducting secret services in a country where they are persecuted. And the view that a moral right is simply what ought to be a *legal* right cannot without emendation explain what it could be to have a moral right to rebel against a tyrannical government. Since the right to rebel against established authority could not be a legal right conferred by the government in power, it could not very well be an ideally legal right. Finally, the analysis of moral rights as mere goals of legislative aspiration cannot make sense out of many homely examples of moral rights on our list of familiar specimens. One might very well acknowledge, for example, a parent's right to be spoken to civilly by his children and a student's right to be graded without prejudice by her teachers, while denying that those undoubted rights ought to be legal rights at all. At least these and similar moral rights, then, cannot plausibly be construed as mere ideally legal or properly legal rights. We think of them as rights against private parties, not necessarily against legislators, and as rights that can be exercised, stood upon, waived, or infringed, quite apart from what the law might say about the matter.[16]

But couldn't Frey, Cranston, Bentham, et al. reply that these examples are cases of conventional moral rights only? They are resistant to the "ideally legal" analysis, they might say, only because they already exist as part of the community's conventional moral code. A better example from our list then would be the right of a suffering terminal patient to active euthanasia from his doctor or friend. This right is not yet part of our conventional code, but is plausibly claimed to be a moral right by Professor Yale Kamisar, who proceeds to argue in his famous article[17] that it *ought not* to become a legal right because of the possibilities of mistake and abuse. One might, on the same grounds, argue that it ought not even to be a conventional moral right. Yet is arguably a critical moral right for all that.

Bentham's use of the "There ought to be a law" gambit is somewhat different from that discussed so far. Unlike Frey, he does not argue "generously" that although ascriptions and claims of moral rights make no sense, people *seem* to be making sense when they ascribe or claim them, so what they must mean (or what perhaps they do mean) by "moral right" is simply "what ought to be a legal right," the latter notion making perfectly good sense. Rather Bentham argues in the opposite direction. If people mean by a moral right simply "What ought to be a legal right," they ought to say so. That would not be objectionable.[18] But when they fall into the language of moral rights they inevitably are led to assume that what ought to be a legal right in our system of laws already is a right actually in force in some ghostly cosmic system of laws parallel to but superior to our own, and this is both muddled and pernicious. "All such language is at any rate false . . . or at the best an improper and fallacious way of indicating what is true."[19] Bentham then concludes with characteristic rhetorical overkill: "Reasons for wishing there were such things as rights are not rights; a reason for wishing that a certain right were established is not that right; a want is not supply; hunger is not bread."[20] To be sure, a reason for wishing a right is not the same thing as a right, but it taxes credulity to represent the couple cowering in bed as the Gestapo boots are pounding up their stairs as having no greater moral claim in that situation than a reason for wishing they had a protective legal right! That is all the moral standing Bentham will allow them, all the content he will grudgingly concede to their moral rights. At least Bentham understands, unlike the generous Professor Frey, that the genuine belief of moral rights advocates, no matter how muddled or pernicious it might be, is that moral rights are actual rights, existent and in force, and not merely what ought to be contained in our conventional norms.

L.W. Sumner in his recent excellent work on the theory of rights, sympathizes with Bentham's contempt for the muddled idea of a ghostly cosmic system of legal-like rules from which actual moral rights are derived. He tries to avoid that conception in his own account of moral rights, but his accurate understanding of Bentham's motives is well expressed in the following passage:[21]

> Although a skeptical argument like Bentham's cannot show conclusively that the very idea of a natural [i.e. moral] right is incoherent, it would be strengthened if some alternative explanation could be given for the persistent belief in the existence of natural rights. Suppose that the legal system governing us has denied us some legal right which we believe we ought to have, and that we wish to make a case for being accorded that right. Since we believe that we ought to have the right then we believe that in an ideal legal system we would have it. It is then but a short and

> tempting step to claiming that an ideal legal system exists in which we *do* have the right, and then to saying that the right conferred on us by this ideal system constitutes our case for having the same right conferred on us by our actual system. The mechanism at work here is projection. As a corrective to the deontic imperfections of the actual world we invent a deontically perfect world in which individuals possess just those rights which, morally speaking, they ought to have, and then we treat this invention as though it were real....[22]

Positing moral rights then turns out to be an instance of mere wishful thinking, and that is what Bentham thinks explains the widespread and persistent belief in them.

How does Sumner himself manage to defend belief in the existence of moral rights without projecting his "wishes" into some ghostly cosmic system? He defines a moral right as a "a morally justified conventional right."[23] "I have a moral right," he says, "just in case my possession of the corresponding conventional right is morally justified." At times he suggests that a moral right is a species of a conventional right, so that I cannot have a moral right unless I already have the conventional right with the same content, that conventional right itself amounting to a moral right if its inclusion in a conventional code or legal system is morally justified. But on the whole, I think that the best interpretation of his intentions is to say that a moral right is either an actual conventional right that is morally justified or what *it would be morally justified*, in the strongest sense, *to adopt as a conventional right* in case it is not a conventional right already. Either the conventional rule system in question already recognizes the moral right or it does not. "If it does then what must be justified is the continued recognition of the right . . . If it does not, then what must be justified is altering the system so that it comes to recognize the right . . . We may call each of these options — either maintaining an already existing right or creating a new one — a social *policy*. A moral right exists when a policy of either sort is [morally] justified for the relevant rule system"[24] usually a system of laws.

The major advantage Sumner claims for this analysis is that it explains what the moral credentials of a moral right are and why it has moral force, the answer being of course that it includes the requirement of moral justification. What is to be justified, however, is not a moral claim made by the right-holder in the face of some threatened infringement, but rather the social policy of maintaining or introducing a rule in a conventional system. This feature, Sumner contends, has the added advantage of making "no references to a ghostly realm of natural moral rules," since "the only rules referred to are conventional."[25]

Sumner's definition of "moral right" seems to be a more refined version of what I have called the "There ought to be a law" analysis. His version is stronger than most in that it does not restrict the relevant class of justified conventional rules to legal rules. By virtue of this enlargement, his version of the theory preserves the possibility that some moral rights exist because it would be justified to maintain or introduce them into a system of conventional moral rules even though it would not be justified to include them as elements of a legal system. This move renders the theory immune to such counterexamples as the child's right to a voice in family decisions, a parent's right to be spoken to civilly, and so on. Moral rights of this class would not be justified as legal rights, but they might well be justified as rights conferred by conventional morality, and thus would qualify as genuine moral rights in Sumner's view. Moreover, Sumner's analysis would please Bentham by its avoidance of any apparent commitment to a ghostly realm of legal-like rules (I too share Bentham's ontological squeamishness in this matter). The failure of Sumner's account, however, lies in its failure to capture a central feature of moral rights, the fact that they are taken to be actual rights at the moment they are asserted, "in force," generating other people's moral duties, capable in many cases of being exercised, and in all cases capable of being either respected or violated. The categorical claim that I have a right to use contraceptives or to marry a woman of another race is not fully translated into any number of hypothetical claims that certain social policies would be justified. If it is a claim about justification at all, it is the categorical claim that interference or noncooperation with me in certain specifiable ways is not justified, that others have a real duty, subject to my control, not to interfere in those ways.

It would appear then that an adequate definition of moral rights should satisfy at least two tests: (1) It should not be committed to a ghostly realm of legal-like rules ripped from their normal connection to actual legal institutions, and (2) it should preserve the directness and categoricalness of moral rights that are part of their normal conception. The way to do this, I submit, is to bypass an intermediate step in Sumner's derivation of moral rights. What is to be morally justified in Sumner's theory is a kind of legislative act of creating institutional or other conventional rules. I would substitute a simpler account in which what is to be directly justified is not a hypothetical legislative act or policy, but rather the claim of moral right itself.

There are as many as six elements in Sumner's more complicated analysis:

(1) The candidate moral right;
(2) The rule purporting to confer that right;
(3) A system of conventional rules requiring, permitting, or prohibiting certain kinds of conduct, e.g. a legal system or a conventional moral code;
(4) A legislative context: the actual circumstance in which the candidate rule would operate at the time of which it would be maintained or introduced into the system (now). ("Moral rights which exist under some social conditions may fail to exist under others." This leads to "a certain relativity in the concept of a moral right."[26])
(5) A hypothetical act/policy (1) of maintaining or introducing (2) the candidate rule into (3) the conventional rule system.
(6) The correct principles of moral justification whatever they may be (e.g. the principle of utility, a contractarian principle, the principle of autonomy, Kantian universalizability.) The candidate moral right (1) turns out to be a genuine moral

right if and only if the act/policy of maintaining or introducing the rule conferring to it (2) into the system of conventional rules (3) in the actual present social circumstances (4) is justified by the correct principles of moral justification (6).

The simpler account I propose would make reference only to two of the elements in Sumner's test: a statement of the purported moral right and the correct principles of moral justification. On this simpler and more natural reconstruction, a purported moral right is a genuine moral right if and only if it is validated as such by correct moral principles. In a parallel way, a purported moral duty (like the duties not to act cruelly or deceitfully) is a genuine moral act if it is certified as such by correct moral principles. If this simple derivation of duties is untroublesome, conjuring up no visions of a spooky cosmic legal system, why shouldn't the correspondingly simple derivation of rights be equally untroublesome? The advantage of this simple derivation of moral rights is that it explains how we can have moral rights in the same direct and categorical way we have moral duties, how the two come from the same source, and why they are called "moral" whether or not they are recognized by the conventional rule systems of particular communities. If a correct moral principle entails that I have a right to be free from arbitrary arrest and detention then that right exists as a moral right binding on public and/or private individuals.

But where do the "correct moral principles" come from if not from some ghostly realm? I cannot here attempt to give a complete metaethical grounding or even an identification of ultimate moral principles, but I can urge that they not be understood on the model of legal rules. They are not the legal-like statutes of some cosmic legal system, or some partial analogue of a legal system without its own charter or constitution, without its own institutional structure, without its own offices and office holders, without its own procedural structure, without its secondary rules for changing the primary ones, without its own mechanism for making new rules, without its own legislation, without public promulgation, without its own trial courts and courts of appeal, without its own sanctions, and so on. This obscure conception is "spooky" because it posits a legal system that is not quite a real legal system like our earthly examples, the same perhaps in some quite essential respects as a legal system, but different in certain other equally essential respects.[27] There is no reason to think of moral principles in that way. Rather they are in essential contrast to legal rules of all kinds whether those of human institutions *or* those of celestial counterparts.

I cannot forbear from concluding this section with a *tu quoque*. If Sumner's appeal to moral principles in justification of legislative acts and policies does not implicate him in the ghostly domain so scorned by Bentham, why should my appeal to such principles (possibly even the very same principles) implicate my account? The only difference in our appeals to critical morality is that he invokes moral principles to justify legislative acts, or policies toward maintaining or introducing conventional rules, whereas I invoke them to justify truth claims on behalf of some statements of rights that have nothing necessarily to do with the rules of human institutions. I think we are both guiltless of the common error or reinterpreting essentially noninstitutional facts as if they were special-institutional facts. But my simpler account has the added advantage of preserving the direct and categorical character of rights-claims, assumed at least in our time and culture by moral common sense.

3. *Doubts about the Value of Moral Rights.* Many other philosophers who are skeptical about moral rights are less concerned to deny that moral rights exist than to doubt the value or importance they would have if they did (or if they do) exist. Such skepticism is easy to come by. Imagine again the cowering couple awaiting the peremptory knock of the Gestapo at their door. A legal right to due process would do them some good, but only if that right's correlative duty were reliably enforced. The legal right without enforcement would give them no protection. What good would it do them in that case to have a moral right? Such a possession would give them control over the moral duties of their persecutors but what good would that moral power do them without physical power to back it up? With a moral right they would have the "satisfaction" of knowing that they were being wronged and not just suffering through their own fault or through the capricious occurrence of some natural accident. This would give them the opportunity to feel righteous and morally superior while they are whipped and clubbed. A moral right in these circumstances is like a "moral victory" (so-called) in a game that is hopelessly lost. Every honest supporter of moral rights, it seems to me, must concede this point to the skeptic. Even if moral rights are valuable commodities in general, they are not sufficient to reward their possessors so some degree in all circumstances. One can say in their behalf only that the world is better off generally for having them; that they do in many cases confer subtle benefits, but at most they are necessary not sufficient for one's overall good, and in no case are they guaranteed protections.

Philosophical writers who doubt the value of moral rights can be divided into two groups: those who charge that rights have an actual *disvalue*, and those who reject the claims of positive value that their defenders make for them. In the former group are some (but not all) feminists, some (but not all) Critical Legal Studies theorists, and communitarians both of the left, following Karl Marx, and of the right, following among others, Edmund Burke. Common to all these writers is the view that rights function to separate people rather than drawing them closer together in tighter communities, that rights are both an expression and a reinforcement of individual selfishness, and a threat to social solidarity. Jeremy Waldron, after carefully interpreting Bentham, Burke, and Marx, writes that "the great recurring theme in all three of these attacks is that the rights of man embody as the be-all and end-all of politics a demand for the immediate and unqualified gratification of purely selfish individual desires . . . For all of them, human life, to be bearable, involved a substantial commitment to living together in community that is belied by the abstract egoism of a theory of human rights."[28] Assuredly, rights claims are demands for things the claimant desires; if a person doesn't want something, then why make claim to it? It hardly follows, however, that the only desires any person ever has, and thus the only desires whose satisfaction he ever lays claim to as a matter of right, are "purely selfish" ones. In fact the desires protected by the most fundamental moral rights, the human and civil rights mentioned in the leading manifestos, are precisely those most plausibly designated as natural, understandable, and *unselfish.* It is morally absurd to accuse the teenage bride in the Cairo slum of a purely selfish desire not to have her sex organ mutilated, or to charge the Indian widow with a purely selfish desire not to be burned alive, or to level similar charges against the suffering terminal patient for insisting that he be released from his struggle, the Baha'i worshiper for desiring to practice his religion, or the Gestapo victims for claiming a moral right to due process, or third parties for judging with them that they do indeed have such rights. Do such judgments, which can be made in the first, second, or third person, really serve primarily to make people selfishly unconcerned with one another? The very opposite would seem to be closer to the truth.

Perhaps some moral rights, property and contract rights in particular, are instruments of and contributors to a kind of righteously callous self-centeredness. Among the more prominent uses of such rights, after all, is their employment as counters in acquisitive commercial strategies, and we are all familiar with the sort of person who, although affluent himself, thinks that taxation for the support of the needy is a kind of theft — a violation of his sacred property rights. People to whom the words "mine" and "thine" come readily to the lips, and are frequently uttered with emphasis and passion, are hardly social paragons, contributing to the sense of community among the rest of us. But we must remember that those of us who would rather own some things in common and cooperate rather than compete, and to whom the words "we," "us" and "ours" come more readily to the lips than "mine" and "thine" will nevertheless treasure *our rights* and the possessions held in common that *we* have. A sense of community does not render rights obsolete, it just assigns some of them collectively to groups who then can assert them collectively against outsiders or against individual members who would harm the collective good. The group has a right not to have its facilities damaged or its treasury pillaged by anyone, and this right contributes to its general cohesiveness. It can hardly be the case, therefore, that rights by their very nature serve to separate people.

Moreover, moral rights often resemble those legal rights that blend claims against others with what are called "powers." A power is a capacity under the rules to create, alter, or extinguish legal or moral relations (or "positions") both of oneself and of others. So, for example, my claim-right against you corresponds to your duty to me, but in addition I have the power of altering, suspending, or extinguishing your duty by choosing, for example, to waive my right and thus release you from your duty. In short, rights give us *control* over other parties' duties to us and (sometimes) to third parties. How we exercise this control is morally up to us, which is to say that we are morally at liberty to release or not release the other party from his duty as we see fit. There is no reason why we can't exercise our power wisely, compassionately, or cooperatively if we choose. We don't have to demand our pound of flesh just because we have a right to it. So again we can see that rights, even if morally necessary, are by no means morally sufficient. Virtues of good judgment, sympathy, and considerateness are necessary too, if the rights are to be used constructively. These excellences of character are an essential part of morality too. But there is nothing in the very nature of a moral right that militates against acquisition and cultivation of these gentler social virtues.

The main point in response to those who condemn moral rights as selfish and divisive, however, must rest on our specimen list of moral rights. The German citizens made subject to Gestapo arrests, detention, torture, and death were up against the whole massive force of the totalitarian state, condemned by a transformed community moral code and the explicit content of the state's enacted laws. "On 26 August 1942 the dummy-Reichstag had voted a law conferring on Hitler's discretionary powers in the administration of justice. The preamble to the law read: 'At present in Germany there are no more rights [conventional rights] but only duties...' A few days later, in his weekly, 'Das Reich,' Goebbels made clear what lay ahead: 'The bourgeois era with its false and misleading notion of humaneness is over'...."[29] It was evidently Goebbels' ideological conviction that a system which includes citizen rights against the state is *morally inferior* to a system in which a united citizenry eagerly accept duties assigned by the state but never consider making any claims of their own against the state, or of supporting the claims made by any other person against the state. How admirable, chorused Nazi philosophers, what self-denying devotion to duty, how pure and uncorrupt! To those of us who react with repugnance and horror to this conception of social morality, it seems plain that when a community becomes highly cohesive and tightly organized, where togetherness prevails and dissent is muted, that is *precisely where there is the greatest need for moral rights*, their acknowledgment, and their enforcement.

What does it mean after all for a person or his conduct to be selfish? A selfish person is not simply one who is devoted to the pursuit of his own ends. If that were true, then we could all be called selfish. In contrast, a genuinely selfish person is one who cares *unduly* or *supremely* for himself, whose conduct manifests an *excessive* concern for his own welfare, and who pursues his own comfort or advantage, etc. in *blamable disregard of or at the expense of others*. It is grotesque to apply this word to victims of the Nazis whose final desires and hopes were directed only to their own bare survival. Charging those who with trepidation and alarm point to what they call human rights violations against themselves or others with being selfish, socially dangerous persons, and citing their pliant conforming fellow citizens as moral exemplars, selflessly devoted to community values, is a transparent moral perversion. It is good that we have heard the last of it from the evil Nazis. Now it would be welcome if we could stop hearing similar perversities from respectable well-intentioned intellectuals.

I turn now to the second group of those who doubt the importance of moral rights if there are any. These are philosophers who deny the case that others have made for the value of moral rights without going quite so far as to assert their actual disvalue. The proposition these philosophers deny is one I have defended, which we can call "the moral impoverishment thesis." I borrow this term from Richard Wasserstrom, who as a Justice Department attorney was a leader in the movement to implement the Civil Rights Act of the 1960s in the southern states. Wasserstrom found that there were some older blacks who had adapted so well to their assigned role under the old system as second-class citizens that they were wary of the equal status conferred on them by their newly declared constitutional rights. Writing in 1964 he states that "To observe what happens to any person who is required to adopt habits of obsequiousness, [and] deferential behavior in order to minimize the likelihood of physical abuse, arbitrary treatment, or economic destitution is to see graphically how important human rights are and what their denial can mean."[30] If this is what tends to happen to people when they have no legal rights and lack a belief or even a conception of their own moral rights, what would the consequences on human character be generally of a normative system which assigned no rights to anyone even though it did impose duties on people of a more privileged class to treat their inferiors decently? Wasserstrom replies that "Such a system would be a morally impoverished one. It would prevent persons from asserting those kinds of claims . . . which a system of rights makes possible."[31]

In my 1970 article "The Nature and Value of Rights," I tried to provide further content and support to Wasserstrom's moral impoverishment thesis. A good part of the argument is empirical; people who must live as slaves tend to become servile simply as a survival mechanism. The situation of rightless dependence on more powerful persons naturally breeds a servile character, imprinted with fear and characterized by obsequious flattery, flaunted obedience, submissive cringing, fawning and meanness. The servile person is also likely to have a clever manipulative side; he turns his false humility off when he is with his own kind and will bully the less powerful. As C.S. Lewis put it, he is "alternately fawning and insolent."[32] People who are confident of their own rights are less likely to develop servile characters. They are not forced to secure their needs by begging "favors" from masters who have no relational duties to them, on the one hand, or by stealing and cheating, or resorting to plain force on the other. To say they have moral rights is to say that morally they are in a position to *claim* what they want as their due, what they have coming, and what the other party is under a moral obligation *to them* to provide. A claim is different from a mere demand like that of a gunman for your money or your life, and it is different from begging, imploring, or beseeching, for to claim is to invoke the authority of governing rules or principles by producing reasons certified by those principles as relevantly applicable and binding. The claimant has control over the claimee's duty which he activates by making the claim, but which he has the power to alter or even suspend as he wishes, as he has the physical power to turn on or off a light by pushing a switch one way or the other. The right-holder has more dignity than a mere beggar who is not in a position to make claim to what he wants, or a highwayman who, in abandoning the moral posture altogether, forfeits, in large part, any claim he might have had to moral respect. I concluded that to respect a person is tantamount to respecting his rights, that is to thinking of him as a prospective maker of weighty moral claims. If a person is thought to have no rights, not even the basic moral rights, he is by the same token thought to be unworthy of respect, and if he thinks of himself that way he can only cringe and beg, or cheat and steal, and will lack the virtue of self-respect. No wonder that a whole human population without rights, lacking even the concept of a right, would be "morally impoverished."

A great many critics registered their disagreement with this analysis. Most of them countered that a world full of moral duties of fairness and benevolence could dispense with rights. William Nelson, following Jan Narveson,[33] asks "Why does Feinberg think that people who do not regard themselves as possessors of rights but [do] regard others as having obligations and duties towards them, will be unable to demand that those others perform their duties and discharge their obligations? Why should they not be able to stand up, look . . . [the] other in the eye and complain just as loudly as anyone else when someone behaves toward them in a way which he was obligated not to behave?"[34] Nelson anticipates my reply when on a later page he writes that "when Feinberg suggests that in morals someone who lacks rights is prevented from claiming or complaining he surely does not mean that he opens his mouth but no sound comes out ..." Exactly so. If *A* has a duty to treat his slave *B* decently, but *B*, being a mere slave, has no right that *A* do his duty (or any other right against *A* for that matter), and *A* proceeds to violate his duty by treating *B* cruelly, then *B* will be "able to demand" that *A* proceeds to violate his duty be treating *B* cruelly, then *B* will be "able to demand" that *A* do his duty in the sense that if he opens his mouth to utter words of complaint the intended sounds *will* come out, or if he merely speaks to remind his master, with the utmost tact of his duties (say) under a code of *noblesse oblige*, those sounds *will* come out. If he chooses incredibly to look his master in the eye and "complain loudly" that the master is neglecting his duty, even those sounds will come out. But it isn't a question of *B*'s physical abilities; it is a question not of what he *can* do, but of what he *may* do under the accepted rules that govern his conduct and *A*'s, and under those rules any claim he may make will be infirm; he will have no legal or moral *power* to affect his master's duties or his own; he will be *able* to complain but not *entitled* to complain; he will in a sense "have a complaint" but he will not have a genuine moral *grievance*; since he had no rights against *A*, he could not be *wronged* by *A*'s conduct but only hurt or harmed by it. If he tries to voice a grievance anyway, he is vulnerable — morally vulnerable — to *A*'s cogent reply: "What business is it of yours whether or not *I* perform *my* noble duties? The rules that govern our relations do not make me answerable to you." That reply does not exactly express respect for *B*, and under the rules, *B* is not worthy of respect. So adding to *B*'s moral repertoire a moral claim-right correlative with *A*'s moral duty to him, does make a moral difference.

This analysis has a further advantage of a practical kind: It provides us with a test for distinguishing cases where one party has a right against another from cases in which he merely stands to gain from the performance of the other's duty to help him or from the other's superogatory act of beneficence toward him. Let us consider two kinds of cases in which that distinction is unclear and controversial. In both of these examples, it is agreed that *A* ought to have helped *B*, that it would have been a good thing and indeed the morally right thing for *A* to have done, and maybe even *A*'s duty to have done, but the question then arises after *A*'s failure to do it: did his failure to assist *B* violate *B*'s right? The first example is the problem of third-party beneficiaries of promises made to second parties. In one clear and uncontroversial example, a life insurance company, *A*, promises *B* that if *B* pays the agreed upon premiums then upon his death an enriched sum will be paid to *C*, his designated beneficiary. *C* may not even know of the existence of this agreement. Still when *A* dies, *B* is under an obligation to *C* to pay him the agreed sum, and *C* has a correlative right against *B* that puts him in a position validly to claim that amount from *B*, even though *B*'s original promise was not made to *C*, the beneficiary, but to *A*, the policy holder and promisee. If *B*, the company, refuses to pay *C*, the third-party beneficiary, then clearly it will be violating *C*'s right, for the money is owed to *C* even though the promise was made to *A*.

In contrast, suppose *B* promises to *A* to do something which, as it turns out, will incidentally benefit some total stranger, *C*, and *C* learns of the deal and eagerly looks forward to, even acts in reliance upon, his expected lucky windfall. *B* then breaks his promise to *A*, thus incidentally ruining *C*'s hope of profit. In that case, clearly *C*, the would-be third-party beneficiary of *B*'s promise to *A*, has not had his own rights violated since he did not have a personal right in the first place that *B* keep his promise to *A*.

I am not interested now in deriving the grounds for the distinction between the two cases, although that seems an easy enough thing to do in these clear instances. Instead I wish to propose a phenomenological test for determining whether or not a person who believes that a benefit to one party was wrongfully withheld by another party is committed by his other judgments and moral responses to the further judgment that the unhelped party suffered a violation of his rights. It isn't sufficient to generate that belief that one already holds the belief that the one party was *wrong* not to behave in the way that would have been helpful, that he *ought* to have so behaved, indeed even that he had a *duty* to behave in that way. We can believe all that and still deny that the unhelped party had a right violated by the wrongdoer. How does one tell, if one is confused about the concept of a right, whether one holds the further belief that a right was violated? I suggest, applying the analysis adumbrated in Part Two above, that one does in fact hold that further moral belief if and only if one also believes the following:

(1) *C* could have appropriately *claimed* in advance the assistance from *B* as his own due (by saying upon the fulfilled of the agreed conditions "You owe me as my due...).
(2) *C* can voice a grievance against *B* afterward (by saying to him appropriately "You wronged me by violating your agreement with *A*).
(3) At any time during the life of the agreement *C* can (has the legal or moral power to) release *B* from his duty if *C* pleases.
(4) It is for *C*'s sake that *B* has his duty to act in the agreed upon way and not merely for some extraneous reason unrelated to *C*.
(5) Whether or not *B* does his duty is *C*'s "business," his proper moral concern.

If you believe that all five of these statements are true of a given transaction, then and only then do you believe that the third-party beneficiary in that transaction had a right to the benefit in question. These five statements do not provide a full and useful criterion for deciding whether *C* had a right; instead they constitute a test of whether an outside judge is committed by his other judgments and moral responses to that belief. And the interesting thing about this test for our present purposes is that several of the elements in it, particularly being in a position to make claims and afterward to voice grievances, are the grounds of the greater dignity and self-respect that are associated with the role of right-holder.

The other example is that of the notorious bad samaritan. Unlike the more celebrated Good Samaritan of the New Testament, the bad samaritan lets an injured person, a stranger to him, lie where he fell on the street after being beaten and robbed, even though getting assistance for the battered victim would have cost him little more than minor inconvenience. Most commentators on this matter agree that morality imposes a duty on the "samaritan" even though the injured party is a stranger, to assist him if he can, but there is great disagreement over whether the battered stranger has a *right* against the samaritan to his help. If you agree with the duty judgment but are not sure whether you hold the further right-judgment or not, I suggest that something like the five-part test proposed above will tell you whether you have that belief or not. If this test is undecisive, it follows that you have no belief at all on the matter, and should apply the appropriate criteria, whatever they are, to the facts to help you make up your mind. But if the test tells decisively one way or the other, it follows that you already have a belief on the question, entailed by your other moral beliefs, and you were confused about that only because of uncertainty about the meaning of the expression — "a right."

I have argued that the test shows that most of us, whatever we may say, do in fact believe that the crime victim had a right to the stranger's help. Suppose, first of all, that you were a friend or relative of the battered victim lying there with no life-threatening injuries of your own but with a serious disablement, say two broken legs. You ask the samaritan's assistance for your unconscious friend whose very life in endangered. When the stranger hesitates you are surely in a position, morally speaking, to make claim to his assistance for your friend. "You can't just leave him there to die!" you might say. Clearly you are not in such a position, morally speaking, that you can only beg or implore the stranger for help; rather you and the friend you represent are in moral control over the other's duties, a role that confers much greater dignity on you than a belief that your friends's life had no value capable of commanding even a stranger's respect.

Secondly, we can ask after the fact whether the stranger's failure to offer help is any business of the one neglected, whether it would be appropriate for him and his loved ones to feel, not just animal anger, but moral indignation against the nonfeasant stranger, and whether they are in a position to voice a genuine moral grievance against the stranger for his neglect of his acknowledged duty. When we agree that passing strangers *ought* to offer assistance in cases like this, indeed that they must offer assistance, I submit that most of us also think that moral indignation on behalf of the recipient of the duty would be fitting if the stranger failed to do his duty. The alternative is just to give the stranger low moral grades, adding that his flaws are no business of the person he declined to aid, nothing that person is entitled to complain about. If some person *A* is pompous, vain, silly, dull-witted, or unimaginative, what is that to *B*, who is a mere stranger, a passive observer? *B* can make these adverse judgments about *A* and avoid his company, but can he claim as a personal grievance against *A* that *A* has these failings? Clearly not, and that is a sign that he has *no right* that *A* be a better person in those respects. That is *A*'s business not his. But the parents (say) of the battered victim will feel understandably and plausibly aggrieved, and we can share that indignation vicariously with them. We would not acknowledge that their child's right was infringed if we thought of the bad samaritan's neglected duty as something like a duty of *noblesse oblige*. But clearly we cannot think of it that way; the persistent sense of personal grievance will not permit it.[35]

Armed with this analysis, we can now return to a charge against moral rights that we considered earlier, that they are in their very nature a threat to worthwhile community. The simplest models of worthwhile community are marriages, families, friendships, and simple partnerships. Confining his attention to marriages and families, Robert Young writes that

> It is frequently when there has been a breakdown in the caring or loving relationships that hold between people that appeals to rights are made. When loving relations break down and the caring for another's interest which is morally proper

> goes by the board, people fall back on the auxiliary apparatus of rights. This is often understandable, but is not morally desirable since it does nothing to mend the ruptured relations.[36]

I have three quick replies to this. I can concede the subordinate role of reciprocal rights *claims* in loving relationships. Having a right does not require one to raise hell every time one perceives an infraction on the part of another. It only "puts one in a position" to make claims or complaints. One can exercise those liberties and powers as one sees fit, and a loving party will see fit to speak softly and gently, to forgive quickly, and so on. Secondly, loving relationships do break down, alas, and probably more often than not, and when this happens rights possession is not merely valuable; it is indispensable if one is to protect one's interests and to preserve one's self-respect. Moreover, there is a real moral value in respecting the other person as a genuine maker of moral claims even — Kant might say "especially" — in the absence of affection. But most important, thirdly, rights are more than a "fall-back auxiliary apparatus," for they are as necessary to love as affection itself is, even during the period when affection flourishes. Part of what is involved in caring for a person is a concern that she have those things that she just happens to have a right to anyway — consideration for special sensibilities and handicaps, fairness in the distribution of labors, freedom from arbitrary hurts and embarrassments, and so on. The rest of what is involved in caring is a concern that the loved one have more than that minimum she could claim as a matter of right — unexpected delights, unique tenderness, gifts, favors, symbolic gestures. Love may demand more than respect for rights, but it cannot survive with less.

Young quotes with approval a passage from Simone Weil meant to show how poorly rights serve a genuine community of reciprocally caring individuals. The very notion of a right, Weil claims, "has a commercial flavor, essentially evocative of legal claims and arguments. Rights are always asserted in a tone of contention; and when this tone is adopted it must rely upon force in the background or it will be laughed at."[37] A twofold reply can be made to these bold contentions. In the first place, it is plain false that rights are always asserted in a tone of contention.[38] Rights, in fact, can be asserted calmly, automatically, with dignity and calm, or with embarrassment, regret, or apology. Indeed they can be asserted without uttering words at all, as when a person makes claim to his coat by presenting his coat check token to the coat room attendant.

An especially interesting example comes from a syndicated newspaper column by Zeke Wigglesworth, defending the quality of food service on international air flights by citing the many difficulties the airlines must surmount in order to serve hot meals at all. After an enumeration of these difficulties, he adds another one — "Then there is always some clod who tries to go to the washroom while the meals are being served, creating a traffic jam and demanding loudly that the stews (stewards or stewardesses) get the trolley out of the way."[39] I have on occasion played the role of the "clod" myself, and it is very embarrassing. The clod either forgets to stop in the restroom before boarding the plane or is so rushed he has no opportunity. By the time he feels the call of nature, it is too late; the luncheon trolley already fills the aisle and there is no room to squeeze by. Fortunately, there is a well-understood moral convention governing situations of this kind. The clod has the right of way, given that his natural need can be presumed to be more pressing, and the stewardesses must back their cart out of the way, thus delaying the service. Both the stewardesses and the clod understand that he has the right to proceed and they have the duty, under the convention, to get out of his way. But the clod need not assert his right by "demanding loudly" that the trolley be removed. Right-possession is not a license for vulgarity. He can assert his right without speaking at all, except for an embarrassed mumbled "sorry" as he passes the stewardesses. His right-assertion in that case would consist in his signaling his intention clearly, and his confident goal-directed strides toward the barrier, with the demeanor of a person who knows his rights and proceeds without hesitation, and with as much dignity as he can muster. Claiming in these circumstances is simply exercising a legal-like, conventional moral "power," as if one were thereby pushing a routine button that creates or "lights up" the other parties's duties. This *can* be done apologetically, regretfully yet firmly.

Weil's other point is about the impotence of rights claims, even when "asserted in a tone of contention," if they are made in the face of superior physical forces and thus are incapable of being enforced. If Salman Rushdie were captured by the Iranians and presented to the Ayatollah, he could on that occasion contentiously assert his right of free expression, and righteously demand to be released. The Ayatollah is not known to laugh easily, but Weil refers in her quote to the laugh of derision not the laugh of amusement, and Rushdie's situation would not be very dignified if he were dragged off by burly guards to be imprisoned. The truth is that rights may be necessary for respect and dignity but, except in the case of Stoics[40] and other heroes, they may not be sufficient. It also helps to have the rights recognized by the other party or even backed up by some physical or military force.

Moral rights, then, do not help much, or not at all, in the face of machine guns manned by the lackies of powerful immoralists or other unimpressed antagonists, even from the point of view of moral dignity. But before one dismisses moral rights for that reason, consider the alternatives. The dissident couple seized in their home by the Gestapo have at least three options. They can affirm their moral rights calmly and firmly, thus triggering derision and cruelty, or they can abandon moral language to make idly heroic demands, as if *they* had the monopoly of force in the situation, or they might prostrate themselves and beg for mercy. Surely, the hopeless assertion of right is not any *less* consistent with dignity than its alternatives, although all three are hopelessly doomed. My analysis of rights as claims, in any case, implies only that the right-holder by virtue of his right is in a *moral position* to make claims against others, not necessarily that he is in a physical or political position to make claims without having his face kicked in. For this "moral advantage" to be a genuine advantage it is necessary that those to whom rights-claims are made have some capacity of moral recognition and at least some minimal moral responsiveness. It is no wonder that Gandhi maintained his impressive moral dignity even in the teeth of superior force from his enemies in British India. The Nazis would have allowed him no moral dignity at all.

Moral powers, so-called, without backup physical power will be impotent against physical force unrestrained by moral responsiveness. But before leaving this depressing topic, we should look at the idea of a "moral power," a little more closely. Moral and legal powers are not just alternative techniques — like nuclear power, hydroelectric power, psychological power, persuasive power, and political power — for producing the same kinds of effect within the physical world. Rather they are ways of producing their own distinctive types of effect within their own distinctive realm — effects on people's duties, liberties, claims, immunities, liabilities, and further powers — and these distinctive effects are produced, not by some other kind of natural power, on a par with electric power or military power, but by offers, acceptances, transfers, acts of consent, and so on. Between two parties who are in some way potential competitors, yet have not rejected the whole moral game in favor of physical force, rights-claims, more than any of their alternatives, dispose the parties toward reasonableness. Carl Wellman makes this point well: "Claiming is an appeal to one's title or to the grounds of one's rights, and thus an appeal to reasons rather than to mere force."[41] In the case of moral rights of the sort listed at the start of this paper, appeal is not made literally to titles, chits, receipts, warranties, and so on — these are *legal* reasons — but to moral reasons, "statements that imply some moral conclusion."[42] Then

> to say that a model right such as the moral right to travel, exists, is to assert the truth of some set of moral reasons and to assert also that they are relevant to human conduct in the appropriate sort of ways. Since neither the truth nor the [probative] relevance of moral reasons depends upon social recognition or promotion, moral rights can exist independently of these also. Where moral rights go unrecognized or unaccepted in a society, they will be ignored and unpractical in that society. But it does not follow, however, that the moral right is infirm as a right, but only that the practices of the society are defective from the moral point of view.[43]

4. *Moral Rights and the Constitution.* If by "the founding fathers" we mean that group of patriots which prominently included the signers of the Declaration of Independence, then there should be little doubt that the founding fathers, or anyway most of them, believed that there *are* moral rights and that many, at least, of those moral rights are incorporated into the Constitution whether explicitly mentioned there or not. Shortly after Jefferson's famous phrase about our

being endowed by our Creator with the "unalienable rights" to life, liberty, and the pursuit of happiness, there occurs the critical passage that it is also a self-evident truth that "to secure these rights, Governments are instituted among Men...." This clearly implies, or so it seems to me, that the crucial rights in question are taken to exist prior to and independently of government enactment, and that they are therefore what were frequently called "natural rights" in the eighteenth century or "moral rights" in the sense I have given to that expression. Now if the protection of these moral rights is the purpose for which we have a government in the first place, it would be very strange indeed if the recognition and endorsement of those rights were not part of the basic law of that government. The very point of having a government — of founding a political state — is to secure these rights. How then could they fail to be a part of the legal framework of the government the founders constructed for that purpose?

The Constitution does mention a number of specific rights, many of which could be construed plausibly as incorporated moral rights: the exclusive right of authors and inventors to their respective writings and discoveries (Article I, Section 8), specific rights in the sense of immunities, for example to the suspension of writs of habeas corpus, to bills of attainder, and ex post facto laws (Article I, Section 9); the famous First Amendment rights to the free exercise of religion, free speech, free press, and freedom of assembly; the right not to have soldiers quartered in one's house without one's consent; the right against unreasonable searches and seizures; the right to just compensation for property taken by the state; the rights against double jeopardy, excessive bail, cruel and unusual punishments, and involuntary servitude except as criminal punishment; the right to vote regardless of race or sex; and the famous Fourteenth Amendment rights to due process and equal protection, to name only some. A few of these rights are claim-rights conferring control over other parties' duties; most, however, are immunity-rights rendering legally void certain types of government action and legislation. Some are held against private parties, but most against the state. Some are relatively precise and specific; some are quite abstract requiring considerable interpretation; some contain terms of the kind often called "essentially contested concepts," like "unreasonable," "due," "just," "excessive," and "cruel," requiring the interpreting judge to provide the appropriate standards for the application of these moral terms. Some of the mentioned rights could without difficulty apply in a state of nature prior to the establishment of civil society but most are specifically claims against governments which would have no use before governments even existed. They could still be construed as moral rights, however, but conditional ones, rights that would hold against any government that might ever eventuate. As conditionally formulated in that way they could exist and be known before there was any point in asserting them, and thus validating reasons for the rights would not include references to the enactments of any government actually in existence.

The rights to life, liberty, and the pursuit of happiness are not names of still other specific rights that are included in the Constitution. Rather, they are category labels for classes into which a large miscellany of specific rights can be placed.[44] To say that all persons have rights in these categories does not tell us much about what these rights are. Moreover, the category labels themselves were obviously selected in part for their rhetorical impact and are extremely vague. The right to liberty, for one, is an excellent example of this vagueness. Most of our legal rights to liberty, including some that could be construed as also genuine moral rights, are conferred on us by particular statutes and precedents, these being permitted by the Constitution but not clearly required by it. Our legal right not to be abducted or falsely imprisoned are examples. Most of the liberties conferred on us by the Constitution are indirect liberties derived from the Constitution's "nullification in advance" of any criminal prohibitions or other coercive restrictions that are contrary to our moral rights. These advance nullifications or legislative disabilities often take the verbal form — "Congress shall make no law...."

Not only are the category labels vague, they also tend to be somewhat arbitrary in the sense that they provide no guidance to the classification of a given right that seems fittingly includable in more categories than one. Almost every right, for example, seems to be a right to the pursuit of happiness; and many rights protected by constitutionally valid criminal statutes can be interpreted as rights to liberty, for example, the rights to be free from assault, battery, rape, even murder. (After all, when one loses one's life, one loses one's liberty too.) Similarly, the constitutional rights imposing limits on what the government can validly do to a citizen (freedom of religion, freedom of speech, freedom from unreasonable searches, and so on) are virtually all classifiable as rights to liberty.

The final shortcoming of the traditional categories is that they are not only uninformative, vague, and somewhat arbitrary; they are also slipshod and perhaps incomplete. The urge to conceptual tidiness makes us want to classify some clearly identifiable species of the right to the pursuit of happiness as rights to property, and since property rights are often in apparent conflict with the personal liberties of others (where your property begins, my liberty of movement ends), some constitutional rights could better be understood as belonging to the property category than as members of the liberty grouping.

The reason for my interest here in the traditional taxonomy of moral rights is that a new posited generic right-category has in recent years generated a furious controversy that is not without its philosophical aspects. I refer of course to the "right of privacy," endorsed by the Supreme Court in the famous case of *Griswold v. Connecticut* in 1965, and applied as a label hitherto unnamed set of generic moral rights that were said to be tacitly incorporated into the Constitution. These rights, though given a new name, are actually like the other specific rights in the Constitution, the First Amendment rights, for example, that protect private liberties to behave in a certain way by imposing legislative disabilities against the valid creation of legal duties *not* to behave in those ways.

What was at issue in *Griswold* was the validity of a Connecticut statute prohibiting the use "by any person" of contraceptives, and permitting any doctor who counsels their use to be prosecuted and punished as if he were the principal offender. To those justices in the majority who declared the statute constitutionally void, the right of married couples to use contraceptives is as clear an example as one can find of a *moral* right — the kind of right governments are instituted among men to secure. Most of the minority, on the other hand, presumably agreed with Justice Stewart that the statute was "an uncommonly silly law," but found silliness to be no ground for unconstitutionality in the absence of an explicit constitutional declaration of a right to use contraceptives or of a right of a more general kind that would imply a right to use contraceptives. Justice Douglas maintained that several explicit guarantees in the Bill of Rights do imply or presuppose privacy rights, and in any case, said Justice Goldberg, the Ninth Amendment declares that "The enumeration in the Constitution of certain rights shall not be construed to deny or disparage others retained by the people." The Ninth Amendment leaves open the question of whether the unenumerated privacy rights are retained by the people in virtue of their prevailing conventional moral code, or whether the rights in question are among those natural rights that governments are instituted among men to secure, but the latter interpretation has the founding fathers' general philosophical orientation behind it, and to most of us who find it morally outrageous that the state should presume to tell couples what they may and may not do in the privacy of their marital bedrooms, the defect of the law is not mere "silliness," but an arrogant invasion of rights, whatever the past or currently prevalent conventional morality may say.

It is by now commonplace among commentators that the constitutional right of privacy has been misleadingly named. The Connecticut statute invalidated by the *Griswold* decision was not constitutionally infirm because it restricted privacy in the usual sense of the term (a liberty to enjoy one's solitude unwitnessed, unintruded upon, even unknown about in certain ways). For even if, as Justice Douglas suggested, the Connecticut legislature replaced the objectionable statute with one that did not forbid the *use* of contraceptives, but only their manufacture and sale, thus giving the police no warrant in Douglas's words, to "search the sacred precincts of marital bedrooms for telltale signs of the use of contraceptives,"[45] and thereby protecting privacy in the usual sense, there still would be a violation of a very stringent moral right. Couples would still be deprived of the opportunity to use contraceptives if they choose, and this would importantly infringe their moral autonomy, for it would diminish their capacity to decide for themselves in what would otherwise be a zone of discretion, that of choices related to marital sexual intimacies and reproductive decisions. As many have suggested, the moral-hence-constitutional right in question would be better named "the right to autonomy" than "the right of privacy." As such, it is a category of rights to liberty distinguished from other rights to liberty by the content of the choices it protects, such pivotally central life decisions as those concerning the sexual intimacies, the home, the family, marriage, motherhood, procreation, and childbearing.[46] The list is open-ended, and could include other basic life-decisions, and even, through classificatory overlapping, freedoms of religion. To repeat, which category we place the moral right in is a matter of no importance. What is significant is that privacy rights, so called, are as vital to those who treasure them, even, as the rights to free speech, due process, and free exercise of religion — which, after all, are parallel in their structure, being rights to liberty conferred in the form of immunities to governmental restriction in other vitally important areas of life.

A large number of commentators have criticized the Supreme Court's privacy decisions on one ground or another, but there is one line of attack in particular which rests on a deep skepticism about the existence of moral rights and is therefore worth discussing here briefly. I refer to the theory of constitutional interpretation sometimes called "originalism," sometimes "interpretivism," sometimes "value-free constitutionalism." Whichever the name used, this theory is that which received its definitive statement in the works of Professor John Ely[47] and Judge Robert Bork,[48] and numbers among its more influential advocates Chief Justice William Rehnquist[49] and former Attorney General Edwin Meese.[50] Justice Sutherland defined the doctrine forcefully in a 1934 case: "The whole aim of construction as applied to a provision of the Constitution is . . . to ascertain and give effect to the intent of its framers and the people who adopted it."[51]

How would an originalist have decided the *Griswold* case? He would first scrutinize the black letter text of the Constitution to see whether the original framers or amenders expressed any strictures there about the use of contraceptives. Following that easy inquiry, he would peruse the text again for any explicit reference to a more abstract right of unregulated sexual intimacy, or reproductive options. Again, finding nothing explicit in the text, he would seek out language in the document (particularly in its provisions of various liberties and immunities) that could be interpreted as expressing the authors' and ratifiers' intention to create a right of sexual privacy, that is discretionary freedom or autonomy in sexual matters not affecting third parties. Here he would ask himself what specific applications they were known to have in mind, which applications from among those they did not have in mind they would have been prepared to accept, or what their larger purposes were in choosing the language they used. The inquiry to this point would have been entirely factual — historical, empirical, and neutral — and its results would be entirely negative. No right to privacy; no remedy against the arbitrary interference of a silly statute; no sex without the risk of either pregnancy or arrest. This mode of interpretation "assumes that the doctrinal content of the Constitution was completely determined when it was adopted and that constitutional doctrines can be identified by a value-free factual study of the text of [its] 'original intent.'"[52] When legislative disabilities cannot be located by this method, then of course there is no ground for overturning the corresponding legislation; it must stand as originally enacted by "the people's representatives," who are empowered to create any kind of law, however silly, that does not contravene the immunities declared in the Constitution.

Why can't a Supreme Court justice simply declare that there is a moral right to personal autonomy (privacy) in the predominantly self-regarding realm, and absent a compelling public interest, that the abstract right to autonomy entails a more concrete right to free choice in sexual and reproductive matters? The originalist replies that that would be to project the judge's own personal "value preference" into the Constitution where it is not otherwise to be found, and the Constitution itself gives courts no valid power to do that. Professor Ely, who is not quite as restrictive of the Court's powers as Bork, when "left with the choice, in the exercise of judicial review, between [what he calls] 'the judge's own values,' and the values of the legislature . . . chooses the legislature's."[53]

Moreover, there are no moral rights anyway, and that which masquerades as such are really just the subjective preferences or "value choices," as Bork likes to put it, of the judge. In Bork's usage, as David Lyons points out,[54] a "value choice" is not a value *judgment*; rather it is as personal and arbitrary as a raw wish, and is incapable in its very nature of being rationally supported. It follows that a judge's use of his own value preferences in interpreting the Constitution is partisan and "unprincipled," and that when two judges disagree about which rights governments are instituted among men to secure, there is no rational way to settle the dispute and one opinion is as good as the other. Bork's value skepticism is apparently unlimited. The conscientious judge, therefore, is restricted to the facts. He may implement the "values" (themselves mere "preferences") which he finds as a matter of fact in the Constitution or in the authenticated intentions of its framers. But implementing the value preferences of others is not the same unprincipled activity as making a value choice of one's own. When the judge therefore is faced with a conflict between those of her own moral judgments (and even those which ascribe moral rights are mere "value preferences") which she is so satisfied with that she wants to read them back into the Constitution, and those equally arbitrary and rationally indefensible value choices of a legislature as indicated in its express statutory language or manifest intentions, she *must* choose those of the legislature, even those of the Connecticut legislature of the 1880s.

The Appellate justice who, like Judge Bork, is a decent person, would in her private capacity, presumably condemn Connecticut's interference in marital birth control, but bravely do her higher judicial duty, recognizing her own moral judgment to be, like all moral judgments, a mere subjective preference, unsupportable by reason. Any other path to a decision would be "unprincipled," because it would be to take sides, without constitutional warrant, in a social conflict between a minority pressing its alleged rights and a majority whose value preferences are expressed in a valid statute. The satisfaction of a preference Bork calls a "gratification" or a "pleasure," so the "unprincipled" judge who arrogates the power of taking sides, will be choosing between the gratifications of the two groups,[55] arbitrarily favoring the gratifications married couples would derive from having their wishes for protection (which they may call "their rights") granted, over the gratification of outsiders who disapprove of what the other group wants, and would therefore take pleasure at restrictions of their liberty. The judge's preference for either one of these competing gratifications would be rationally indefensible, hence arbitrary, since there is no objective ground for preferring one to the other.[56]

David Lyons has an even more telling example: "Prior to the Fourteenth Amendment, Bork would presumably respond to a suit seeking invalidation of a law banning Jews and Catholics from certain professions [by reiterating that] 'Where the Constitution does not embody the moral . . . choice, the judge has no basis other than his own values upon which to set aside the community judgment embodied in the statute.'... Bork's express reason for a judicial policy of 'restraint' is that all opposing positions, *including the rejection of bigotry*, are rationally indefensible, so that lacking [explicit] constitutional warrant, a judicial decision favoring one would be 'unprincipled' *just because* any 'preference' for one side or the other *could not* be 'principled.'"[57] Making the point forcefully in his own language of "gratifications," Bork concludes: "There is no principled way to decide that one man's gratifications are more deserving of respect than another's or that one form of gratification is more worthy than another."[58] (In calling such comparisons of conflicting "gratifications" arbitrary, Bork goes even further than Bentham whose theories his views otherwise resemble, for Bentham, as a utilitarian, believed in the objectivity of moral judgments, and would have the judge support the more extensive, intense, and durable "gratifications" in cases of conflict.)

I propose now to argue against Judge Bork's view and in favor of its alternative, the theory of moral rights in the Constitution. The first argument is almost too easy. As a matter of history there is little doubt that Jefferson was speaking for the vast majority of his colleagues, including those who were to become drafters, ratifiers, and amenders of the Constitution, when he declared that there are moral rights in the possession of the people for the securing of which governments are instituted among them. It would be absurd to posit such rights as part of the raison d'être of the state and yet deny that the basic legal structure of the state incorporates those rights. Therefore, the founding fathers, or most of them, as a matter of historical fact, believed that moral rights, whose existence was prior to and independent of their own deliberations and enactments, were part and parcel of the charter of the government they were designing. But according to originalism the "original intent" of the founders is for us the source constitutional law. So it follows that originalism itself is committed to the presence in the Constitution of rights which have a source independent of the intentions of the original drafters. Put in another way, it was the intention of the original framers that their own words and intentions not be the single key to subsequent judicial interpretation. Originalism thus is hoist with its own petard.

The second argument is an ancient embarrassment for a *complete* ethical skepticism. The complete relativist about moral judgments would have to avoid making moral judgments of his own, whether about himself or others, whether about rights or about duties. If he allowed himself, as Bork does for example, to make judgments about the duties of judges, he would have to subject those judgments to the same withering analysis he uses in criticizing the moral judgments ascribing rights and duties to parties in the conflicts between individuals and governments: they are mere subjective preferences, rationally indefensible, arbitrary, and so on. In that case, Bork's own moral judgment would no sooner giveth than his theory would taketh away.

One might evade this traditional argument against moral skepticism by restricting the doctrine to statements of moral *rights*, thus exempting moral duties. Many moral duties, however, as we have seen, are linked logically to other parties' rights, and in many of these cases it seems as plausible to explain the duty as the consequence of the right as vice versa. Moral rights, like their institutional and legal counterparts, typically confer on their possessors "powers" to control the duties of other people, switching them on or off, for example, to facilitate the choices or protect the interests of the right-holder. It would seem arbitrary to concede that the duties exist in these cases but then assert that their beneficiaries lack all control over them, and cannot appropriately claim them as their due, or appropriately express personal grievances when they are left undischarged, in short that the duties are objective facts while their associated rights are mere arbitrary "preferences" of the speaker.

Another part of the originalist argument, common to Judge Bork, Professor Ely, and many others, seems to me to commit a very subtle non sequitur. All of these writers claim at a certain point in the argument that for a judge to make a moral judgment is one and the same thing as her asserting her "own values" or her "own opinion." Professor Ely describes the option of the judge in judicial review, when the constitution is silent or unclear, as a choice between the values of the legislature and the judge's *own* values,[59] and speaking of *Roe v. Wade*, he goes so far as to say that "judges . . . occasionally impose their *personal* values...."[60] Not just their values but their private personal one, or their private beliefs or "opinions" about what is moral. Bork writes scornfully that his academic critics propose "that judges enforce good values or," he quickly adds, "the values that seem to the professor good,"[61] as if the values that *seem* good to someone or other could not, in the very nature of the case, actually *be* good. The subtle fallacy in these formulations consists in an equivocal slide from the interpretation of an expression as a trivial truism to the interpretation of that statement as asserting a serious substantive point that the reader is antecedently likely to consider false. One begins by assuming that when one is asked to make a judgment, one is being asked to express his *own* opinion (who else's?) or what amounts to the same thing, the truth as *he* sees it. When a person makes a reasonable judgment about a matter independent of his own will or impression, it is *his* opinion after all, not someone else's that he expresses. That is the truism: When I make a judgment it is my judgment that I make. The subtle equivocation begins when one qualifies the truism with the belittling words "*merely* one's own opinion," or "*simply* one's own belief," or "*solely* one's own judgment," as if the tautology that expressions of one's opinion *are* expressions of one's opinion necessarily implies that one's opinion is something merely subjective, unrelated to any matter of fact *independent* of itself which may, in the best cases, lend it credibility. The slide continues and becomes more egregious when one moves from the tautology that when I express my opinion it is of course *my* opinion that I express to the conclusion that in all cases my opinion must be an opinion of a very special kind, a private or "personal opinion" peculiar to me and unsupported by any general or impersonal reasons which make no reference to me personally. When I say, for example, that broccoli tastes good, I express a "merely" personal opinion; when I say that broccoli is rich in vitamin C, I make claim to public and impersonal evidence. Surely, it does not follow from the tautology that when I express an opinion it is my opinion that I express that every opinion I ever express is an opinion of the personal kind. In fact, nothing whatever of a substantive and controversial nature can follow from a mere tautology.

The mistake I have been trying to describe is often committed even more blatantly by people attempting to prove psychological egoism, the doctrine that all human motivation is selfish. The steps are well known.[62] The egoist begins with a truistic premise that he presents as if it were a self-evident substantive truth, namely that "Every voluntary action is prompted by a motive of the actor's own." That is the premise that is analogous to "Every opinion a person expresses is his own opinion." The reason why the premise in the argument for egoism is true is that if a person's motive or intention in acting were not his own but rather that of someone else in control over him, we would not call the action *his* — that is, voluntarily his — in the first place. But then the slippage begins, as one slides from the truism that since I always act on my own motives, I am always seeking something for myself, a controversial substantive claim that seems contrary to experience; and from that, one slides to "Every voluntary act is prompted not merely by the actor's own motives (as the truism says) but also by a motive of a very special kind, namely a selfish one." We have gone a long way without logistical warrant from the truism with which we began. We do the same thing in the other case when we move from "an opinion of mine" to "an opinion of mine of a very special kind, namely a 'personal' one."

By means of this logically illicit device, we can relativize everything. We can tell a scientist to appeal in support of his hypothesis only to reasons of a certain kind, say mathematical reasons, and then complain after the fact that he didn't really appeal to mathematical truths but only to what he believed were mathematical truths; he "merely" expresses *his* opinion about what is mathematically true, and a "personal" opinion at that. Hence even judgments of mathematics are merely personal, private, subjective, and arbitrary. Alternatively, we can instruct a Supreme Court judge to admit only reasons of type R, say originalist reasons of the favored Ely-Bork kind, and then after the judge accepts our recommendation, we can complain that she isn't really using originalist reasons at all, but *rather*, what is necessarily different, *what seems to her* to be originalist reasons, therefore her own private personal reasons instead of the objective factual reasons we wanted. Nobody can win *that* game.

When Bork writes that "In a constitutional democracy, the moral content of the law must be given by the morality of the framer or legislator, never by the morality of the judge," he wants us to assume with him that any moral judgment made by a judge can only be his own private personal morality — "the morality of the judge" — and not the impersonal objective morality it may claim to be. Moreover, Bork wants us to transfer the self-evident truth of the tautologous premise to the very dubious tendentious conclusion, as if we had been asleep throughout the transition from the one to the other.

My final criticism of originalist arguments is directed exclusively to Judge Bork who, in his Francis Boyer Lectures on Public Policy, has used an opportunity to refine and amplify some of the views he expressed in the main source of his judicial philosophy, his influential *Indiana Law Journal* article of sixteen years earlier on "Neutral Principles...." In his lecture on "Tradition and Morality in Constitutional Law," Bork turns to what has been called, since Patrick Devlin's famous lecture, the problem of the "legal enforcement of morality." There in his confrontation with Millian liberalism, it is Bork himself, of all people, who accuses his opponents of moral relativism! The liberal position declares illegitimate all criminal statutes forbidding acts contrary to the community's morality except such acts as also cause harm to people other than the actor. So, for example, statutes forbidding homosexual relations between adults in private, even where such conduct is contrary to the prevailing moral conventions, may not legitimately be prohibited. Bork complains that this liberal principle (often called "the harm principle"[63]) would indefensibly restrict what a community, or its majority, "are entitled to regard as harms," since they may prevent physical injuries and economic losses but not what they think of "moral harms." This in turn, he protests, amounts to "the privatization of morality," and "require[s] the law of the community to practice moral relativism." Moreover, it shows the liberal's true contempt for liberty because while it entitles individuals to their moral beliefs, it does not empower them "to express those moral beliefs in law."[64] The latter argument strikes me as exceedingly strange, soliciting our sympathies, as it does, for the majority for having *its* freedom of expression so brutally suppressed, as if mere "expression" were all that is involved when a prohibition backed by criminal punishment is put into a criminal code! According to the liberals who would so callously interfere with the majority's right to express itself by threatening the minority with imprisonment, Bork tells us, "moral relativism is a constitutional demand."[65]

The court opinions Bork criticizes in his lecture are about what I think is properly called "vulgarity," and only misleadingly called "immorality." He quotes from the opinion of Justice Harlan in *Cohen v. California*[66] the oft-quoted sentence "One man's vulgarity is another's lyric." That sentence in the majority opinion makes the liberal claim that "The Constitution leaves the matter of taste and style . . . largely to the individual." The Court thereby reduces the entire question of unorthodox style, Bork complains, to a matter of private preference.[67] Can this be the same Judge Bork who asserted sixteen years earlier that judgments of moral rights are indeed mere expressions of personal preference?

As a liberal, I also disagree with Bork on the question of state regulation of taste, style, and manners. It may thus seem that both of us are inconsistent, each of us implying that one realm of morality is a matter of mere personal preference and another realm of morality a matter of objective judgment properly enforceable by law. There is nothing wrong with distinguishing the two realms, as we both agree, but from the point of view of common sense, Bork does it in such a way as to turn the truth upside down, for his view appears to be that the immorality of vulgarity is a matter of objective moral judgment enforceable by the state, whereas some seriously harmful conduct is condemned only as a matter of private preference. On the other hand, the moral rights theory that I have been expounding maintains that Gestapo-style early morning arrests without due process violate moral rights; that prohibitions of contraceptives violate moral rights; that preventing a competent adult couple who love one another from marrying one another because one of them is of the wrong race is a violation of moral rights; whereas vulgarity in dress and manner is *not* a violation of moral rights unless it should somehow be seriously harmful to vital human interests in the manner of the rights-violations mentioned above — which seems unlikely. In a nutshell, Bork seems to hold that issues of human rights are matters of taste about which there is no disputing; whereas obvious matters of taste and style, on the other hand, are, as issues of human rights are normally thought to be, questions for objective judgment and legal enforcement. There will not be many converts, I suspect, to that antipodean moral outlook.

5. *Conclusion.* In conclusion, I should like to recommend that people have more respect for their own considered moral judgments. Legal powers to make raids and arrests as they pleased were conferred on Gestapo agents by constitutionally valid German statutes and decrees, so they were not contrary to enacted law. Nor were they contrary to the thoroughly cowed or enchanted public opinion behind the new Nazi "morality." Yet who can deny that they were morally wrong anyway? Moreover, they were wrong because of the unconscionable harms imposed on their victims for no acceptable moral reasons. Identifying with the victims, we can intuitively apprehend and appreciate the moral claims they had

against their oppressors, which were of course totally ignored, and on behalf of the victims we can, without shame or embarrassment, voice genuine moral grievances and feel genuine moral indignation. These are the chief criteria for the application of the word "rights." So it follows not only that the Nazi actions were morally wrong, but that they violated moral rights and that is *why* they were morally wrong. The moral rights in turn did not stem from legal enactment and were in fact unrecognized and unprotected in both the governing legal and moral codes. Holding independently then of the accepted conventional rules, the rights were moral rights, and since they were moral rights held equally by all of us they were human rights.

To deny these truths is to deny the appropriateness of moral indignation, a moralized emotion expressing outrage not only to our feelings of human sympathy, but more centrally to our sense of fairness, and our respect for autonomy. Much the same could be said about a state's prohibition of the use of contraceptives, of interracial marriage, or of unfettered international travel, though the harms done in these examples fall short of the Nazi example. In all these cases the restrained victim of arbitrary legislation will insist that what he does in the area in question is *his* business, not the state's, not the public's, not his neighbor's, and not the legislature's. Some claimed moral rights, of course, are controversial, and others even more spurious, but that should not prevent us in these paradigmatic cases from acknowledging the rights being claimed. Anyone can distinguish a genuinely believed judgment ascribing moral rights from a mere expression of an arbitrary wish or preference. Those who express their wishes and preferences in the language of moral rights cheapen that language and spread skepticism harmfully and unnecessarily. But it is equally harmful to trivialize our authentic rights claims by regarding them as mere wishes. To deny the distinction between the two in that way is to break faith with some of our deepest convictions and to be untrue to what we really believe.

Notes

1. *Griswold v. Connecticut*, 381 U.S. 479 (1965).

2. *Loving v. Virginia*, 388 U.S. 1 (1967).

3. "A historian who said the British agricultural laborer of 1810 had no right to organize in trade unions, would seem to be making a statement about actual conditions which could be judged true or false as it accorded with the facts." S.I. Benn and R.S. Peters, *Social Principles and the Democratic State* (London: George Allen & Unwin, Ltd., 1959), p. 92.

4. The example is from R.B. Brandt, "The Concept of a Moral Right and its function," *The Journal of Philosophy* (1983): 29.

5. Cf. "The Most Wretched Place," a CBS Transcript of *Sixty Minutes*, Vol. XX, No. 5, October 18, 1987. ". . .the slum outside Cairo where the 30,000 people who collect the garbage live . . . They and their families are not city employees. They're a

group of outcasts who have lived from the garbage for more than a century, a completely closed society . . . the most despised people in all Egypt . . . Next to her passion for the young children, Sister Emmanuelle [a visiting French nun] cares most about the women. She says they are forced to bear the children, sort the garbage, and endure regular beatings by their husbands . . . She boycotted this wedding [filmed for TV by CBS] because the bride and her young husband are only fourteen and because of what the young woman must go through. She was circumcised when she was young, a painful mutilation designed to reduce sexual pleasure. If she isn't a virgin, she'll be beaten, even killed. This night, an old woman is sent to test the bride's virginity while the music drowns her screams. The blood on the handkerchief proves she came to the wedding a virgin.": 8, 9.

6. "The practice of killing a favorite wife on her husband's grave has been found in many parts of the world . . . [among] the Thracians, the Scythians, the ancient Egyptians, the Scandinavians, the Chinese, and peoples of Oceana and Africa. Suttee was probably taken over by Hinduism from a more ancient source. Its stated purpose was to expiate the sins of both husband and wife and to ensure the couple's reunion beyond the grave, but it was encouraged by the low regard in which widows were held . . . isolated cases of voluntary suttee have occurred into the 20th century." *The New Columbia Encyclopedia* (New York and London: Columbia University Press, 1975): 2662.

7. R.G. Frey, Interests and Rights, *The Case Against Animals* (Oxford: Clarendon Press, 1980): 7.

8. Still another sense of "natural rights," usually left implicit, refers to rights based on natural *needs*.

9. E.g., W.D. Ross, *The Right and the Good* (Oxford: Clarendon Press, 1930), Appendix I, "Rights,": 48-55.

10. Richard B. Brandt, *Ethical Theory* (Englewood Cliffs, NJ: Prentice-Hall, 1959), Chap. 17: 433-454.

11. Howard Warrender, for example, writes that "A 'right,' as the term is generally used in moral and political philosophy . . . is . . . a comprehensive description of the *duties* of other people toward oneself in some particular respect . . . In this sense, the term 'right' has a rhetorical rather than a philosophical value . . . The rights formula . . . is a loose, summarizing expression that would be useful in an argument where others are denying this right, or where longwindedness is to be avoided, or where its emotional and personal reference is to be emphasized, but as a vehicle of philosophical inquiry, it is insignificant." *The Political Philosophy of Hobbes* (Oxford: Clarendon Press, 1957): 18.

12. Frey, op. cit.: 12.

13. Cf. H.L.A. Hart, "Bentham on Legal Rights," in *Oxford Essays in Jurisprudence,* 2nd series, ed. by A.W.B. Simpson (Oxford: Clarendon Press, 1973), esp. pp. 179-180, and Carl Wellman, *A Theory of Rights* (Totowa, NJ: Rowman & Allanheld, 1985): 91-94, *et passim.*

14. Wellman, ibid., 42-51, 66-68, 147-157.

15. Maurice W. Cranston, *What Are Human Rights?* (New York: Basic Books 1963): 10.

16. The remainder of this paragraph is drawn from my article, "Rights: Systematic Analysis" in *Encyclopedia of Bioethics*, ed. by Warren T. Reich (New York: Macmillan, 1978): 1508.

17. Yale Kamisar, "Euthanasia Legislation: Some Non-Religious Objections," *Minnesota Law Review*, Vol. 4 (1958).

18. If I say that a man has a natural right to [this] coat or [this] land all that it can

mean, if it mean anything and mean true, is that am of opinion he ought to have a political right to it..." *The Works of Jeremy Bentham*, ed. by John Bowing (Edinburgh: William Tate, 1843), Vol. III: 218.

19. *Jeremy Bentham's Economic Writings*, ed. by W. Stark (London: George Allen & Unwin, 1952), Vol. I: 333.

20. As quoted by Jeremy Waldron, *Nonsense Upon Stilts, Bentham, Burke, and Marx on the Rights of Man* (London and New York: Methuen, 1987): 37, from Bentham's *Anarchical Fallacies* in *The Works of Jeremy Bentham*, op cit., Vol. II.

21. Paraphrasing Bentham, *Works* (1840), Vol. II: 501, Vol. III: 221.

22. L.W. Sumner, *The Moral Foundation of Rights* (Oxford: Clarendon Press, 1987): 119.

23. Ibid., 163.

24. Ibid., 143-44.

25. Ibid., 136.

26. Ibid., 147.

27. Note that a "ghost" in folklore and fiction is the same as a human being in some respects — identifiable form and features — but totally different in other equally essential respects — no flesh and blood, no weight, no physical substance, no tangibility. For that reason "ghostly" is an apt term for a special cosmic legal system different in essential respects from all mundane legal systems.

28. Waldron, op cit., 44.

29. Marie Vassiltchlev, *Berlin Diaries* (New York: Knopf, 1987): 78. I am indebted to Professor Ruth Marcus for this reference.

30. Richard Wasserstrom, "Rights, Human Rights, and Racial Discrimination, " *Journal of Philosophy*, Vol. 61 (1964): 636. For an illustration of the sort of thing Wasserstrom may have meant, consider this World War I example from "Billie Dyer," by William Maxwell, in *The New Yorker* (May 15, 1989): 44:

Camp Funston, In Kansas. It was the headquarters of the 92nd Division, which was made up exclusively of Negro troops the Army was not integrated until thirty-one years later by executive order of Harry Truman.

At Camp Funston, a bulletin was read to all the soldiers of the 92nd Division: "The Division Commander has repeatedly urged that all colored members of his commands, and especially the officers and noncommissioned officers, should refrain from going where their presence will be resented. In spite of this injunction, one of the Sergeants of the Medical Department has recently. . .entered a theatre, as he undoubtedly had a legal right to do, and precipitated trouble by making it possible to allege race discrimination in the seat he was given . . . Don't go where your presence is not desired."

Is it possible for a white reader to imagine what it would be like for a black soldier to read this bulletin and *not* seethe with moral indignation? Is it possible that a black soldier could accept the claim that his rights and where the desires of others for his nonpresence, no matter how arbitrary or ill-founded, begin? To imagine such a person is to appreciate what Wasserstrom means by "moral impoverishment."

31. Wasserstrom, loc. cit.

32. C.S. Lewis, *Studies in Words* (Cambridge: Cambridge University Press, 1961): 14.

33. Jan Narveson, *Journal of Value Inquiry*, Vol. 4.

34. William Nelson, "On the Alleged Importance of Moral Rights," *Ratio* (1976): 150.

35. The preceding five sentences are taken from my "The Moral and Legal Responsibility of the Bad Samaritan," *Criminal Justice Ethics*, Vol. 3, No. 1 (1984): 64.

36. Robert Young, "Dispensing with Moral Rights," *Political Theory*, Vol. 6 (1978): 68.

37. Simone Weil, *The Need for Roots* (London, 1952): 18. Quoted by Young, op. cit: 68.

38. Carl Wellman is another who appears (perhaps through inadvertent overstatement) to make this mistake. He writes, for example: "Claiming is striking a blow in a struggle to prevail over one's opposition" Carl Wellman, op. cit.: 209.

39. Zeke Wigglesworth, Knight-Ridder Newspapers, April 16, 1989.

40. See Epictetus, *Discourses*, Book I, Chap. 19 "Of the Right and Treatment of Tyrants."

41. Wellman, op. cit.: 210.

42. Ibid., 170.

43. Ibid., 176.

44. See my *Social Philosophy* (Englewood Cliffs, NJ: Prentice-Hall, 1973): 70-71.

45. *Griswold v. Connecticut,* op. cit.: 486\5.

46. Warren Burger, C.J., in *Paris Adult Theatre, I v. Slaton*, 413 U.S. 49, 65 (1973).

47. See especially his *Democracy and Distrust* (New York: 1980).

48. See especially his "Neutral Principles and Some First Amendment Problems," *Indiana Law Journal*, Vol. 47, No. 1 (1971): 1-35.

49. William Rehnquist, "The Nature of a Living Constitution," 54 *Texas Law Review* 22 (1985).

50. Edwin Meese, "Constructing the Constitution," 19 *UC Davis Law Review* 22 (1985).

51. *Home Building & Loan Association v. Blaisdell*, 290 U.S. 398, 453 (1934) (Sutherland, J., dissenting).

52. David Lyons, "Constitutional Interpretation and Original Meaning," *Social Philosophy and Policy*, Vol. 4, No. 1 (1986): 77.

53. Linda R. Hirshman, "Brönte, Bloom and Bork: An Essay on the Moral Education of Judges," *University of Pennsylvania Law Review*, Vol. 137, No. 1 (1988): 182.

54. Lyons, op. cit.: 97.

55. Bork, op. cit.: 98.

56. Lyons, op. cit.: 98.

57. Ibid., 98.

58. Bork, op. cit.: 10.

59. *Supra*, note 53.

60. Ely, op. cit.: 2-3.

61. Robert Bork, "Tradition and Morality in Constitutional Law," *The Francis Boyer Lectures on Public Policy* (Washington, D.C.: American Enterprise Institute for Public Policy Research, 1985): 8-9.

62. See my "Psychological Egoism," in *Reason and Responsibility,* 7th ed., ed. by Joel Feinberg (Belmont, CA: Wadsworth Publishing Co., 1988): 489-499.

63. See my *Harm to Others* (New York: Oxford University Press, 1984).

64. Bork, *supra*, note 62: 3.

65. Loc. cit.

66. *Cohen v. California*, 91 S.C., 71.

67. Ibid., 4.

Chapter 7

Can Welfare Rights Be Found in the Constitution?

James Nickel
University of Colorado

Many contemporary national and international bills of rights impose duties on governments to ensure the availability of education and a minimum income. The U.S. Constitution and Bill of Rights, dating from an era two centuries ago when governments did — and were able to do — far less in the areas of education and welfare, do not contain such rights explicitly, nor have they been added by amendment. And opposition to the idea that education and a minimum income are human rights has been strong in the United States. Nevertheless, I want to argue that the U.S. Constitution's commitment to a system of protected individual liberties implies a commitment to rights to education and a minimum income. The argument will not depend on a nonstandard conception of the nature or scope of these liberties. Roughly, the argument is that the Constitution's commitment to a legally implemented set of rights to important liberties for all implies a commitment to create and maintain — insofar as possible and affordable — the conditions under which all people can know, exercise and defend their rights. Education and access to some minimal economic resources are so central to the creation and maintenance of these conditions that constitutional claims to education and a minimum income are generated. If I am right about this, at least part of the case for rights to education and subsistence is that they are important to protecting liberty.[1]

I. *Liberty*

Arguments attempting to go from liberty to welfare rights have often defined liberty in such a way that one is not free unless one enjoys such rights or the material benefits they guarantee. The problem with such arguments is that they beg the question. They fail immediately to persuade those who disagree with their definitions or redefinitions of liberty. To avoid this problem I intend to proceed from a conception of liberty that is noncontroversial in the United States. I will sketch this conception of liberty in a few broad strokes.

First, the liberty in question is freedom from interference by government agencies, not freedom from interference by other citizens. This is political rather than social liberty. Second, the liberties to be protected are the standard ones: freedom of thought and religion; freedom of speech and press; freedom of association and peaceful assembly; freedom to acquire, hold and dispose of property; freedom to marry and have a family; and freedom to travel and to choose one's place of residence. Third, liberties of political action and participation are also to be protected. These include liberties to participate in politics, express oneself publicly on political issues, vote, and run for and serve in public office. No doubt there are other things that should be included in our understanding of liberty against government, but this short list will serve for present purposes.

Embodied in the Bill of Rights as amended to date are two propositions that I will use as premises. One is that important liberties should be protected against government in the United States as a matter of effective legal rights. Rights are declared in the Bill of Rights not merely as aspirations or goals; they are in addition set out as legally enforceable norms. The second proposition is that such rights are possessed and are to be enjoyed by all residents (or, in some cases, all citizens). This proposition finds its roots in the amendments passed after the Civil War, particularly in the Fourteenth Amendment's guarantee of equal protection of the laws. Putting these propositions together, we can say that there is a constitutional commitment to an effective system of legal rights to liberties for all.

II. *Components of an Effective System of Liberty Rights For All*

An effective system of legal rights to liberties must contain a number of components that work together to provide guarantees that government will respect individual liberties. Without purporting to offer a comprehensive list of such components, I will mention some key elements of an effective system of legal guarantees of political liberty. All of these elements can be found, at least in part, in the U.S. Constitution and Bill of Rights as amended to date.

First, an effective system of legal rights to liberties must protect people against some of the most common ways in which governments violate liberties. A bill of rights should not only declare some liberties that are to be respected by government; it should also identify and restrain some of the main means that governments have traditionally used to invade liberty. For example, repressive governments have often abused the legal system to kill, imprison or exile their opponents and critics. Due process rights, among others, help to block such abuses of the legal system. Important rights here include: (1) the right of habeas corpus; (2) the right not to be deprived of life, liberty or property without due process of law; (3) the right to a fair trial; (4) the right to assistance of legal counsel; (5) the right against torture and cruel punishments; (6) the right against retroactive criminal laws.

Second, an effective system of legal rights to liberties must make the courts an arena in which remedies for rights violations by government can be gained, and ensure that people have access to the courts. This means giving people the power to sue public agencies and officials, and requires that courts be willing and able to stand in judgment of government agencies and officials. Important rights here include: (1) rights to petition and sue government; (2) rights to seek and employ legal counsel; (3) rights to a fair trial; (4) rights to effective remedies for rights violations.

Third, an effective system of legal rights to liberties must create democratic institutions that allow the public to turn out of office politicians who abuse their positions and violate people's rights. Important rights here include: (1) freedom of speech and press; (2) the right to assemble and to create political organizations; (3) the right to vote in free and regular elections; (4) the right to work in and contribute to political campaigns; (5) the right to run for and serve in public offices.

Fourth, an effective system of legal rights to liberties must restrain governments from blocking the means that people can use to fight back against violations of their rights. This matter is already partially covered by categories two and three above, which concern making both the courts and democratic institutions into means that people can use to protect their rights. Important rights here include: (1) rights that give people access to information and that prevent governments from suppressing information about rights violations; (2) the political rights listed above that allow people to organize opposition to government actions and policies that violate rights; (3) rights that allow people to travel, flee, and seek asylum; (4) rights that allow people to seek support for their causes in other parts of the country and abroad; and (5) rights to acquire resources through work, hold them as property, and use them to fight violations of one's liberties.

Finally, an effective system of legal rights to liberty for all must extend the protection of liberties and rights to everyone, not just to those who are white, male and propertied. This is an area, along with rights to political participation, that was very deficient in the original constitutional system in the United States, and enormous struggles have been required to remedy (or partially remedy) these deficiencies. Rights in this area might be called "equality rights." Important equality rights include: (1) the right to citizenship; (2) the right to equal protection of the law; (3) the right against discrimination on the basis of race, ethnicity, sex or religion.

Equality rights restrain governments from engaging in selective or targeted oppression, i.e., victimizing unpopular minorities or groups that lack the means to resist. Rights of political participation may prevent governments from abusing the rights of all or most of their citizens, but such rights leave open the possibility that government will invade the liberties of an unpopular minority while ensuring the majority that it is in no danger. The implementation of equality rights, together with making the courts into effective means for the protection of rights, help to close off this possibility.

So far we have been concerned with what is involved in creating an effective system of legal guarantees for liberties, but have not said anything about education and subsistence. In what follows I will first discuss the contribution of education to an effective system of legal guarantees for everyone's liberties. I will try to show that education is so indispensable to the creation of such a system that it qualifies as an important constitutional claim. Secondly, I will make the same argument for guarantee of a minimum income.

III. *The Right to Education*

Protection of people's constitutional rights is at least partly a do-it-yourself effort. Legislators, public officials, ombudspeople, and interested fellow citizens can act on behalf of others whose rights are being violated in some cases, but an effective system of legal guarantees for liberty rights cannot rely totally on such parties. Both for practical reasons of effective protection and for theoretical reasons pertaining to equal citizenship, people must be empowered to protect their own rights. A key step in such empowerment is education, providing people with information about what their constitutional rights are, what they mean in practice, and what one can do to protect them. Crudely, since one can't act to defend one's constitutional rights without knowing what they are, what they mean, and what can be done to defend them, an effective system of legal guarantees for liberty rights requires that government provide people with such information. People have a strong constitutional claim to education about their rights.

An effective system of legal rights to liberties for all must prevent people from being deprived of the means of fighting back against violations of their rights. An oppressive system can diminish the ability of victimized groups to fight back by keeping those groups poor and ignorant, lacking in knowledge of their entitlements and lacking in know-how and resources for organizing protest and litigation. This was the position that most blacks were in for many decades after the Civil War. In fact, limited knowledge and resources were supplemented by intimidation and violence directed against those who dared to fight back.

The kind of education that is needed in order to know one's rights and how to protect them is fairly rudimentary. Literacy is necessary, as is a general understanding of the workings of the political and economic system. A high school education would be adequate.

It might be objected that only the leaders, or only the attorneys, of a group need to be educated in order to fight back against rights violations.[2] But there are two responses to this. One is that even in a group context people need to be able to understand where their leaders are taking them and decide whether they want to follow. They may have to decide whether to follow, for example, those who favor slow reform, those who advocate a vigorous program of protest and litigation, or those who advocate violent resistance. The second response is that not all victims of rights violations are members of oppressed groups who have leaders or sympathizers who are willing to act on their behalf. For such individuals to recognize that they have rights that are being violated, and to recognize that they can do something to stop and remedy such violations, they need education. Once they are able to recognize their position and their possibilities, assistance by organizations or by legal aid attorneys is possible.

The claim to education is supported by many good reasons, some of them economic, and hence the U.S. government has long provided free public education to all, even if the quality of what was provided was often poor (the United States has often treated education like the Soviet Union has treated health care). But even if productivity and national competitiveness are the main concerns that come to mind when we think of education, we should not forget that education serves political as well as economic roles. Each person has a constitutional claim to education because knowing one's rights and how to exercise and protect them are essential parts of a system of effective legal guarantees for liberty to every person.

IV. *Subsistence*

There are two ways in which one can defend a claim to a minimum income on the basis of the requirements of having an effective system of guarantees of liberty. One of these arguments piggybacks on the argument for education. It is based on the fact that children who are inadequately fed and clothed are severely handicapped in learning. The second argument, which I will discuss in detail, suggests that in order to be able to fight back against violations of their rights, people need some minimal resources.

It is extremely important to notice that this argument is not claiming that liberty rights are not valuable when one is very poor. It is rather claiming that severe poverty is a substantial handicap in defending one's liberties. Not only are these claims different; they are actually in conflict since one would not care about poor people being able to defend their rights to liberty if such rights were of no value to them. Poverty does not render valueless liberties such as freedoms to choose and practice a religious faith or freedoms to choose where to live and with whom to associate. Further, political liberties are extremely important to groups who wish to seek political assistance in improving the economic and social conditions under which they live.

Legal guarantees of important liberties are important to people who find it difficult or impossible to obtain the necessities of life, and the claims of such people to protections for their liberties must be taken seriously by a system that undertakes to protect the liberty of all. Lack of sufficient income to cover the costs of food, clothing, and housing can prevent one from being able to take the actions needed to fight back against violations of one's liberties. Perhaps the best way to show this is to discuss some examples. All assume that government programs of income support are unavailable.

Nina is unemployed and receives no support from anyone. Sometimes she gets a little money by doing housework. Her 25-year-old son, Howard, was arrested and accused of robbery while traveling 500 miles away. Because of his Islamic beliefs he is subject to harassment by his jailers and by other inmates and he is unable to engage in his normal religious practices and eat in the way his religion requires. A legal aid attorney is handling his robbery case but is too busy to deal with or even take seriously the issue of religious freedom while he is in jail. Nina has no phone, but Howard was able to contact her through a relative. Neither Nina nor Howard has the money to raise bond, nor is Nina able to pay the cost of a trip to visit Howard. Hiring a private attorney for him is far beyond their means. Members of her extended family dislike Howard and are unwilling to do anything for him. Nina heard that she might get help from local civil liberties groups, but she lacks suitable clothing for a visit to a downtown office and in any case getting to that office would require that she use her food money for bus fare. Howard stays in jail, subjected to harassment on religious grounds, until his case finally comes to trial.

Marshall is a 43-year-old street person who sleeps in a cave near the medium-sized town where he was born. He has no living relatives. Intolerance for authority, plus a problem with alcohol, have made it impossible for him to find regular employment. Police in the town where he lives often attempt to reduce the number of street people by putting them on outbound intercity buses, warning them to keep quiet and not come back. Some who have returned in spite of such warnings have received beatings by unknown persons. Late one Thursday night, when he is mildly drunk, Marshall is picked up by police and put on an outbound bus. The next morning he gets off the bus 200 miles from his home, angry and sober. He believes that his liberty to live in his hometown was violated by the cops who put him on the bus, but he lacks the means to get back to that town and is afraid of being beaten up if he returns. The police in the town where he was dumped laugh off his complaint and suggest that he move on down the road. He is unable to locate any civil liberties group in the town where he was dumped, and lacks the money for an attorney. Marshall panhandles enough money for a bottle of cheap wine, and starts looking for a place to bed down.

Stories like these test one's commitment to liberty for all. It is easy to discount the claims of people at the bottom to guarantees of liberty. But the Constitution commits us to taking these claims seriously. These examples illustrate the way in which a lack of financial resources can make it impossible for people whose liberties are being violated by government to fight back. Of course many people without financial resources do manage to fight back: they do so by using their food money for bus fares, by calling on friends and relatives for assistance, by finding religious or charitable or legal aid organizations who will assist them. But the fact that many manage to fight back doesn't make disappear the fact that many don't, that many are literally unable to do anything to seek and gain remedies for violations of their liberty rights. Since some minimal economic resources are strictly necessary to these people's being able to seek and gain remedies for violations of their liberty rights, their constitutional claim to protection of liberty also supports a constitutional claim to these minimal economic resources.

V. *Objections and Rebuttals*

In this section I present three objections to the arguments I have presented and offer rebuttals. These rebuttals develop some of the details of the position I am advocating.

1. *The framers did not intend to create rights to education and subsistence.* This objection goes from the premise that the framers of the U.S. Constitution did not intend to create rights to education and subsistence to the conclusion that there is no basis now for claims to education and subsistence within the Constitution.[3] Responding to this objection could easily lead to an extended discussion of the role of original intention in constitutional interpretation, but I will try to avoid an extended discussion of issues about intent and interpretation.[4] Further, I will grant the truth of the premise about original intent. It is probably true that neither the eighteenth-century authors of the first ten amendments or the nineteenth-century authors of the Fourteenth Amendment consciously intended to create constitutional rights to education and subsistence.

Having conceded so much, my rebuttal will depend on the idea that by intending to create one right it is possible to commit oneself, without being aware of this, to some other right which is necessary to the effective implementation of the first. Since the arguments for the rights to education and subsistence depend heavily on the commitment to protecting the liberty of *all* citizens, the constitutional commitments to which I wish to appeal probably did not exist until after the passage of the Fourteenth Amendment. The authors of the first ten amendments seem to have been less concerned with protecting the liberties of each and every person.

The kind of "presuppositional" argument that I am using suggests that one can intend more than one is aware of. If one commits oneself to protecting everyone's right to liberty, and if in order to do this fully it is strictly necessary that people be provided with education and a minimum income when they are unable to provide these things for themselves, then rights to education and a minimum income are implied by the original commitment, even if the people who made this commitment didn't realize or say this. This sort of argument is common in constitutional interpretation. If the system of constitutional guarantees would not be coherent or viable without a commitment to a right that was not mentioned by the framers (e.g., the right to travel between the states), then a commitment to such a right is taken to be present.

Presuppositional arguments may fail if (1) the inferred right is not strictly necessary to the full implementation of explicit rights but is merely very useful to such implementation; or (2) the costs of the inferred right are so large as to make unaffordable the explicit right (now that its full costs are apparent). The first problem would apply to rights to education and subsistence if these things were merely very useful to implementing legal guarantees of liberty but not strictly necessary. But in fact education and a guaranteed minimum income are strictly necessary for hundreds of thousands of Americans to be able to do the things necessary to have their liberty rights protected. The stories above attempt to illustrate how this is so. The second problem would apply to rights to education and subsistence if these rights were not affordable in the United States. But this is not the case, given that massive programs of education and subsistence are already available and being paid for (although generally not as constitutional rights) in the United States.

2. *The arguments presented ignore the distinction between restraining from depriving and providing.* Although governments should not deprive people of the means to fight back against violations of their liberties, it is not up to governments to provide people with the means to fight back against oppression. For example, it would be wrong for a government to follow policies that deliberately keep a minority group poor and ignorant, but governments are not required, as a matter of promoting liberty, to create programs to help their citizens overcome poverty and ignorance.

The first step in rebuttal is to argue that the Constitution already requires governments at various levels to take positive or affirmative measures to protect people's liberties. For example, the U.S. government is constitutionally required to provide people with an accessible legal system in which effective remedies for government violations of their liberty rights can be obtained. To provide such a legal system is to provide a positive benefit, a resource, a service. For another example, the U.S. government is constitutionally required to provide a system of democratic policies whereby government officials who invade liberty rights can be subjected to complaints, petitions, and political campaigns intended to prevent their reelection. To provide such a political system is to offer individuals opportunities and benefits that they would not have on their own, that they would not have if they were merely "left alone." The point here is that government is already required by the Constitution to provide positive benefits. If these positive benefits were not provided, effective guarantees for the liberty rights of all would not exist.

Ensuring that people have the means of fighting back against violations of their liberty rights is no more "positive" than ensuring that they have available systems of legal procedures and guarantees and systems of democratic policies.

In the absence of accessible courts and democratic processes, some individuals would nevertheless have the power and influence (because of wealth, family ties, or friendships) to protect their liberties. There have always been some individuals whose complaints had to be taken seriously by governments. Accessible courts and democratic processes ensure a modicum of equality in this area; they allow those without wealth or influence to make effective complaints about violations of their rights. They provide a way of taking seriously the liberty rights of those without wealth and influence.

The situation is exactly analogous in the area of education. In the absence of free public education, some individuals would be educated and know how to go about protecting their liberties, but others would be illiterate and know little about what one can do to protect one's rights. To take seriously these people's claims to be able to protect their liberties is to give weight to their claims to the resources and institutions needed to become educated. Providing education is an essential means to protecting the liberty rights of the uneducated and impoverished.[5]

3. *It is not the job of the courts to recognize constitutional rights to education and subsistence.* Creating programs to provide education and a minimum income to Americans who are otherwise unable to gain access to these things is a legislative function rather than one that would normally be handled by the courts. So it might be objected that even if there are grounds within existing constitutional commitments for rights to education and subsistence, it would be not be proper for courts to simply recognize these rights and demand that legislatures organize and fund them.[6] I will respond to this objection in two ways.

First, the premise of this objection about the proper role of the courts is not self-evident and may indeed be unjustifiable. The Constitution is not very explicit about what courts may and may not do; even judicial review is not explicitly authorized in the original Constitution. Congress has often been unwilling or unable to amend our ancient Constitution to provide protections of rights that other contemporary democracies that we admire provide, and hence the courts have often had to choose between tolerating severe injustices and engaging in constitutional innovation. Both Congress and the public have been tolerant of, and indeed have sometimes celebrated, the constitutional innovations of the courts. In response to issues about busing to integrate schools, school financing, and prison overcrowding, courts have sometimes required legislatures to build institutions and fund them in order to satisfy recognized rights. The taboo that the courts can't deal with anything whose remedy might require substantial budget appropriations has been broken.

Second, suppose that I am wrong about this, that the courts should not recognize general rights to education and subsistence. This would not prevent the courts from recognizing that there are serious constitutional commitments in these areas. One way in which these commitments could be given life would be for the courts to call on legislatures to recognize these commitments and begin treating education and income assistance as matters of rights. Since education and income maintenance are already areas in which federal and state legislatures do a great deal, a declaration by the Supreme Court that constitutional rights are involved could do a lot to give an improved status to these efforts and to make clear that their quality and coverage would be subject to judicial oversight. Another way in which these commitments could be given life is suggested by this. Once recognized by the courts, they would exert "gravitational force" on other decisions. They could influence the standards of scrutiny applied in decisions about school financing, levels of funding for income-support programs, and due process in the termination of welfare benefits.

VI. *Conclusion*

A plausible argument runs from a constitutional commitment to protecting standard sorts of liberty rights to a commitment to rights to education and subsistence. The key premise is that both education and access to at least minimal financial resources are often necessary for people to be able to defend their rights, to fight back against invasions of liberty by governments. The courts should recognize constitutional rights to education and subsistence, even if they are unwilling to make wholesale demands on legislatures for the implementation of such rights.

Notes

1. This argument is a version of the kind of "presuppositional" argument presented by Henry Shue in *Basic Rights* (Princeton, N.J.: Princeton University Press, 1980). For a discussion of presuppositional arguments for rights, see James W. Nickel, *Making Sense of Human Rights* (Berkeley: University of California Press, 1987): 102-4. See also Frank I. Michelman, "Welfare Rights in a Constitutional Democracy," *Washington University Law Quarterly* 1979: 659-693.

2. Robert H. Bork makes this objection in "The Impossibility of Finding Welfare Rights in the Constitution," *Washington University Law Quarterly* 1979: 659-693.

3. For any instance of this objection, see Bork, "The Impossibility of Finding Welfare Rights in the Constitution": 696.

4. See Munzer and Nickel, "Does the Constitution Mean What It Always Meant?" *Columbia Law Review* 77 (1977): 1029-1062.

5. For more extended discussions of the distinction between "negative" and "positive" rights see Shue, *Basic Rights*, 51-64, and Nickel, *Making Sense of Human Rights*, 14, 122.

6. Bork makes this objection, "The Impossibility of Finding Welfare Rights in the Constitution": 698-700.

Cases Cited

Index

About the Contributors

Roger Barrus

Associate professor of political science at Hampden-Sydney College. He has published widely on topics as diverse as the history of modern philosophy, American political thought, and the relation of religion and politics.

Robert Bork

Now affiliated with the American Enterprise Institute in Washington, D.C., Judge Bork is a renowned legal scholar who has been solicitor general of the United States, law professor at Yale and judge of the Federal Court of Appeals in Washington, D.C. He has published widely on constitutional issues, interpretive theory and antitrust law.

Richard Epstein

James Parker Hall professor of law at the University of Chicago. He is the leading libertarian legal theorist of our time as well as one of the most important contributors to the field of law and economics. He has published in areas as diverse as public choice theory, antidiscrimination law, and property rights law.

Joel Feinberg

Professor emeritus of philosophy at the University of Arizona. Professor Feinberg also taught at a number of other institutions, including Rockefeller University and Princeton. He has a distinguished list of contributions to moral and legal theory, including a magisterial series of four volumes on the moral foundations of the criminal law.

Charles W. Johnson

Professor of philosophy and liberal arts at Utah State University. He has published on such diverse topics as philosophy of mind, philosophy of religion and philosophy in literature.

Ralph Lerner

Professor and member of the Committee on Social Thought at the University of Chicago. He has published a number of important works on American political thought, especially of the founding period, as well as highly significant studies on and editions of key texts in medieval philosophy.

Harvey C. Mansfield

Frank G. Thompson professor of government at Harvard University. Professor Mansfield has published widely in modern political philosophy, American political thought, and on modern political institutions, e.g. the presidency. He has also edited and translated key works of Machiavelli.

James Nickel

Professor of philosophy at the University of Colorado. Professor Nickel has published widely on constitutional theory, theories of human rights and applied ethics. He is the author of widely cited essays on constitutional interpretation and international human rights.

Kent E. Robson

Professor of philosophy and liberal arts at Utah State University. He is also head of the Department of Languages and Philosophy and outgoing president of the Faculty Senate. He has published in philosophy of religion and ethics and has an ongoing interest in research in the areas of philosophy of history, philosophy of language and philosophy of religion.

Richard Sherlock

Professor of philosophy and liberal arts at Utah State University. He has published in such diverse fields as medical and applied ethics (e.g. abortion, euthanasia, and patient rights), the history of modern philosophy and constitutional theory.